# Hunters of the Steel Sharks
## The Submarine Chasers of WWI

Todd A. Woofenden

Signal Light Books™ • Bowdoinham, ME

Hunters of the Steel Sharks
The Submarine Chasers of WWI

Published in the United States by
Signal Light Books™
422 River Road, Bowdoinham, Maine 04008
www.signallightbooks.com

Copyright © 2006 by Todd A. Woofenden

All rights reserved. No part of this publication may be reproduced or transmitted in any form or by any means, electronic or mechanical, including photocopy, recording, or any information storage and retrieval system now known or to be developed, without permission in writing from the publisher, except by a reviewer who wishes to quote brief passages in connection with a review written for inclusion in a magazine, newspaper or broadcast.

Additional notes and other information at:
www.signallightbooks.com/hunters

See also:
The Subchaser Archives
www.subchaser.org

Hunters of the Steel Sharks
Library of Congress Control Number: 2006907833
ISBN-13: 978-0-9789192-0-7
ISBN-10: 0-9789192-0-3

Cover photo: SC 354 on the mine fields. G.S. Dole Collection.

# Contents

| | |
|---|---|
| Author's Remarks | 1 |
| Prologue | 6 |
| | |
| Chapter 1 – Building the Chaser Fleet | 10 |
| Chapter 2 – Antisubmarine Warfare | 36 |
| Chapter 3 – Crossing the Atlantic | 61 |
| Chapter 4 – American Bay | 77 |
| Chapter 5 – On the Otranto Barrage | 86 |
| Chapter 6 – Post-War Diplomacy and Travels | 108 |
| Chapter 7 – The Northern Russia Expedition | 121 |
| Chapter 8 – Mine Sweeping in the North Sea | 147 |
| Chapter 9 – Homeward Bound | 165 |
| Epilogue – The Impact of the Submarine Chasers | 173 |
| | |
| Appendix I – Distribution of Submarine Chasers | 181 |
| Appendix II – Submarine Chaser Service at Plymouth, England | 183 |
| Appendix III – Submarine Chaser Service at Queenstown, Ireland | 189 |
| Appendix IV – Submarine Chaser Service on the Atlantic Coast | 192 |
| Appendix V – Submarine Chaser Service on the Pacific Coast | 195 |
| | |
| Bibliography | 196 |
| Notes | 201 |
| Index | 211 |

*"I have often thought as we were on the peaceful voyage just completed, and watched the stars keeping time absolute, infallible, and guiding us on our journey in safety, that the steel sharks will not long be allowed to interfere with the beauty and safety of His seas."*[1]

Ensign George S. Dole
1885 - 1928

## Acknowledgements

I am grateful to the many people who helped me in one way or another during the course of this project.

I am particularly indebted to Franklyn K. Brown of Holbrook, Massachusetts, whose endless enthusiasm for the study of the chasers helped inspire this work, and whose wisdom and perspective on this bit of history have been invaluable; and to Jack Hudock, for generously offering his extensive knowledge and expertise in a great many discussions of the details of chasers, equipment and devices.

Thanks also to Dan Treadwell, Arthur Herrick, and many others who helped by directing me to sources and providing me with information, images and other material.

Special thanks to my father-in-law, Paul Wesel, for reviewing and editing the manuscript and making excellent suggestions for improving the structure and flow of the work, and to my wife Lisa Wesel for reviewing and proofreading, and putting up with me all these years.

It has been a great pleasure to have corresponded with many descendants of chaser officers and crewmen, researchers, archivists, historians and others while compiling this work. These conversations on the service of the submarine chasers in WWI help keep the story alive.

## Notes on photographs and illustrations

Except as otherwise noted, all of the photos, diagrams, charts and other illustrations in this book are from Lt. Dole's personal collection. The original photographic prints vary in quality: Some are stunningly clear and crisp, while others are faded, very small, or not particularly clear. Of the 1,400+ photographic prints in his collection, I have selected about 100 representative photographs for this work.

I have also included several photographs from my own collection of period prints. These come from different sources, including several photograph albums compiled by chaser men. In all cases, these images are taken from original period prints.

In illustrating the equipment and tactics of the chaser, I have presented drawings and diagrams from tactical manuals and documents that were used by the chaser men. While some of these are rather rudimentary, they strike me as being more authentic and interesting than modern drawings would be.

There are several other sources of photos and illustrations:

The subchaser Plan and Profile drawings are based on the USN Booklet of General Plans for the 110' submarine chaser. Drawings and sections of drawings from the Booklet have been digitally combined and extensively modified; and the hand-written text labels that appear in the original drawings have been removed and replaced by new labels and a key to identify features.

The images of early ASW devices are from the archives of the Raytheon Company in Waltham, Massachusetts, a collection that includes several folios of images of early Submarine Signal Company devices.

The photographs of radio telephone equipment are from the New England Wireless and Steam Museum in East Greenwich, Rhode Island, which has in its collection a radio telephone set of the type used on the subchasers.

The illustrations of the Standard Motor Construction Company engines are from the engine manual produced by Standard Motor in 1917 for use by chaser engineers.

One engine room photograph is from the National Archives.

# Author's Remarks

When the United States resolved to enter the arena of the Great War, the submarine menace was regarded as a serious threat to the Allies. As the war in the trenches wore on, and the count of dead and injured grew to monstrous proportions, the enemy began to focus greater attention on the sea. The prospect of England being starved into submission through the sinking of merchant shipping grew into an alarmingly plausible scenario.

*U-boat UB 92, an example of a German coastal torpedo attack submarine, type UB III.*

Earlier in the war, the German U-boat had proven itself to be a formidable offensive weapon, engaging in a strategy that came to be known as *unrestricted submarine warfare,* in which any vessel regardless of its type was subject to being sunk. The U-boats attacked military transport vessels, merchant ships and private ships alike, the most notorious example being the Cunard Line steamship RMS *Lusitania,* torpedoed and sunk on 7 May 1915 by the German submarine U 20. In this incident 1,198 people died, including 124 Americans.[2] Among the Allies, the sinking of *Lusitania* grew into a symbol of the indiscriminate ruthlessness and inhumanity of the enemy.

The killing of innocent Americans, both in this incident and in several others, created increasing political pressure on the administration of President Woodrow Wilson to take military action, but in 1915 the problem had not yet grown to sufficient proportions to prompt a declaration of war. Moreover, German military authorities halted the practice of unrestricted submarine warfare soon after the sinking of *Lusitania.* This was a controversial move among German military strategists, seen by some as a reflection of weakness and lack of resolve and by others as a necessary step to quell the growing public outrage that threatened to draw the United States, a fresh enemy, into the war.

For almost two more years the United States maintained official neutrality. Then in February 1917, Germany resumed its policy of unrestricted submarine warfare, and two months later, on 6 April 1917, the United States declared war on Germany. Soon a massive naval buildup was under way, in no small part motivated by the popular American sentiment that the U-boats had to be stopped.

*Conning tower of UB 92. Probably at Inverness, Scotland, in 1919. (T. Woofenden Collection.)*

In addressing the U-boat menace, the convoy system would become what Rear Admiral William Sowden Sims, commander of U.S. Naval Forces in Europe, called a "defensive offensive,"[3] a strategy for protecting merchant and passenger shipping as well as troop transports while increasing the chances of flushing out and attacking enemy subs. A convoy of merchant and military ships presented an attractive target to the U-boats, and thus by accompanying the convoys, Allied destroyers and other warships would have a better chance of engaging enemy subs while providing protection for merchant ships.

But Adm. Sims was convinced that the U.S. Navy should also be engaged in a purely offensive strategy against the U-boats, to hunt them down. The submarine chaser would come into existence as a tool for putting this plan into action.

The American submarine chasers took part in several components of the antisubmarine warfare (ASW) effort, including patrols in Allied waters, participation in convoys, and barrage line duties. Barrage lines were one of the tactics for putting the U-boats in check. These barriers in key seaways were intended to contain enemy submarines and deny them access to open waters. The most massive and notable barrage, the North Sea mine barrage, consisted of a series of mine fields crossing the North Sea from Scotland to Norway. But in some areas the installation of mine fields was impractical or altogether unfeasible. This was the case at the mouth of the Adriatic Sea, where the waters were far too deep for tethered mines. Thus the Otranto Barrage, intended to prevent Austrian and German submarines from passing through

U-boat U 126, an example of a German minelayer submarine, type UE 2. Shown post-war, under Allied command.

the Strait of Otranto and gaining access to the Mediterranean Sea and open ocean, consisted initially of a line of trawlers deploying antisubmarine nets intended to hamper passage of submarines. Later, mine nets were employed as well; and in June 1918, American submarine chasers entered the barrage line, equipped with listening devices and depth charges. Twelve units of chasers – thirty-six in all – were assigned to the Otranto Barrage.

Subchaser SC 93, a typical example of this new type of vessel, was commissioned in December 1917, in New London, Connecticut, armed for action against enemy submarines, soon to be assigned to service on the Otranto Barrage. The chaser was fitted with a 3"/23-caliber deck gun, a depth charge launcher, machine guns, small arms – and a crew that would spend long, difficult days on rough seas in remarkably close quarters. The wood-hulled vessel, at 110' length and 15' beam, was a long, slender boat powered by three 220-hp gasoline engines. It was designed to provide exceptional seaworthiness and reasonably good speed – and no comfort whatsoever. Its commanding officer was Ens. George S. Dole, Olympic-gold-medal-winning wrestler, Yale graduate and amateur yachtsman. A U.S. Naval Reservist, he had experience serving on USS *Malay* (SP 735), a converted yacht assigned to patrol duty in the North Atlantic, but SC 93 was his first command.

His mission: to hunt down the steel sharks and help end their dominance of the seas.

George S. Dole was the identical twin of my grandfather, Louis A. Dole. He and his brother were close throughout their lives. They attended Yale together and shared their passion for sailing, fishing and wrestling. At wrestling the two were evenly matched, and both gained considerable fame in their collegiate wrestling careers. The family story has it that a coin toss won Louis the trip to London for the Olympic Games in 1908, but an illness kept him home, and George took his place. George went on to enter the record books as the first collegiate winner of a gold medal.

Both his father and his brother expressed enthusiastic support for the American war effort, but following in his father's footsteps as a Swedenborgian minister, Louis's passion was for the pulpit. Thus as the United States geared up for war, the paths of the two brothers would diverge for a time, and Ens. Dole would return in 1919 as Lt. (jg) Dole, having earned an additional half-stripe and an award of the Navy Cross.

This is an account of the subchaser offensive based heavily on my great uncle's tour of duty. In a sense, it is the story of Lt. George S. Dole. But it is also the story of the chasers and the men who served on them. It includes an account of the development of early ASW tactics, the use of new listening devices on the subchasers, and the role of the subchasers in the sea war.

Lt. Dole's service provides a notable and comprehensive picture of the overall subchaser story. As commanding officer of SC 93, he was in the first convoy of chasers to set out from the United States, in February 1918. He then served in the Otranto Barrage for the full duration of the American chasers' involvement there, engaging in ASW, hunting and attacking enemy submarines. Following the Armistice in November 1918, he participated in diplomatic missions, representing the United States. Then as commanding officer of SC 354 he led a unit of chasers on a mission to Archangel, Russia, to assist with the evacuation of American troops stranded amidst the turmoil of the Russian Revolution. He then returned to England and assisted in what was probably the most dangerous component of his tour of duty, the post-war clearing of the North Sea mine barrage, for which service he was awarded the Navy Cross.

Lt. Dole performed another service for his country and for history by preserving an extensive collection of documents. As a commanding officer of a submarine chaser, he had access to confidential military papers including classified orders, tactical manuals, telegraphs, nautical charts and requisition forms. He was an avid amateur photographer, taking many hundreds of photos of the chasers and their work and collecting others from his colleagues; and he was conscientious about writing home. Fortunately for those of us with an interest in WWI naval history, he saw fit to keep a large collection of these documents and photos. This book draws extensively from this collection.

What has drawn me to this story – other than the role of my great uncle and the characteristics he shares with his identical twin, my grandfather – is the story of young, enterprising and ingenious American men embarking on what must have seemed like a fool's errand, to cross the Atlantic Ocean in wooden motorboats packed with TNT and chase enemy submarines. It was in many ways an improvisational effort, for there was not yet an established science of ASW. The commitment to the cause shown by these men, and what they endured in an effort to secure peace, is remarkable. "...To make the last sacrifice is but a trivial matter in comparison to the speedy restoration of peace, order, and sanity," writes Ens. Dole during the first leg of his journey to Corfu. "The price is cheap at any cost of life or treasure, and must be paid."

This is the story of the chasers and the men who set out on them, ready and willing to make the last sacrifice.

Todd A. Woofenden, Bowdoinham, Maine

## Prologue

24 October 1918: Unit E, The Otranto Barrage. It was early morning, and Unit E was on duty south of the Strait of Otranto. Aboard SC 90, Lt. Oscar Borgeson was in command of the unit of three submarine chasers. His wing boats were SC 92 and SC 93, under the commands of Ens. Joseph H. Mundy and Lt. (jg) George S. Dole. The chasers had been working a rotation of four days on the barrage line and four days at the base in American Bay on the island of Corfu, Greece, and this was day two on the line.

Enemy submarines from bases along the coast of Albania had to pass through this relatively narrow channel between Greece and southern Italy in order to reach the Mediterranean Sea and proceed to the seaways around England or other destinations. The role of the chasers was to detect them, hunt them and attack them, to block their passage through the strait.

At 6:40 a.m. with engines off, the men on SC 93 put the K Tube hydrophone listening device over the side and waited for the triangular frame and the boat to drift apart until the tether was taut. The listener put on his headset and turned the dial to adjust the bearing, sweeping for the telltale sound of submarine propellers. All was quiet. This was not unusual. Tracking submarines was a matter of patience and perseverance. The listeners reeled in the K Tubes, and the unit continued its pattern of listening, moving along a course and listening again.

Two hours had passed when a report was received of a distress call from a French seaplane. SC 90, closest to the estimated location, was ordered to assist. Lt. Borgeson sounded bells to the engine room, and SC 90 left formation to head out on a search. As the morning wore on without any contact with the downed plane, SC 92 and SC 93, still detecting no submarine activity, joined in the search.

At 2:00 in the afternoon, Lt. Dole paused to take a sextant reading to determine his position: Lat. N 39° 08', Long. E 18° 45'.[1] They were in the Ionian Sea, roughly fifty miles southeast of Cape St. Maria di Leucca on the boot-heel of Italy, and sixty miles southwest of their base on Corfu. Before long, the men sighted an object on the horizon, and Lt. Dole set a course for it, thinking it might be the plane they were looking for. Then at 3:20, as they approached, the crew recognized the object. This was no French airplane, but the forward deck of what appeared to be an Austrian type IV submarine on the surface, six miles dead ahead.

Lt. Dole sounded general quarters, and crewmen raced to their stations. As the submarine began to submerge, realizing that it had been spotted by the chasers, the gunner on the deck of SC 93 aimed the deck gun and fired

*Section of nautical chart used on SC 93 during submarine hunts, showing the location of the attack on 24 October 1918. Place names and marks added for emphasis.*

off a round. It was a wild shot, but when hunting a sub, one didn't waste an opportunity, however slim.

There was too much static to use the radio telephones, so the signal man set the bearing indicator above the pilot house to send a visual signal to the unit leader. Sub sighted, bearing 340°. The chase was on. The men on SC 90 relayed the signal to SC 92, and in the engine rooms, bells rang for full speed ahead, all engines. The engineers in each chaser tipped the air valves, turning over the engines, and the machines roared into action. They moved the throttle levers to full speed, and the three slender boats sped off toward the target.

At 3:37, Lt. Borgeson's boat reached the oil slick of a submarine's trail, and Lt. Borgeson gave the order to drop charges, set to explode at a depth of 150 feet. The men in SC 90 felt the low, booming impact of the explosions, as charges of TNT detonated, sending huge spouts of water hurtling upward. Crew members strained to see through the spray as the shape of a submarine's bow heaved up into the air. As it crashed back into the sea, a heavy film of dark, yellow oil bubbled up to the surface, and pieces of wood appeared floating nearby. Cheers went up as the men of Unit E realized their attack had found a target.

The men aboard the wing boat, SC 92, were in a good position to see the action. Edward J. Williams, Coxswain, reports, "The second bomb and last I noticed, lifted about twelve feet in the air an object of a submarine's stern similar to those I have seen on French, Italian and English submarines. The object was black and solid and its shape, leading diagonal from the water. The stern of the submarine was similar to that of UC 22-70 type shown to us by Mr. Mundy." Seaman John J. Murphy, looking through binoculars at the time, reports seeing "an object in the midst of the water thrown up by the explosion. Could not make out what it was. It appeared dark and about the size of the bow of a submarine." Seaman 1st Class Jeffrey Cormier reports, similarly, seeing "a dark object above the water shaped like the stern or bow of a submarine in a diagonal position." Gordon Ellis Tessman, Ship's Cook 3rd Class, who had come up on deck at the general quarters call reports, "I seen a large object come up as if it were lifted on end."

But subs were wily. Reports of the destruction of subs had frequently been proven groundless, when days or weeks later, Allied radio men intercepted transmissions from the sub in question, or a spy in a German port sent back word of its arrival, intact. The men of Unit E stopped the engines and lowered the hydrophones. Soon the listener on SC 93 picked up a signal. The sub was still moving, but the sound was faint, and the listener had trouble figuring the correct bearing. In an attempt to get the sub to speed up and reveal its position, Lt. Dole ordered two depth charges to be dropped. The unit continued its listening periods, but no further contact was made.

Had they sunk a sub? Was the faint sound of the sub its last gasp? As usual, it was nearly impossible to tell. If there was any evidence, it was lost on the bottom of the ocean. Without a live prisoner or a piece of the sub itself to bring back to base, it was unlikely that Unit E would be officially credited with a sinking. Maybe the sub had limped along to its demise somewhere along its course, or maybe it had gotten away clean. But in any case, Unit E had shown a U-boat reason to fear the dangerous firepower of the subchasers. Spirits were high.

Lt. Dole, showing characteristic modesty in a letter to his brother Louis, remarks simply, "Was in action on October 24." To his father and stepmother he offers similar understatement, "Oct. 24 was a fine day for me."

In just a few weeks from SC 93's final submarine pursuit, the Armistice would become effective and the chasers would be in American Bay firing salutes and celebrating the Allied victory. Yet the end of the war would not mark the end of Lt. Dole's "fine days at sea," but only about the halfway point. He would not return to New York harbor until November 1919, a full year later. In many respects his work following the Armistice would be more dangerous and more interesting than his duty on the Barrage line.

To appreciate these challenges and the unique piece of history occupied by the American submarine chasers of WWI, we need to start at the beginning, in the second half of 1917.

## Chapter 1 – Building the Chaser Fleet

*"The submarine situation in April 1917 was briefly this. Germany had constructed 213 submarines; she had lost 55, leaving her a total of 158 underwater craft, with which in April she sank 875,000 tons of shipping. She was building an average of six or seven per month, while her losses averaged but three or four."*[1]

Ens. John Langdon Leighton
Intelligence Section staffer under Adm. Sims

**Designing the American Submarine Chasers**

As the United States prepared to enter the war, a new fleet of American vessels was under construction, hundreds of boats hastily being built by many different shipyards for the purpose of hunting and destroying U-boats. Adm. Sims, who was to become commander of the U.S. Naval Forces in Europe, was committed to putting U.S. Navy forces into the war arena in an offensive response to the U-boat campaign. His staffer, Ens. John Langdon Leighton, explains, "He took this stand because he believed that the antisubmarine forces needed help more critically than the other units," and "He believed that the American people would prefer to have their forces in Europe primarily fighting submarines because the submarine war had been the cause of America's entry into the struggle."[2]

More specifically, public outrage had grown at Germany's strategy of unrestricted submarine warfare, in which virtually any ship, civilian or military, was targeted and sunk without warning. The sinking of the ocean liner RMS *Lusitania* had long since become a symbol of this sentiment in Europe, and as the number of American citizens and American ships lost to submarine attacks mounted, the United States abandoned its efforts to remain neutral, and Germany faced a new, fresh enemy.

In planning the deployment of the chaser force, Adm. Sims was insistent on using the chasers only to hunt subs, a policy that persisted throughout the war. This was reflected in organizational documents including those circulated to the chaser commanding officers:

## Employment of Subchasers

The following principles shall, in general, govern the employment of subchasers.

    (a) That they shall be used for hunting submarines in areas where submarines are most likely to be encountered.

    (b) That they shall not be used for escort or similar duty except in cases of emergency...[3]

It was an ambitious undertaking to build a new fleet to wage this offensive. What was the ideal design for a small vessel that would hunt enemy subs? Naval tacticians already knew enough about the U-boat to have some good ideas. To chase a submarine, a vessel would need to be fast, heavily armed and capable of deploying modern technology such as new listening devices; and it would need to be highly maneuverable, able to stop and start quickly. The specific design – how big, how fast, what features – was a matter of considerable discussion, but in the end, pragmatic considerations would drive much of the design process.

Already in the arena was the British Motor Launch (ML), an American-made, 80-foot long, wood-hulled boat – small, fast and maneuverable.

*British Motor Launch ML 223.*

*Subchasers at sea, SC 95 in the foreground.*

There were already hundreds of these ML boats in action. But the American designers set their sights on a larger design that could accommodate more equipment, more men and more provisions.

While this would allow greater self-sufficiency and the potential to remain at sea longer than their smaller British counterparts, the decision to build a larger vessel would offer an unexpected additional benefit, for these new boats would prove ideal for the deployment of new ASW technology.

Ultimately each would be fitted with a Y-gun (depth charge launcher), a complement of a dozen or more depth charges each containing 300 lbs. of TNT, a deck gun and a set of listening and tracking devices that represented the state of the art in detecting enemy submarines. The design included quarters and room for provisions to support a crew of two dozen men on missions that could keep them at sea for weeks at a time.

The design finally settled upon was a single-hulled wooden vessel of 110' length and 14' 8¾" beam, rather similar in appearance to the British ML, but larger. The principal architect of this new design was Lt. Comdr. Albert Loring Swasey, a U.S. Naval Reservist and yacht designer in Boston, Massachusetts, working under Comdr. Julius A. Furer of the Construction Corps, USN.[4]

Swasey's new design was a long, slender motorboat with a full-load draft of under 6', and a pilot house which, ironically, would be mistaken on more than one occasion for the conning tower of an enemy submarine.

## Building the Chaser Fleet

On 4 March 1917, the U.S. government authorized the construction of

*Subchaser SC 151, Azores.*

these "submarine chasers,"[5] and as time was of the essence, the navy contracted with shipyards all across the country, each shipyard receiving a contract of a size it could handle in a short time frame. For some of the smaller shipyards, this meant a contract to build only one or two chasers. This distribution also resulted in numerous minor construction differences among the chasers, such as in the run of the hull planking, the fine details of pilot house construction and the size of the port holes.

On a rapid timeline, 441 submarine chasers were constructed. Of these, 403 were completed and launched during the war, including one hundred built for France. Four were transferred to Cuba on 4 November 1918, but since they were under U.S. control until one week prior to the Armistice, they may be counted as part of an American wartime force of 303 subchasers.[6]

The chasers' hasty construction was blamed for frequent leaks, probably due to the use of unseasoned wood. This caused the vessels to be put into dry dock several times during the war for the seams to be caulked. But in spite of having persistently wet bilges, these small vessels proved remarkably seaworthy. Of the 303 chasers in the American force, only six were lost during the war, two to fire (SC 117 and SC 219), three in collisions with other vessels (SC 60, SC 132 and SC 187), and one, SC 209, was mistaken for an enemy submarine and shelled and sunk by the USN freighter USS *Felix Taussig*.[7] In post-war duties in 1919, three more were lost to fire, SC 58, SC 256 and SC 343, for a total of only nine lost in connection to service in WWI.

The chasers of Unit E, SC 90, SC 92 and SC 93, were among sixteen built by Elco Co., in Bayonne, New Jersey, the same company that had manufactured hundreds of MLs for the British navy. These chasers were delivered to the

Brooklyn Navy Yard in New York in November 1917[8], bound for the U.S. submarine base in New London, Connecticut.

In December 1917, as he and his crew were aboard SC 93 and becoming familiar with this new vessel, Ens. Dole describes to his father his early impressions of the seaworthiness of the craft.

> You may be interested in the fact that the boat behaves in great shape at sea. She is wet as a duck and rolls so you cannot keep anything on deck or below deck that is not lashed, and lashed in good shape. But the boat is on top of everything, and what water does come on deck, and we get considerable green water, does not stay there long. She shakes it off and is ready for another before the next one comes, which pleases me muchly.[9]

**Construction of the 110' Submarine Chaser**

Viewed in profile, the major feature of the chaser was the pilot house, built just forward of the center of the boat. (See diagrams on pages 16-19.) The main mast with a crow's nest was located just behind the pilot house. Below decks, the officers' stateroom and the radio room were located directly under the pilot house, and forward of that was ammunition storage and crew's quarters. Toward the stern from the officer's stateroom were the engine room, crew's quarters and the galley. The fuel tanks were under the officer's stateroom, and storage lockers of various types were scattered throughout.

*Leisure time on deck of a chaser, showing an open hatch. The 3"/23-caliber deck gun is shown covered by canvas, upper right.*

The identification markings on the chasers varied from region to region. Generally "SC" and the vessel's number were painted on the hull on each side of the bow and on the crow's nest canvas – as in "SC 93" – but sometimes letter codes were assigned, and the vessel's hull number would be located on the flying bridge canvas, the bridge wing canvas or in some other location.

Among the earliest uses of hull markings other than the chaser's number were convoy letters, used to aid in signaling other vessels in the convoys as the chasers crossed the Atlantic and to assist in holding tactical maneuvers and target practice.[10] Later hull markings appear to have been arranged locally by base staff needing to maintain order in the ports, accounting for the variations at different times and locations throughout and after the war. Lt. Dole's second chaser, for instance, was marked "SC 354" on the bow most of the time, but bore the marking "AU" for a time, and was marked "BT" during the Northern Russia Expedition. Generally, these designations were simply assigned alphabetically in series: "AR," "AS," "AT," "AU" and so on.

**Engines**

To fit the boats with engines was a difficult undertaking. The sound-detecting devices soon to be fitted to the chasers wouldn't be of much use with the engines running. The engines for a chaser would have to be stopped and silenced quickly to allow for quiet listening periods, then started up again equally quickly to pursue a detected sub. Moreover, in selecting a source for production of the engines, consideration had to be given to the ongoing work of building engines for other, larger war vessels.

After reviewing several proposals, the Bureau of Steam Engineering selected a gasoline engine produced by Standard Motor Construction Company of Jersey City, New Jersey. The Standard 220-hp engine was already widely in use in the ML boats and had a record of adequate performance. The designers of the ML boats had considered using lighter, faster engines, but after some debate they settled on the heavier, slower and more powerful Standard 220-hp engine, in order to provide greater power in heavy seas.[11]

For the 110' American chasers, use of the Standard 220-hp engine would mean installing three engines per chaser instead of two, to deliver the 600 hp called for in the engineering design. But the timing was right, in that the manufacturers were nearing completion of their orders for British and Italian boats, and were geared up for production. The cost of installing an additional engine and the increase in the need for spare parts and maintenance seemed more than offset by the advantage of availability, so Standard Motor Construction Company was awarded the contract.[12]

## 110' Submarine Chaser Deck Plan

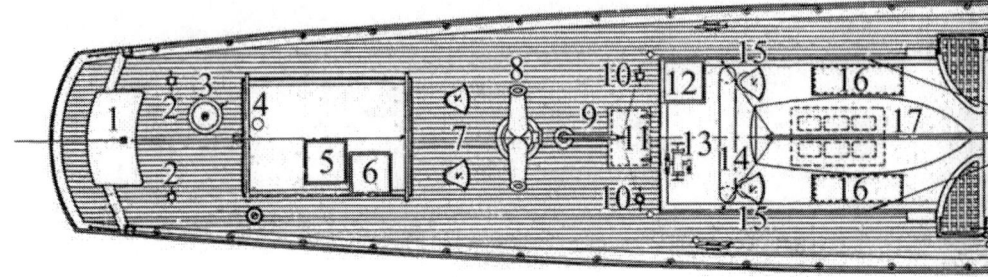

1. Rudder quadrant cover.
2. Mooring bitts.
3. Manhole to lazaret (food storage).
4. "Charley Noble" vent stack for galley stove.
5. Hatch to galley.
6. Hatch to aft crew's quarters.
7. Cowl ventilators for aft crew's quarters.
8. Y-gun. Initially a Davis non-recoiling gun was mounted here on some chasers.
9. Crane for loading depth charges.
10. Towing bitts.
11. Hatch to stowage.
12. Hatch to engine room.
13. Bilge and/or fire fighting hand pump.
14. Life raft, stowed on edge.
15. Cowl ventilators for engine room.
16. Lockers. Not present on many chasers.
17. Wherry, with skylight to engine room below.
18. Gratings for machine gunner footing, and machine guns mounted on bridge wings.

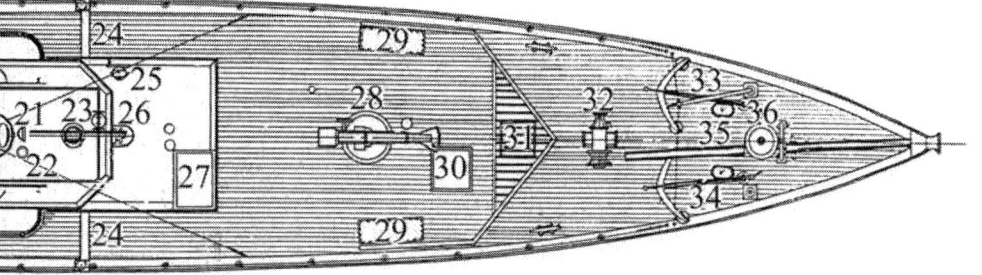

19. Cowl ventilators for engine room.
20. Crow's nest.
21. Signal light.
22. Pelorus.
23. Bearing indicator represented by the line over the circle.
24. Rudder cable covers. Cables ran inboard or outboard of the life line stanchions.
25. Gasoline transfer hand pump.
26. Safety shield for radio antenna lead-in.
27. Hatch to radio room, officers' quarters and magazine/listening room.
28. Deck gun. Under the barrel is the cowl ventilator for crew's quarters (partially obscured).
29. Storage lockers.
30. Hatch to forward crew's quarters.
31. Crib for stowage.
32. Anchor windlass.
33. 250 lb. anchor.
34. 150 lb. anchor.
35. Chain trough.
36. Manhole to stowage.

## 110' Submarine Chaser Inboard Profile

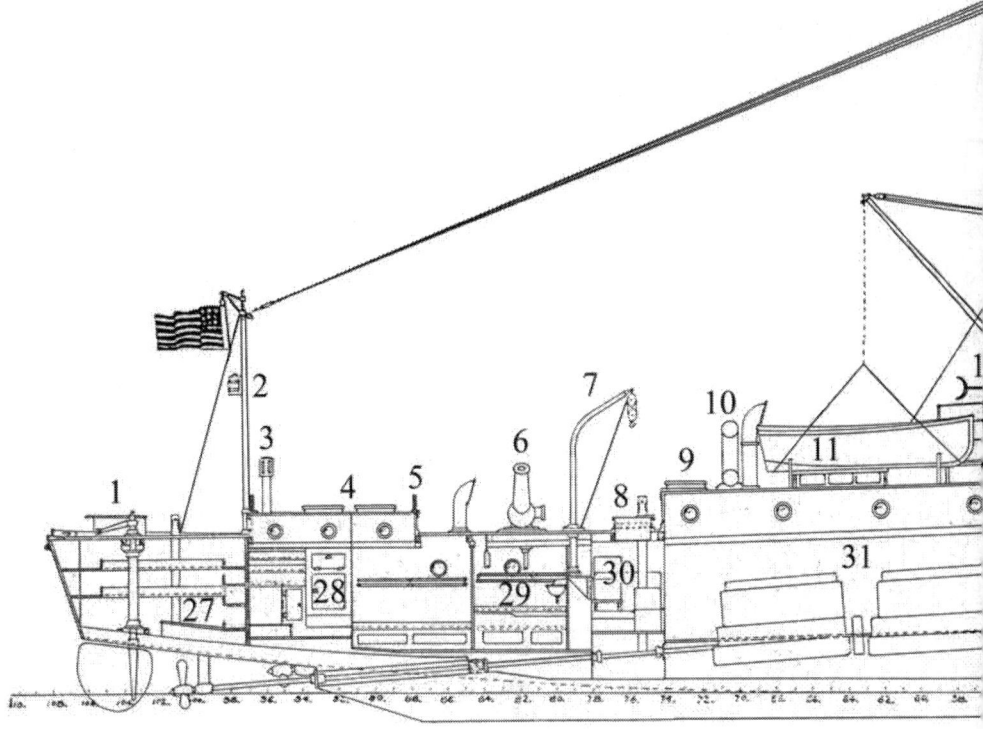

1. Rudder quadrant.
2. Stern light.
3. "Charley Noble" stack for galley stove.
4. Hatches to galley and aft crew's quarters.
5. Cable guides for towing, fore and aft on deck house.
6. Y-gun.
7. Crane for loading depth charges.
8. Hatch to stowage.
9. Hatch to engine room.
10. Life raft, stowed on edge.
11. Wherry, with skylights to engine room below.
12. Machine gun (Colt or Lewis).
13. White masthead light.
14. Twin red lights, located six feet from the top of the mast. The white masthead light and these red lights were used for nighttime maneuvering signals.
15. Wireless telephone antenna. Connected to upper yard (not visible from this perspective). Sometimes a "pig stick" was affixed to the aft side of the mast below the upper yard, where the commissioning pennant was flown.
16. Crow's nest and mainmast range light. The lower yard was typically just below, but its location varied.
17. Pelorus on stand, signal light and bearing indicator.
18. Ship's bell. Location of the bell varied.
19. Pilot house. Sometimes a canvas visor

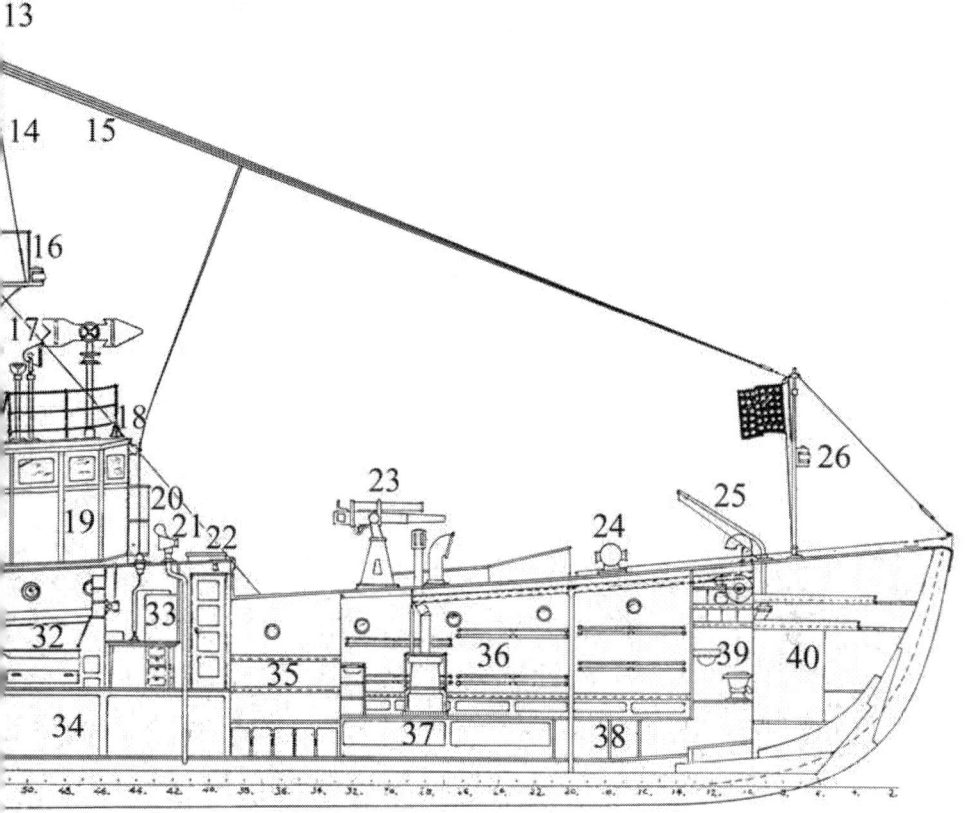

was installed above the windows.
20. Safety shield for antenna lead-in.
21. Bilge vent.
22. Hatch to radio room, officers' quarters and magazine/listenting room.
23. 3"/23-caliber deck gun. Some chasers had a Hotchkiss 6-pound Single Purpose gun here. Under the barrel is the stack for coal-fired heating unit.
24. Anchor windlass.
25. Anchor davit.
26. Forward range light.
27. Lazaret.
28. Galley.
29. Aft crew's quarters. Bunks represented by horizontal lines.
30. Stowage of depth charges and other items.
31. Engine room. Center engine aft of starboard/port engines. Air tanks, stacked, forward, for starting the engines.
32. Officers' state room. Hatch to pilot house, above.
33. Wireless room and radio man's quarters.
34. Gasoline tanks.
35. Magazine, and listening room.
36. Forward crew's quarters.
37. Fresh water tanks.
38. Anchor chain locker.
39. Crew's toilet.
40. Stowage.

This was seen as a compromise by some, who considered the theoretical top speed of 18 knots that these engines would deliver to be less than ideal. Moreover, gasoline engines were not widely used in shipbuilding, and some of the refinements that would later be regarded as essential – such as electric start and closed crankcase design – weren't available yet in a mass-produced marine engine. But time wouldn't permit the design of a new engine. Each chaser would be fitted with three Standard engines.

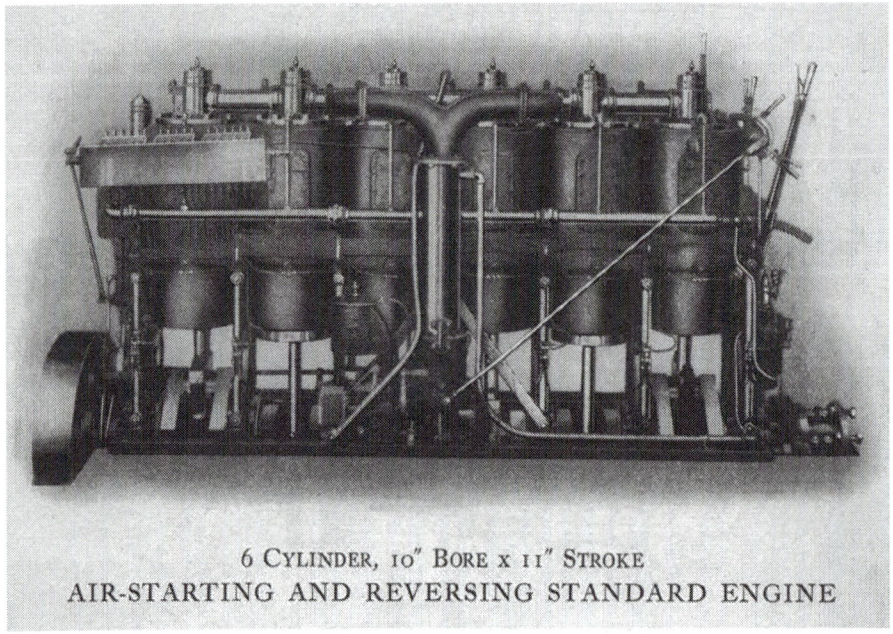

6 CYLINDER, 10" BORE x 11" STROKE
AIR-STARTING AND REVERSING STANDARD ENGINE

*The Standard Motor Construction Company 220-hp engine.*

To meet an increased demand for engines due to a doubling of the initial order for submarine chasers, Standard Motor subcontracted some of the production work to Lyons-Atlas Company of Indianapolis, Indiana. Each completed engine was tested by Standard Motor for economy, power and reliability.[13]

This three-engine arrangement also meant that to run the engine room would require, in addition to a chief petty officer in charge of the engine room, a minimum of three men per shift to operate the engines. These men were known as the "black gang," and the working conditions of the engine rooms made them look the part: The men worked in choking, stifling smoke for hours at a time, and emerged after a watch blackened with oil, grease and exhaust. The Standard 220 was an open crankcase engine, a crude affair compared to

*Engine room of a chaser, looking aft, showing the three 220-hp engines.. National Archives, RG-165WW.*

the enclosed engines we are used to seeing in cars. A lubricating oil reservoir was filled by hand, using a funnel and strainer. From the reservoir, seventeen pumping units forced oil through seventeen feeds to various lubrication points. Excess oil collected in an open pan under the engine.

The design intent was that as the engine speed changed, the pumps, driven by cams powered by the engine, would self-regulate, increasing and decreasing the oil flow. But the engineers had to monitor and adjust the lines individually, refill the reservoir periodically to keep the engine from seizing, and empty the pan under each engine regularly to prevent the oil from spilling over the top of the pan into the bilges. In high seas this task was nearly impossible.

Whether the seas were calm or stormy, any time the boat was under way the engines required constant attention, oiling, monitoring the throttle position to keep the engine operating at peak efficiency, and monitoring wear-and-tear parts such as bearings to avoid overheating. Even when the boat was not under way, the black gang was kept busy with maintenance and repairs. Nobody wanted to be at sea with an engine out of commission.

In addition to the three main engines, each chaser was equipped with a two-cylinder gasoline-powered auxiliary engine, also manufactured by Standard Motor Construction Company. The auxiliary engine generated electricity to power the batteries for the radio equipment, fans, electric heaters and other electric devices on board, and generated compressed air for starting the engines in the event the main engines' compressed air tanks should fail.

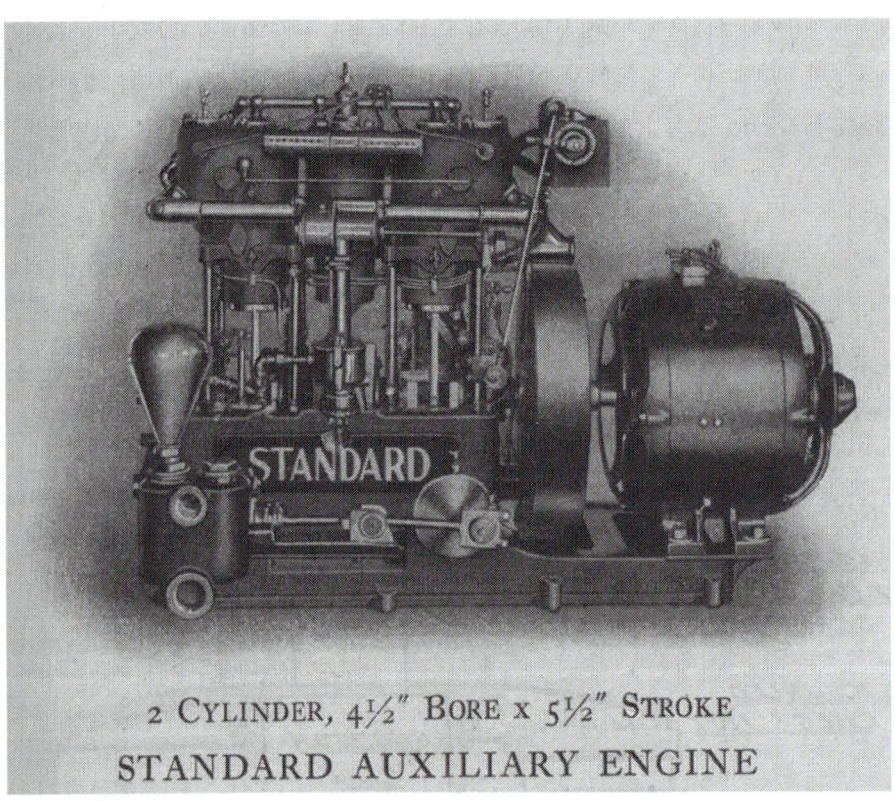

*The Standard Motor Construction Company auxiliary engine.*

This arrangement led to serious unintended consequences for many chasers: explosions and fires in the engine room. The engine rooms were equipped with ventilation fans, but because the auxiliary engine was not always in use to power the batteries, and the explosive nature of gasoline fumes wasn't widely understood at the time, the ventilation fans weren't always in use when the main engines were running.

It is hard to imagine working under those conditions without ventilation. Even with the fans on in these tiny rooms, breathing must have been difficult, with hot engines emitting burning oil fumes, exhaust and gasoline vapor. Engine room explosions and fires would be a persistent problem for the duration of the chasers' duties during and after the war, taking the lives of some chaser men, and resulting in severe damage or loss of several chasers. As late as 2 July 1919, the navy published Circular Letter D-2, warning chaser crews that "Recent frequent explosions and fires on submarine chasers lead the Bureau to believe that the hazards on board all vessels using and maintaining a supply of gasoline are not sufficiently understood,"[14] and cautioning them not to allow explosive vapors to accumulate in enclosed spaces.

The engines were difficult to operate, even setting aside the issue of the open crankcases and the fumes. There were no clutch and shift levers to allow the engineers to disengage the propellers or shift from forward to reverse on the run. Instead of operating on a system of gears to turn the drive shaft in one direction or the other, there were two complete sets of valve cams, one for forward and one for reverse. Moreover, whenever the engine was running, the propeller was turning. To move ahead from a cold stop, the engineers primed

*Engine Room, probably SC 45. (T. Woofenden Collection.)*

the engine by pouring some gasoline into the cylinders, then the so-called "reverse lever" was set to the forward position, which shifted the cam shaft so that the forward cams were engaged, and the engine was started. To stop required shutting off the spark and throwing the reverse lever into neutral, a position which stopped the engine short, ideally with a charge of unburned gasoline in one cylinder so the engineer wouldn't have to re-prime the engine each time a change in direction was ordered. To put the engine into reverse the engineer would then pull the reverse lever back, engaging the reverse cams, and throw the spark lever on to re-start the engine and drive the crankshaft the other way.

Further complicating the process was the lack of an electric starter. It was an air-started engine, meaning that compressed air was injected to turn it over and start it. While the engine manual assured the engineer that in re-starting a warm engine, "nine out of ten times an ignitor trips and fires in some cylinder and the engine starts automatically without using compressed air,"[15] this certainly wasn't a reliable way to restart. The fallback plan was to use more compressed air; and if there wasn't enough compressed air, then the auxiliary engine would have to be used to replenish the supply. This meant a delay, which could pose serious problems in maneuvering the vessel.

More often than the crews might have liked to admit, stopping was accomplished by slamming the boat into the pier, or into another ship. In January, SC 93 experienced this firsthand, when SC 143 ran into its stern, carrying away the flagstaff shroud and bending stanchions.[16] Then a few weeks prior to their departure from New London, Ens. Dole found himself on the other side of the issue. He tells the story to his brother Louis as follows:

> I am in trouble at present. Rammed another boat. It was not my fault but the responsibility falls upon me. In getting away from dock I gave bells port engine slow astern. The bell was answered half speed ahead. I rang full speed astern on all three engines and got full speed ahead out of the port motor. The center and starboard engines did not take and I plunked the boat ahead of me (No. 90) and did considerable damage to her stern. I thought I was going to cut her in half. This boat suffered no material damage. They have a lot of gold braid making an investigation at present, as far as I can make out. Expect to get some present as a result. I have a good case as far as law is concerned, but that does not go in the Navy. May get removed from command and set ashore, but think when the smoke clears away, I will still be holding down my present job. Will let you know as soon as I get anything definite.[17]

Military authorities reviewed many similar incidents among other chasers during this early training process, and presumably understood the challenges inherent in rapidly training many new officers in the command of a new class of vessel. Ens. Dole retained his command.

Because the chasers would be required to be at sea for days or weeks at a time, fuel consumption was a logistical problem. During convoys, chasers had to re-fuel at sea, a tricky feat even in calm seas. To save fuel, the chasers were designed so that they could run on two engines instead of three; but if the engineers were simply to stop the center engine, the stopped center propeller would have created enormous drag. Therefore, to run on two engines the engineers would crank a hand screw to tighten a brake band on the drive shaft of the center engine, stopping the shaft from turning. They would then loosen a coupling and disconnect the shaft, then release the brake band, allowing the propeller to rotate freely, disconnected from the engine.

Another advantage, probably not an intentional design feature, was that in a pinch the crew could shut down the center engine and use it for parts. This was handy on long voyages, or any time they were out of range of a repair ship.

## Coming Aboard SC 93

As the production and delivery of new submarine chasers proceeded, the navy undertook the work of training men to take command of these new vessels. They needed men who could navigate, who could command a crew of up to 24 men and who could quickly learn the emerging science of ASW, such as it was in 1917.

Many of the men called for this duty were members of the U.S. Naval Reserve Forces, George S. Dole among them. Dole had served on USS *Malay*, a converted yacht that patrolled the north Atlantic coast, but in 1917 as the American war movement developed, he was working in an administrative capacity, tracking the locations and duties of officers. "Work from 9 to 5," he tells Louis, in the fall of 1917. "These are the shortest hours I ever worked."[18] Dole was restless. He was receiving good reports, and was being primed to take charge of the Assignment to Duty department. "I can't see myself in that job, tho," he tells Louis, "and have requested sea duty." Chaser service would soon offer him the opportunity he was looking for: a command of his own, a tour of duty overseas and the promise of the experience of a lifetime.

Since well before his navy service, Dole had been a skilled navigator. With his father, Henry Clinton Dole, and his brother Louis, he had spent summers sailing and fishing.

To prepare for chaser service, Dole attended Cadet School at the

*Crew members on USS Malay. George S. Dole with pipe.*

Massachusetts Institute of Technology, where he received training in deck duties, navigation, mathematics, armament and many other skills related to commanding a navy vessel. Cadets were required to understand the use of navigational equipment, to show a knowledge of signaling systems and tactical methods, and in general to demonstrate a knowledge of seamanship.[19] This was of necessity a crash course. There wasn't time for the chaser men to acquire years of experience, or even to attend a typical officer training program.

Commissioned as an ensign, Dole was given command of SC 93, which was docked at the navy yard in New York for preparations, soon to sail for New London, Connecticut, where the men would engage in a second phase of crash-course training, this time in the new science of ASW.

Some accounts of the American chasers are highly critical of the lack of regular navy men in command positions, and some of the accounts of men who served on subchasers illustrate the difficulties officers faced because of their inexperience. But for the chaser men themselves, it became something of a mark of distinction. Ens. Alexander Moffat, for instance, commanding officer of SC 143, titled his autobiographical account of life on the chasers, *Maverick Navy*, paying homage to the relative lack of customary military order on his command.

Ens. Dole came to the job with some distinct advantages over some of the other chaser commanding officers. First, he had significant experience in navigation, more than adequate for the work of handling a submarine chaser. He knew how to read nautical charts, how to figure his location using a sextant, and how to operate small vessels. Being an Olympic-gold-medal-winning wrestler must certainly have been another mark in his favor. While some of the other chaser officers complained of being unable to keep their crews under control, Ens. Dole had no such problems. An unsigned poem, probably written by a student during his days as wrestling coach at Milton Academy, Milton, Massachusetts, sizes him up:

A Mr. Dole has come to town,
Wears collars size nineteen,
Each afternoon he gets me down,
And sits upon my bean.
He twists my arm with hammer-lock,
He bends me till I creak,
He turns me up upon my block,
I cannot even squeak

Every little movement has a meaning of its own,
This is guaranteed to break the strongest human bone.
And as with scissors he gently squeezes
While the victim just grunts and wheezes,
Then the toe hold he fondly seizes
With a movement that's all his own.[20]

It is also to the credit of Ens. Dole, his crew and the other subchaser crews stationed in the north Atlantic, that they rose to the task as admirably as they did. Their trial started the first day they set foot aboard the chasers. The sheer physical endurance and will power required for this service became readily apparent, for the winter of 1917 was among the coldest ever recorded. The harbor was a mass of ice chunks, the boats white with frost inside and out because of inadequate and largely non-functional heating equipment. Yet in spite of the relentless, bitter cold, these green officers and seamen were actively engaged in the serious business of training for duty against the enemy. With American subs as training targets, the men practiced submarine hunting, formations and tactics, sub-zero weather notwithstanding. Sometimes this meant passing through miles of ice to reach open ocean before exercises

*Subchaser SC 93 anchored off of New London, Connecticut during the harsh winter of 1917-1918. This was the last anchorage of SC 93 in American waters prior to its departure for duties overseas.*

could even begin. In a letter home in December 1917, Ens. Dole describes living in these conditions.

> It is a cold day, 14 below. All the exposed metalwork, bolts, steel plates, port fittings etc. in the quarters, is covered with ¼ inch of frost. The pilot house windows coat with frost faster than it can be removed, so they have to be kept open when under way. Had motors warmed up and ready to start at 6:00 a.m. Came up from the experiment station to sub wharf alongside subs. The weather was thick owing to the water giving off a dense vapor. Could just see the masts of the vessels lying in the harbor when close aboard. Had to just crawl along with steerageway. The subs are waiting for the sun to clear the fog when we will proceed. There is considerable wind loose, and expect we will be busy cutting ice from decks as soon as we get outside. It is quite a job to keep the wheel ropes clear, as they are exposed for ½ the length of deck.

In addition to the cold, the crew was adjusting to life in close quarters. "It is now about noon and I am in my palatial quarters," Ens. Dole informs his brother. "Can stand with my heels together, and without turning touch the four walls with my hands and the ceiling with my elbow. When I get comfortably located in the only chair, and the desk open, the room is occupied, and it would take a small mouse to find his way in to keep me company." The enlisted men might not have seen the humor in his remarks, for their quarters were even tighter.

But overall, Ens. Dole was impressed with the vessel. "I believe the design of these boats is about as near perfect for the work intended as they well could be," he writes home. "They can not be expected to be comfortable, but I believe they will take considerable punishment. They are hard to steer in a sea way but you could expect nothing else from a boat this size."

While the chaser was at anchor, Ens. Dole's time was spent preparing the vessel for the voyage overseas and reviewing and training his crew. "At present the time is pretty well filled making out requisitions orders, answering communications, and following them up," he tells Louis. "The work is far from monotonous. We can profitably fill every hour of the day. I think I have an Executive Officer with all the earmarks of a real sea-dog," he remarks, referring to Ens. Frank A. Snow. "He is a year older than I am, and has had considerable sea experience. He does not know much about navigation, but I am working with him daily on the subject and he is progressing in good shape. Am fortunate to have him with me."

**Learning the Ropes**

SC 93 was commissioned on 4 December 1917, but would remain in the frigid waters of the north Atlantic coast for another two and a half months

*Subchaser SC 80 in choppy seas.*

before making the journey overseas. Ens. Dole and his crew spent the time training and becoming accustomed to the equipment and personality of this new kind of vessel. They faced a long list of obstacles: stray cables fouling the propellers, a persistent lack of adequate heating and ventilation, the challenge of trying to operate the boat in high seas, and an ongoing process of fitting the chaser with listening devices and armament.

In a letter home, Ens. Dole notes some of these difficulties, and how his crew was taking on the responsibility of maintaining the chaser.

> Several things have happened since I last wrote. The principal thing is that I had to get hauled out of the water before I could get the propeller clear. There was some mess of wire on the wheel. An inspector was supposed to be present to look things over. Sent a crew over the side and had the wheel cleared before the boat was out of the water. When the inspector arrived he had nothing to report. One wheel was badly bent as we struck some ice. Another wheel was slightly bent. Got out some sledges and straightened them out in good shape, put files on them and smoothed them so that they are as good as new now. Had this done before the inspector showed up. We were ready to go into the water about 30 minutes after we had the propellers clear and reshaped.[21]

Ice, as usual, was a serious problem. "The bow was scored by the ice," he writes. "I told them that the ice was pretty thick, but they would not change the orders. It is lucky that we did not spring a leak. ... Had to chop ice off the decks and knock it off the rigging." The only respite from the cold came when the chaser was hauled out for fitting the listening tubes, and the crew was able to hook up a line to an electric power source on land, offering reliable and steady power to run the electric heaters. They had tried to use portable oil stoves, but found that in all but a calm sea they were impractical, and even then they emitted acrid fumes, making the severe cold seem a better option, on balance.

Installing the listening equipment required only about three days, and all too soon they were back in the water and the electric heaters were off again. Things were back to normal, cold and wet, and they discovered another challenge of their upcoming service: To operate the listening devices required stopping the boat, which meant that they were left to roll with the waves. They couldn't run across the waves as they could when under way. Ens. Dole describes the experience in a letter home:

> When we stop to use the detectors, the boat rolls to the gunwales on either side, and you have to hang on tight to stay with the ship. It almost looks as

if the man in the crows nest could get a dipper of sea-water from the next wave. He has to tie himself in, and gets wet when we get any headway. Water comes into the pilot house so charts cannot be kept there. I expected to see the pilot house go several times, but it is still on deck. It has taken some terrific wallops. I do not think that you would have much luck trying to push it over. However I am not sure the sea can not do it if it is caught on the side. Do not expect the glass will last long, but have plenty on board to fit out several times.[22]

Photos of chasers with the pilot houses lashed down with cables and planks reveal that not all the chaser commanding officers were as confident of the integrity of the structures.

Much has been written of the Archangel Expedition, the chasers which rounded North Cape and experienced the rigors of the White Sea in the land of the midnight sun. To the chaser men who went farthest North are respectfully dedicated these photographs of Division C, taken in January, 1918. Where? In Block Island Sound, N. Y.

*A photo and caption in the "Subchaser Post" newsletter, January 1921, depicts the icy winter in New York, paying humorous homage to the Northern Russia Expedition of 1919.*

In spite of the weather, the learning curve and all the other difficulties, the crew was enthusiastic, cheerful and well fed. "The cook used to cook aboard a dining car of the N.Y., N.H. & Hartford R.R., and that means he is accustomed to close quarters, and is also some good," Ens. Dole writes in a letter home. He lists a menu of bacon, eggs, French fried potatoes, toast and jam for breakfast, lamb chops, mashed potatoes, beans and gravy for lunch, and Irish stew, biscuits, cheese and peaches for dinner. In a few months the crew would come to miss this rich fare, faced with months of spilled coffee and "canned willie" (corned beef). But there was still time before the adventure would start in earnest, and at the end of 1917 the men were able to enjoy a fine Christmas dinner.

## Final Preparations

As the year 1917 came to a close, the men on the chasers were anxious to get into action. There were rumors that a period of intensified training was about to begin. This would be a welcome change for Ens. Dole, for the weather in New London continued to be brutally cold, and life aboard SC 93 was an ordeal, both physically and mentally.

Ens. Dole writes to his parents of the cold, the tedium of paperwork, and the prospects for a change in the intensity of the work:

> According to promise we will be very busy from now on. Hope so but do not see any indications of it at present. Put in a report on heating system the day it was completed. A hot water system is now being installed, and it promises to be fairly satisfactory. I scraped considerable frost off the present "heating" apparatus, situated over my bunk so that in case of thaw I would have a dry place to sleep. Every bit of exposed metal painted or unpainted looks like part of an artificial ice plant. Am going to wrap the pipes with canvas tonight, also take a shave so the frost will not collect on a week's growth of whiskers. Am enjoying what little work I have to do that does not include clerical work. Have about 30 reports to get out by the first of the year. These reports include everything from clothing outfit of men and officers to detailed description of Radio Installation. There are the usual monthly reports of supplies consumed and needed in addition. Monthly pay accounts, and transfers also come in for attention. Expect to have them done and off on time...[23]

There was also a heightened sense of urgency around preparing the vessels for the journey overseas. The commanding officers of the chasers were responsible for seeing to it that their vessels were properly fitted and ready, which sometimes required persistence. In a requisition follow-up to the Bureau of Navigation, Ens. Dole urges, "...The need of the instruments

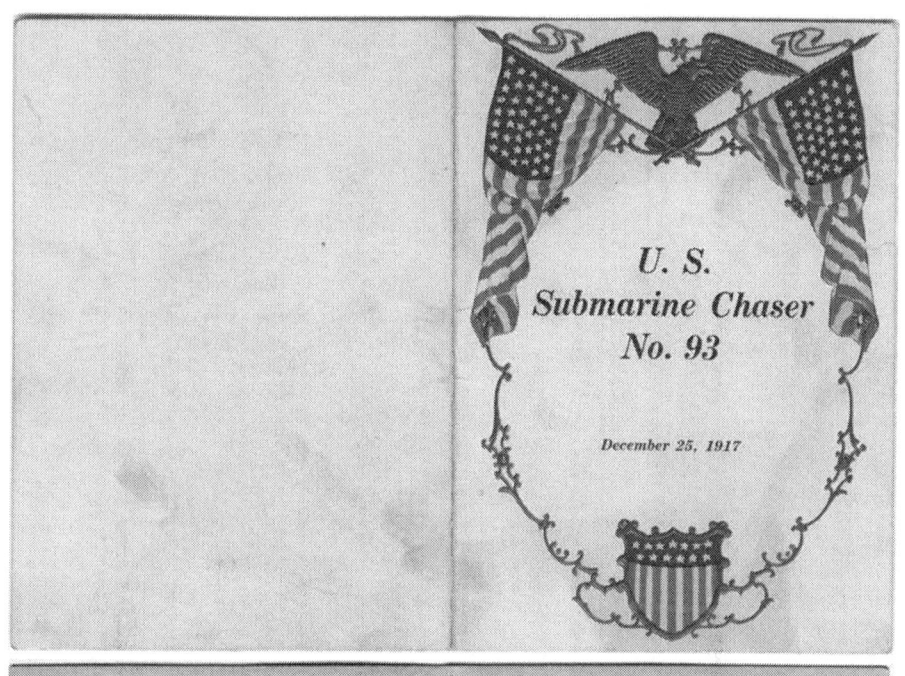

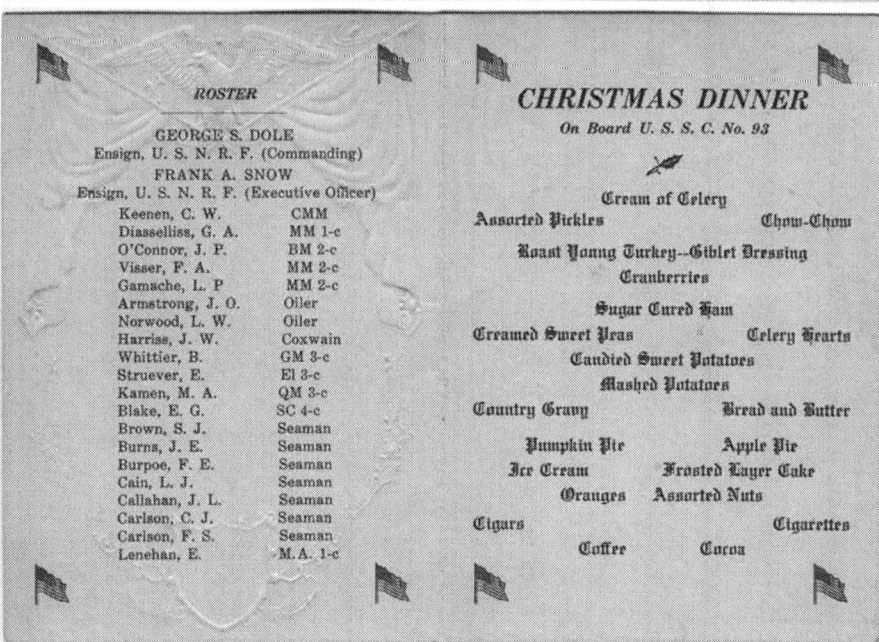

Christmas Dinner card from SC 93, cover / inside panels.[24]

listed in the requisition is urgent. This boat will not be ready for duty until the instruments are supplied. We are greatly handicapped in maneuvers and drills from lack of proper instruments. We are expected to be ready for duty in a few days and the need for the instruments above noted, which we properly rate, is consequently most urgent." Sometimes several of these "urgent" notes were required to produce a result. The little chasers, it seemed, didn't command the attention given to the destroyers and other large vessels.

But eventually SC 93 received its equipment, and attention turned to learning how to use these new tools effectively. There was much to learn, and the chaser officers attended a series of lectures on shore. In addition to practical matters such as the ins and outs of storage batteries, they learned how to use an array of new technological tools including the wireless telegraph and telephone, and new, top-secret devices for detecting and tracking enemy submarines.[25]

As anticipated, there was a sudden increase in activity in mid-January 1918. All liberty was cancelled, and the chasers began intensive training, with multiple days at sea at a stretch. The cold weather persisted and the seas kicked up. On 20 January, Ens. Dole writes to his brother Louis, "The boat is able on the sea. She rolls badly, seems not to be contented till it puts the rails under, and seems insulted if it can not put out the galley fire, also clean off the stack on the furnace. It does not very often take on green water but when she does, all fires give up the ghost." Of the weather, he remarks, "Just returned from maneuvers. The decks were covered with ice, it is some job to stick on deck. Skates would help considerably."

Their maneuvers were made all the more punishing by a driving snow that brought visibility down to nearly zero. On one day's maneuvers, they were able to locate their position off Point Judith, Rhode Island, only by fog signals, arriving late at night at Block Island, New York, relieved to find the jetty. Ice patches, in some cases more than two feet thick, became such a problem that a few days later he had the chaser hauled out and the bow sheathed with sheet iron. Even so, it was a hazardous business, and on more than one occasion he found himself in tight spots. "Tried to run inshore," he tells Louis of one such experience, "but the ice field closed in and we had to get out of that place in a hurry to prevent being caught in a jam. The tide was terrific, and the ice was shelved in many places. We had to steer clear of such places as it must have been about 10 ft. thick in places." But he seemed to take it with good humor. "After this winter I believe I will take a polar expedition to keep warm," he writes, foreshadowing a later part of his tour of duty when he would lead a unit of chasers above the Arctic Circle to northern Russia.

Even travel on open waters was a trial. "On the way back we were bows to the seas and the spray froze as soon as it hit the deck or ports," Ens. Dole writes. "Had to keep two men wiping ports so we could see. It was some job to stick on the top-sides. Salt water ice is just soft enough to be more slippery than grease."

Finally on 20 February 1918, Ens. Dole and his fellow chaser commanding officers received Movement Order No. 1 from the commander of the detachment.[26] A dozen chasers including SC 93 would be getting under way soon, under the command of Lt. Comdr. W.M. Falconer, captain of the converted yacht USS *Wadena* (SP 158).

On 23 February, SC 90 (unit leader of Ens. Dole's unit) was caught in an ice floe, and suffered a broken rudder, damaged propeller blades and bent shafts.[27] This reduced the count of chasers in the first crossing to eleven. SC 90 would follow several weeks later.

On 24 February, the chasers left on the first leg of their journey. Present in the convoy were four units of chasers (minus SC 90 of the first unit):

SC 92, SC 93
SC 349, SC 225, SC 327
SC 255, SC 256, SC 143
SC 177, SC 148, SC 244

They would comprise the first group of American submarine chasers to set out across the Atlantic to employ the new tactics of ASW.

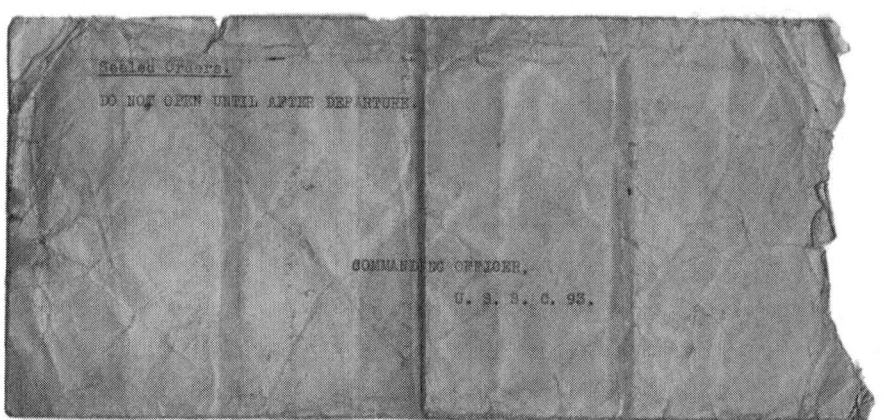

*Sealed Orders envelope from SC 93.*

## Chapter 2 – Antisubmarine Warfare

*"The submarine presents a problem such as the world at large has never dreamed of before. The Kaiser's deep sea monsters represent the most perfect engines of evil genius man has been able to devise."*[1]

Ens. George S. Dole

Naval commanders knew enough about submarines to put together a rigorous program, but they also understood that this new, untried science was subject to adaptation as theories were put to the test. As such, they allowed for revision by the chaser men in implementing the new tactics. "Officers and men of all ranks and ratings are given a certain independence in the execution of the tasks assigned and are expected to show initiative in meeting the different situations as they arise," writes Captain Lyman A. Cotten, commander of the subchaser detachment at Plymouth, in a tactical manual.

While some of the newly commissioned officers had experience at sea, many of them did not, and hardly any had experience in a command position in the navy. Recognizing this, Capt. Cotten notes, "Officers and men of limited sea-going experience may be forgiven for errors of judgment in professional matters, but not for any shortcoming in zeal, loyalty and activity, nor ignorance upon any matter covered by written instructions or orders."[2] A little leeway would be allowed, but only when an infraction could be attributed to being inexperienced in matters of seamanship. Moreover, written instructions were plentiful and highly specific, in spite of the newness of ASW tactics. Every detail of the hunt was documented and circulated to the chaser officers. They were expected to acquire a quick, comprehensive knowledge of the full array of equipment and tactics, and to be ready to employ them effectively.

**Submarine Detection Equipment**

The tactical objective in ASW was to locate enemy submarines and destroy them. Early on it was assumed that deck guns would be used to attack submarines on the surface, but this notion was quickly dismissed when it became clear that the more likely scenario would be detection and pursuit of a submerged submarine. The depth charge, not the deck gun, would become the primary ASW weapon on the chasers. But before any type of attack could be made, the submarine had to be located.

Lt. Alfred Y. Lanphier, an expert on the development of ASW devices and later the commanding officer of the USS *Patterson* Special Hunting Group, offered lectures on detection, and compiled a document for distribution to the commanding officers of the chasers, describing the secret devices on the chasers: the "tubes," the bearing indicator, and a set of tools for plotting the course to a point of attack.[3] These were the state of the art in the budding science of ASW.

***The S.C. Tube hydrophone*** was a T-shaped listening instrument used to detect the sound and bearing of an enemy submarine. It was one of several variations of the C Tube hydrophone design of the Submarine Signal Company, a scientific instrument company (later purchased by Raytheon Company) that had been developing underwater navigation and communications, and maintained a testing facility during the war at Nahant, near Boston, Massachusetts.

Among the versions of the C Tube built by the Submarine Signal Company were the S. and S.C. versions, for Submarine and Sub Chaser, respectively. Thus the technical designation for the device as used on the chasers was the S.C. C Tube, but it was commonly referred to by subchaser crewmen simply as the S.C. Tube. The two models were almost identical except that the submarine version was intended to extend above the top of a submerged submarine, while the subchaser version was inverted to extend below the hull of a chaser.

The vertical section of the S.C. Tube's inverted tee penetrated the hull of the chaser through a water-tight mounting assembly, so that the horizontal part of the tee, below the hull, could be deployed by lowering it into the water beneath the boat when in use, and retracted up against the hull when not in use, protected in a channel mounted low on the starboard side of the hull near the keel.

At each end of the horizontal section of the tee was a rubber bulb, and at the top of the vertical section – inside the chaser in the listening room – a stethoscope device conveyed the sound from one of the bulbs to one ear of the listener and from the other bulb to the other ear. The entire inverted T could be rotated by the listener by means of a hand wheel. A graduated dial showed the orientation of the tubes relative to the axis of the boat, so that the magnetic compass bearing of a detected sound could be determined by correcting the angle shown on the dial to account for the heading of the chaser. The device did not indicate the depth of the submarine.

***The M.B. Tube*** was a modification of the C Tube design concept. In this case, the horizontal tubes extending from the vertical tube were of non-equal length, the goal being to aim the longer end directly at a source of sound. Imagine if the horizontal ends of the tee were the same length, as with the S.C. Tube, and one end of the pipe were aimed directly at a source of sound. In that case, sound traveling through the forward pipe's rubber bulb would reach the center (vertical) pipe sooner than sound traveling through the rearward pipe,

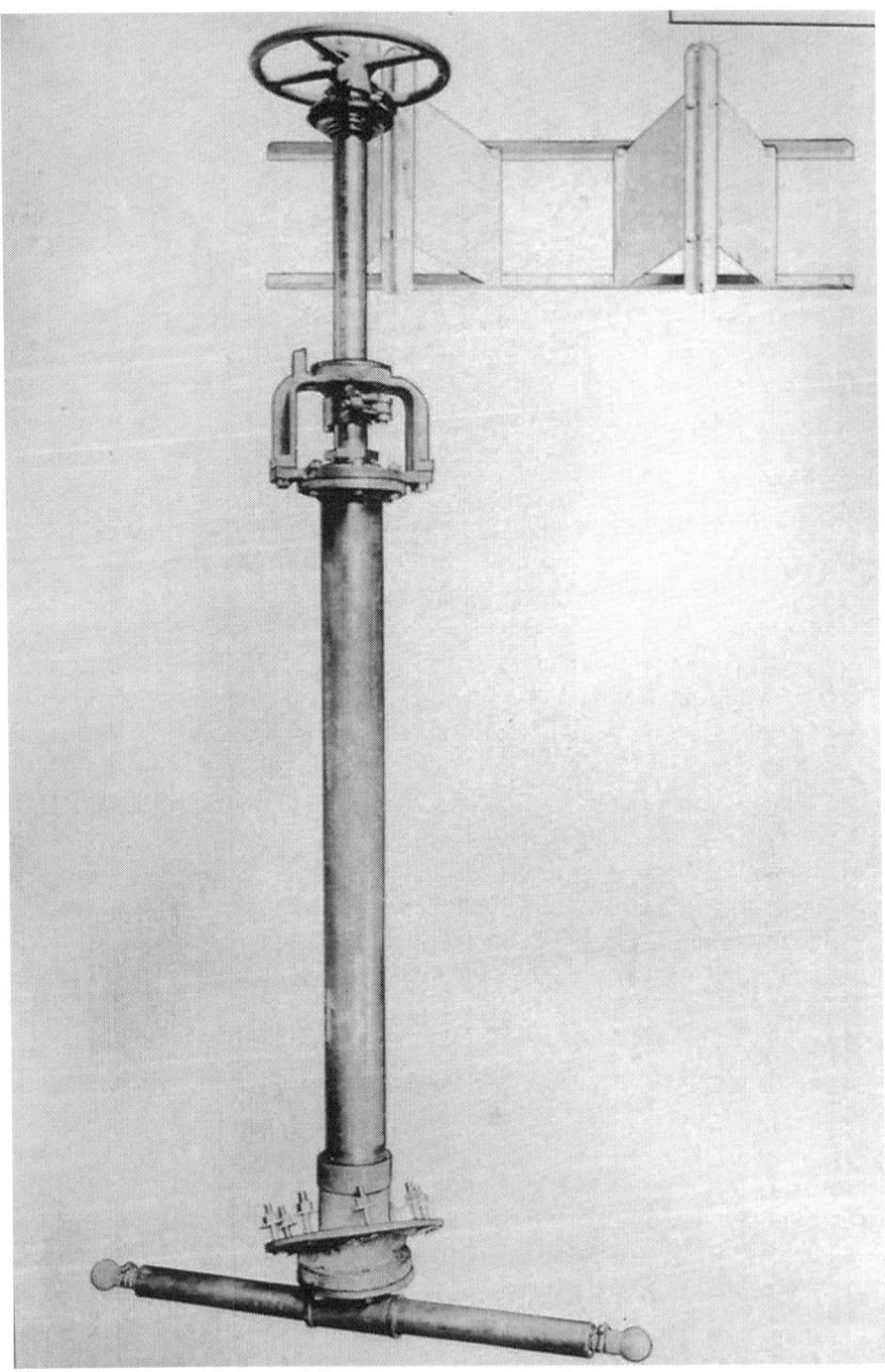

*The S.C. C Tube Hydrophone. (Raytheon Company Archives.)*

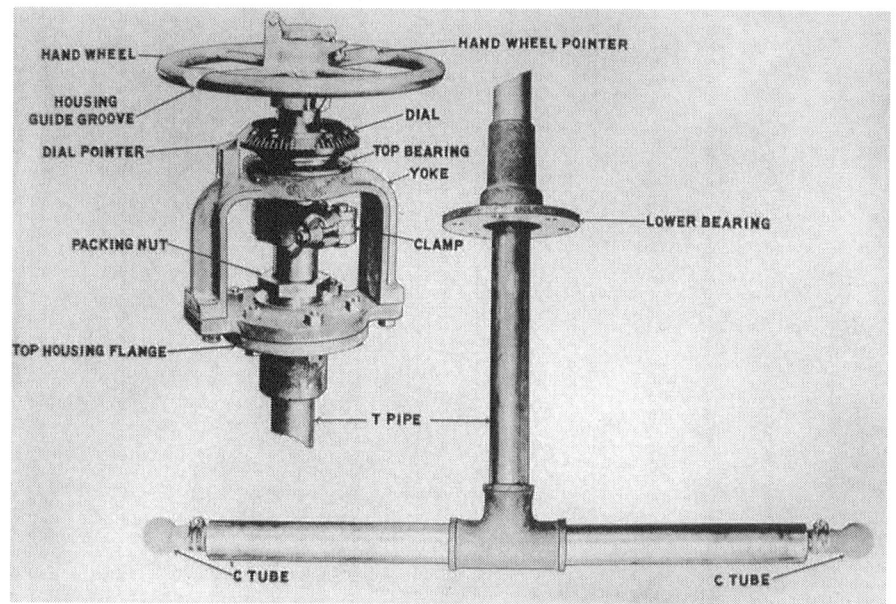

*The hand wheel apparatus and tee assembly of the S.C. C Tube. The horizontal section is 44" long. (Raytheon Company Archives.)*

because the latter would have to travel the length of the forward and rearward pipe before reaching the rubber bulb. Since sound travels faster in water than in air, the M.B. Tube was designed with tee ends of calculated, unequal length, so that when the longer forward pipe was aimed directly at the source, the sound waves would reach the bulb on the shorter, rearward pipe at the right moment to allow the sound to travel through the rear pipe and reach the center pipe at the precise moment that the sound traveling along the forward pipe reached the center. Thus the sound from both ends would travel up to the listener's ears at the same time, resulting in a clear, strong sound.

**The K Tube,** another device designed and manufactured by the Submarine Signal Company, was not actually a tube at all. Rather, it was a large, triangular frame with a microphone sealed in a waterproof rubber casing attached to each tip.

The triangular frame was lowered overboard on the windward side, and as the boat drifted away, the frame was held in a horizontal plane at a fixed depth by means of cables on the frame connected to a float. It was connected to the receiving apparatus on the chaser by a tether cable, which also contained the wire leads from the microphones.

The receiving apparatus, the *compensator*, was used to control the signals

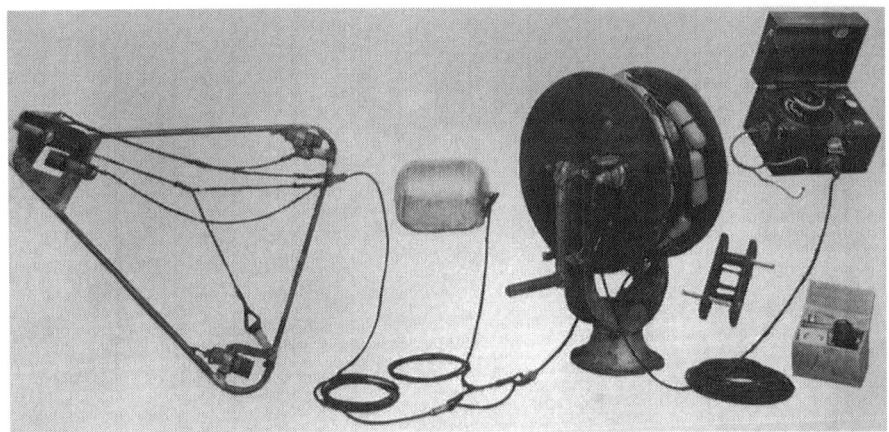

*Complete K Tube device. Left to right, the triangular frame, the main float, the tether line reel with small floats on the line, the hand reel (for the line between the compensator and the main reel), the compensator box (top right) and spare parts box (bottom right). (Raytheon Company Archives.)*

*Compensator box, open to show internal components. (Raytheon Company Archives.)*

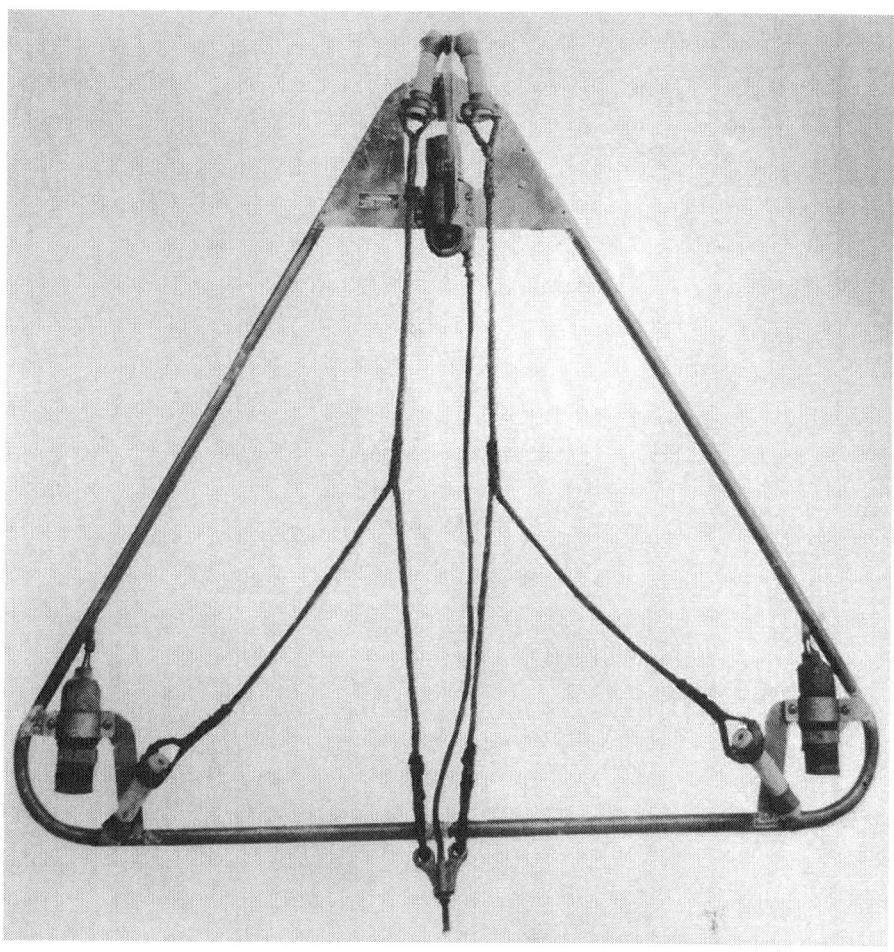

*The K Tube frame detail. (Raytheon Company Archives.)*

from the microphones and to determine the direction of the sound source. The microphones were used in pairs, only two of the three microphones active at a given time. A set of two telephone receivers in the compensator box converted the signals from the two active microphones to sound, and directed the two sound streams separately to the ear pieces of a stethoscope device, so that the listener heard the sound picked up by one microphone in one ear and the sound picked up by the other microphone in the other ear.

Since the distance from a sound source to each of the microphones would be slightly different, the time required for the sound stream to reach each ear would also be slightly different. The compensator was the device used to compensate for this slight difference, advancing one sound stream slightly as it retarded the other, until the two streams reached the ears at the same time, resulting in a clear sound. Tuning the sound in this manner was accomplished by turning a hand wheel on the compensator box, which finely adjusted the length of the air passage from the receivers to each ear, lengthening one as it shortened the other. A scale showed the amount of movement of the wheel, which corresponded to the angle of bearing of the sound relative to the position of the K Tube frame.

To measure the bearing of a detected sound, the listener would first take a reading using one set of two microphones, and mark the angle of the sound source. He would then switch to a second pair of microphones and take another reading. These two readings were used to confirm the angle of the sound and to determine if the angle of the sound relative to the position of the K Tube frame was to the right or left of perpendicular. A third reading, from the third pair, could be used to double check the result.[4]

*Listener using K Tube hydrophone on submarine chaser SC 93.*

A set of floats on the tether line allowed the chaser men to observe the bearing of the K Tube relative to the boat, so that by correcting the listener's results to account for the bearing of the boat, the magnetic bearing of the detected sound could be calculated.

For use on a submarine chaser, the K Tube frame was built of nonmagnetic metal, brass and bronze, so that it could be lashed to the front of the pilot house without interfering with the ship's compass.[5]

***The Trailing Wire*** was a reel of phosphor-bronze wire, used to detect submarines sitting on the bottom. A weight was attached to the end, either a length of chain insulated from the wire or a wooden triangle weighted on one corner, and the wire was reeled out and dragged across the ocean floor. If the wire came into contact with a metal object, a small electrical current traveled up the wire to an electric annunciator, signaling to the crew that they had

*Reel of phosphor-bronze wire on a chaser. (See this image in larger context on page 71.) The "X" on the stern is probably a convoy identification marking.*

found something. They would then throw a marker buoy overboard and sweep from the other direction, throwing another marker buoy overboard when once again the annunciator sounded. The true location of the object should then be centered between the buoys.

***The Bearing Indicator*** was a large, wooden arrow, painted white on the tip and red on the feather, with a light on each end. It was mounted on a post

*Obverse of the bearing indicator on submarine chaser SC 90, showing the lights mounted on the tip and feather, for nighttime signaling.*

*Reverse of the bearing indicator, showing hand-wheels and graduated dial used to position the arrow. (T. Woofenden Collection.)*

on the flying bridge, and could be rotated using a hand wheel, a graduated dial showing the angle of inclination. It could also be turned to display the illuminated side of the arrow to the unit leader – the lead vessel in a unit of three chasers – whether the unit leader was on the port side or the starboard.

This allowed the wing boats – the chasers on either side of the unit leader – to indicate to the unit leader the bearing of a detected sub. The radio telephone, a new device for the navy ships of 1917, would prove the more efficient tool for this purpose, but in the early days of training the expectation was that the chaser crews would use the radio telephone as little as possible, and rely instead on visual signals as the primary means of ship-to-ship communication.

**The Position Plotter** was a device used to determine the correct bearing of a chase and the likely distance of the target. The unit leader in a three-chaser unit would receive three sets of sound bearings: one from each of the wing boats and one from his own listeners. He would then triangulate the location of the sound's source using the position plotter.

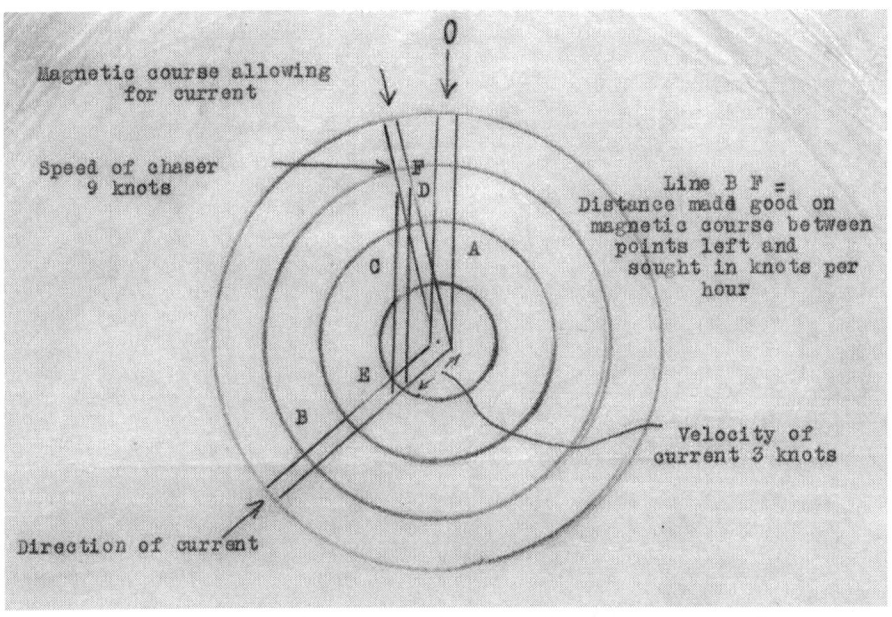

*Illustration of the use of a position plotter to show an estimation of course and distance allowing for current.*[6]

The device consisted of glass plates with celluloid pointers used to mark the bearings reported by the listeners. Concentric circles on the upper plate represented distance, and while the bottom plate was fixed, the top plate could be rotated to correct for the chaser's bearing. The convergence of the three pointers marked the location of the enemy sub.

The device also could be used for other types of calculations of distance and course, such as to compute an approximate course and distance to a location, compensating for currents.

***The Course Protractor*** was a round, transparent card made of celluloid with a slot in it, used as an aid in plotting on paper each course computation during a chase. Marks radiating from the end of the slot served as protractor lines, so that each successive segment of the chaser's course could be plotted relative to the last by positioning the card over the paper, lining up one end of the slot at the end of the last segment, and drawing a new line in pencil to represent the next segment. The result was a map of the chase.

In addition to these tools for detecting, hunting and attacking enemy submarines, there was plenty of paperwork. Every sighting and pursuit was reported to the naval base. These reports indicated the location of the attack, the time, which chasers were engaged and the precise actions taken, including the number of depth charges dropped and whether or not they exploded.

The report form included a blank page on which the commanding officer of the lead chaser could illustrate the course of the attack. To confirm the sinking of a submarine was extremely difficult. Often the only evidence of success was the set of reports itself, insufficient to result in official recognition of a submarine kill.

**Organization of Chaser Units**

Ens. Dole's chaser would serve on the barrage line as a wing boat in a three-chaser unit, Unit E, under the command of Lt. Oscar Borgeson, commanding officer of SC 90 and senior-ranking officer in the unit. SC 90 was thus the unit leader, and would typically operate with SC 93 on one flank and SC 92, under the command of Ens. Joseph H. Mundy, on the other.

This three-chaser unit arrangement was not the initial conception for the chasers. Early in the planning process, several different theories for organization of chasers had been considered and rejected. At the outset, for instance, there was an assumption that chasers would always operate accompanied by a destroyer. Presumably the idea was that the chasers would engage in the hunt, using their new listening and plotting devices, and the destroyer would be on hand to finish the job when a sub was located, and to support the little chasers at sea. This idea was abandoned when it became clear that groups of chasers could work efficiently on their own.[7]

Another early theory was that chasers ought to be organized into units of six, with three serving as a "tactical unit" and three as a "patrol unit." In the event of the detection of an enemy submarine, the tactical unit would engage in a chase, while the patrol unit would remain in position to detect any other hostile forces in the area.[8] This plan was rejected on similar grounds of inefficiency. Three chasers could both plan and execute an attack. By the time the thirty-six chasers of the Otranto Barrage had reached Corfu, it was three chasers to a unit, a configuration that persisted for the duration of the war.

## Elements of Sub Chasing

The subchaser officers drilled their crew in three elements of the hunt: the search, the chase and the attack. Each element involved its own unique tactics and procedures.

**The Search.** In hunting for enemy submarines, local conditions were the greatest tactical variable. Sometimes U-boats were spotted by aircraft, for instance. In this case, the commanding officer of a chaser might receive orders to hunt for the sub in a particular localized region. In other cases his unit would be engaged in general patrol, hunting for subs by canvassing large tracts of open ocean to detect any enemies lurking beneath.

In general, there were three different methods: anchored patrol, drifting patrol and running patrol.

The idea behind *anchored patrol* was to engage in long listening periods, unburdened by the need to perform maneuvers. If a unit were on anchored patrol, the engineers of all three chasers could keep their engines off, and the listeners could concentrate on listening for extended periods.

*Drifting patrol* was intended to be used to find subs lingering on the bottom or known to be located in a given area. For example, if Unit E were to receive a report of a submarine in the vicinity that had been sighted by a passing aircraft, Lt. Borgeson might order a drifting patrol. The three chasers would be at the ready for immediate action, hence anchors aweigh. But the engines would be off so that, as in anchored patrol, the listeners could engage in uninterrupted listening periods.

*Running patrol*, probably the most common tactic actually employed by the chasers, was used to cover a large area. The chasers would run forward for a given distance, fall silent for a fixed listening period, and run forward again. These listening periods were in principle to be observed by all ships on the barrage line. In practice, it took months of coordination and adjustments of the chasers' locations relative to the other ships to achieve the goal of quiet intervals when subs could be detected, uninterrupted by the masking noise of some other ship trolling through the listening period.

The standard formation during the search was for the three chasers to run line-abreast. In Unit E, Lt. Borgeson's vessel would operate in the middle, with Ens. Dole and Ens. Mundy at equal distances on either flank. Aside from the obvious need to have sound bearings from multiple angles in order to triangulate the source of the sound, there was a practical advantage to this formation. If Ens. Dole and Ens. Mundy merely had to keep their chasers in a straight line at a fixed distance from Lt. Borgeson, it was much simpler to stay in proper formation.

Ship-to-ship communications took several forms, depending on the type of information and the need for speed. Radio telegraphs operated from the

*Signal flag lockers ("flag bags") on bridge wings, bearing indicator on flying bridge concealed by canvas cover, and shape signal raised.*

radio room were used for ordinary, non-emergency message transmittal. During hunts, two-foot tall shape signals – top, cross and drum – were used in various combinations for daytime communication of formation and distance. For instance, the cross shape at half mast indicated "prepare to attack." A cone fully raised indicated "under way."

At night a set of dot and dash codes on the white light on the truck and red lights mounted on the mast six feet lower were used in place of the shape signals. These lights, called "maneuvering lights" or "hearing lights," were operated by a set of switches in the pilot house, one for the white light, one for the red

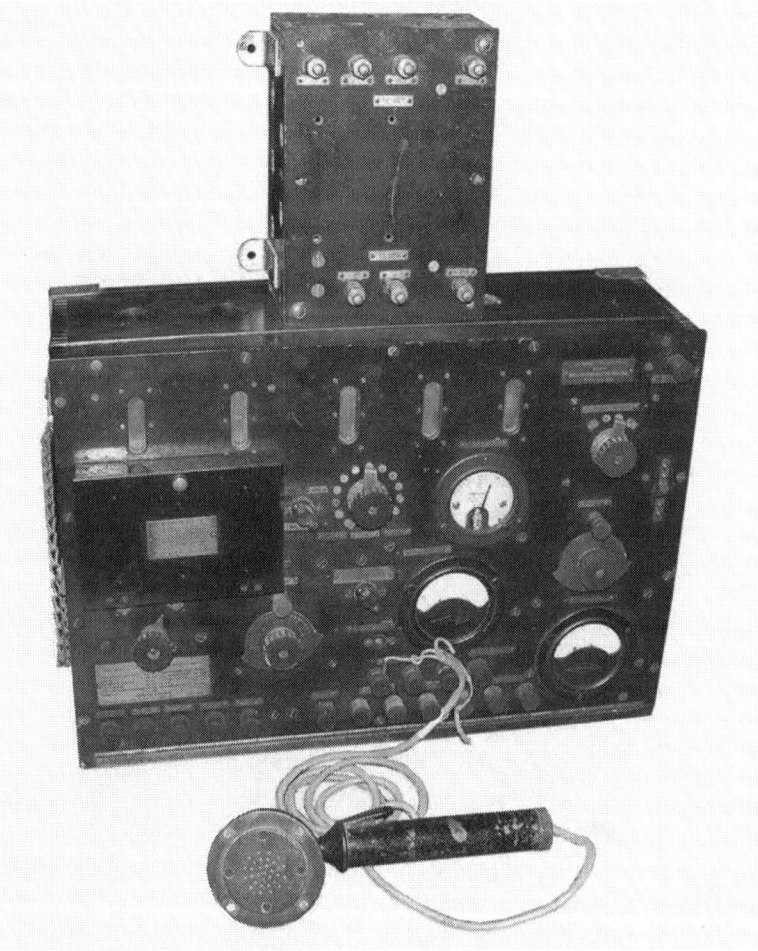

*CW 925 Radio Telephone Transmitter/Receiver, a component of the CW 924 set designed by Western Electric and installed on the chasers. (New England Wireless and Steam Museum, East Greenwich, RI.).*

and one to operate them simultaneously. For instance, flashing white and red lights three times indicated "prepare to attack." A steady white light indicated "under way."

To report the bearings during a hunt, there was the innovative bearing indicator and a new radio technology, the radio telephone. To send a signal by bearing indicator, the arrow was pivoted to face the other chaser, and the bearing of the detected sound shown by rotating the arrow to the angle of the bearing. The lights on the bearing indicator were used for nighttime bearing signals.

The subchasers were among the first U.S. Navy vessels to receive radio telephones, a new device for ship-to-ship voice communication. That the chasers were fitted with them had nothing to do with normal priority, however. Typically the chasers seemed to be last in line, the larger vessels receiving a greater share of attention from the supply depots. But it was clear that fast communication would be particularly critical when hunting U-boats, so even

*Internal components of the CW 925 Transmitter/Receiver.*
*(New England Wireless and Steam Museum, East Greenwich, RI.)*

before many larger warships received radio telephones, they were installed on the chasers.

In the early stages of their ASW service, the crews were admonished to use this new technology sparingly, and instead to be well drilled on the use of visual signals as the primary means of ship-to-ship communications when on the hunt. This was partly out of a sense that the radio telephone technology needed to be fully tested before it could be relied upon, but at least in the early stages of chaser deployment it was also a practical matter. The tubes used in the receivers were not readily available in large quantities at the navy bases, and tubes burned out quickly under certain conditions, such as when using the radio telephone set to receive radio telegraph messages – a practice that precisely for this reason was to be employed only in an emergency.[9]

The practical reality was that chaser men had to be ready at all times to use every means of sending and receiving bearings and hunt orders. The radio telephone was clearly the fastest and most efficient method for ship-to-ship communication, but sometimes – as in Unit E's attack of 24 October 1918 – the radio man couldn't establish a clear signal, so the bearing indicator had to be used, and used efficiently.

Lt. Borgeson on SC 90, as officer of the deck on the unit leader, would have the greatest responsibility in Unit E in this regard. His signalmen would receive the listeners' bearings from the two wing boats, and combined with the bearings reported by his own listeners he would triangulate the position of the enemy sub using the position plotter. He would then plot a course to the target, and his signal men would return bearings for the chase to the wing boats.

**The Chase.** Having received orders to engage in the chase, the listeners would haul in the tubes and the three chasers would run forward based on the bearing established by Lt. Borgeson, the wing boats closing in on the unit leader as they approached the target location.

The standard formation in the chase was the *60 degree method*. In this formation, Lt. Borgeson's chaser would be in the center, positioned with the sub dead ahead. Ens. Dole and Ens. Mundy would be in line with Lt. Borgeson, at equal distances on his flanks such that the two wing boats and the sub formed points on an equilateral triangle, the angles being 60 degrees.

Detection of a sub might inspire thoughts of a fast race to the kill, but the commanding officers of the chasers were advised not to be over-hasty in their pursuit. First, the listeners' bearings had to be tested for accuracy. Lt. Borgeson would need to receive several sets of bearings, each taken at precisely the same moment, so that he could be certain of a good read on the sub. Second, so that he could project where the sub would be when his unit reached the attack

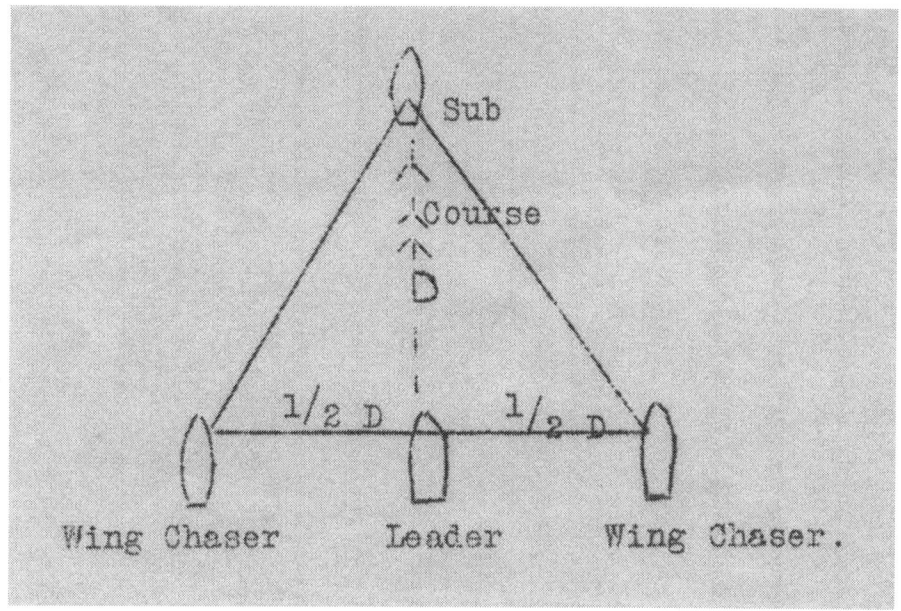

*Illustration of the 60-degree Method in subchaser tactical document.*[10] *The geometry is rough-and-ready. If the formation were a perfect equilateral triangle, the distance from each wing boat to the unit leader would be a bit more than ½ the distance from the unit leader to the target. But at sea during a chase mathematical accuracy wouldn't be feasible anyway. The goal was to move into a formation that would allow deployment of an optimal pattern of depth charges over the target location.*

point, he would need to know whether or not it was changing course and how fast it was moving. The listeners were encouraged to pay close attention to the sound of the propellers and even to attempt to count revolutions, so that they could estimate the speed of the sub. And third, the accuracy and range of the listening equipment were greatest when detecting sounds forward or abeam, and diminished significantly when trying to detect sounds aft. If Lt. Borgeson's calculations caused his unit to overtake the sub, he might lose track of it altogether. Therefore, the recommended tactic was to engage in multiple short runs, stopping at predetermined moments, listening, re-computing the bearing, and again pursuing, ideally until the target was within a few hundred feet, and then attacking.

There were a couple of notable exceptions: First, if any chaser in the unit were to gain visible contact with an enemy sub, the commander was to order an attack immediately, without wasting precious moments to signal the other chasers. Second, if the officer of the deck on the lead chaser felt that the unit was at risk of losing the sub, such as in high seas when listening might be hampered, he might order a fast run to the detected location and an immediate attack.

A potential vulnerability of the tactic of stopping at set intervals was that a savvy submarine commander could pay attention to the runs of the chasers, and resort to silent running each time chasers stopped to listen. The countermeasure for the chasers was to have one chaser stop shortly before the other two, so that the listeners in the first chaser could have the gear down and ready to detect the sub immediately upon the cutting off of the other two chasers' engines, perhaps detecting the submarine before its commander ordered silent running for the next period.[11]

**The Attack.** When the chase had led the unit close enough, ideally within 300 yards of the enemy sub, it was Lt. Borgeson's role in the unit to call for an attack. His wing boats would then close in to 100 yards from SC 90, and as the three chasers raced forward across the path of the sub, they would drop a pattern of depth charges, known as "ash cans" because these 300 lb. charges

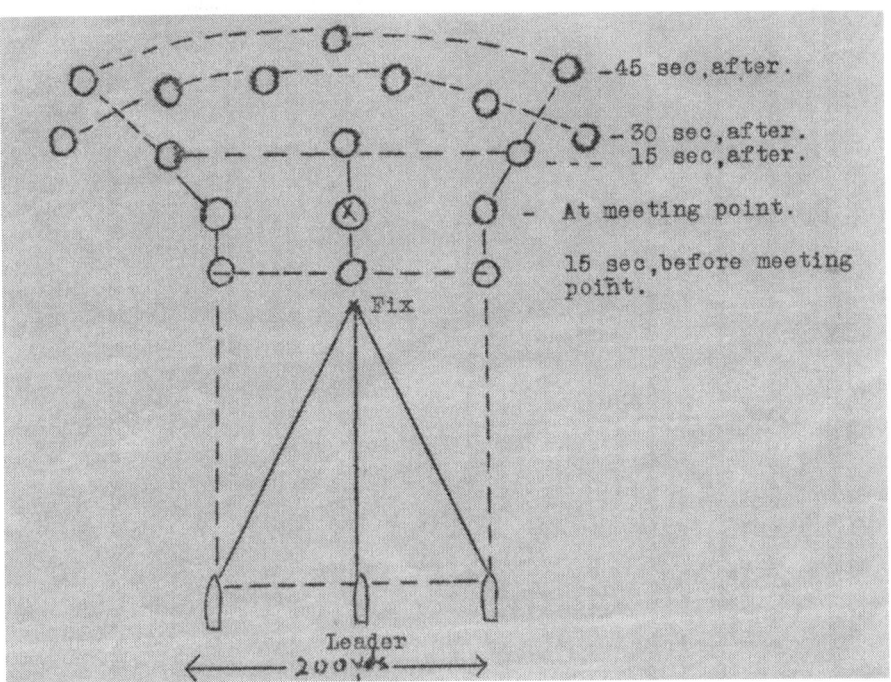

*Attack pattern diagram from subchaser tactical document, showing deployment of eighteen depth charges covering a large target area.*[12]

looked like large metal cans.

The textbook attack involved a pattern of eighteen depth charges, four dropped off the stern of each chaser and two launched from the Y-gun, for a total of six charges per chaser. The pattern was five drops spaced at 15-second intervals, one charge per drop except for the fourth drop, when the Y-gun would be discharged, launching two depth charges from each chaser.

Rolling a depth charge off the stern of a chaser didn't present a problem, assuming the chaser was running at adequate speed to be well clear of the explosion. But the Y-gun launched the charges over the sides of the vessel, one to each side. For this reason, as the chasers crossed the point of the fix on the sub the wing boats would turn about twenty-five degrees away from the unit leader to allow adequate distance between chasers before firing the Y-gun.

A chaser could carry up to about eighteen depth charges, although sometimes fewer were carried. This created a limit of two or three attacks, based on the

*Capt. Charles "Juggy" Nelson (left), commander of the subchaser detachment at Corfu, and Lt. Borgeson (right), commanding officer of SC 90 on board a subchaser, standing near the Y-gun with depth charge in place.*

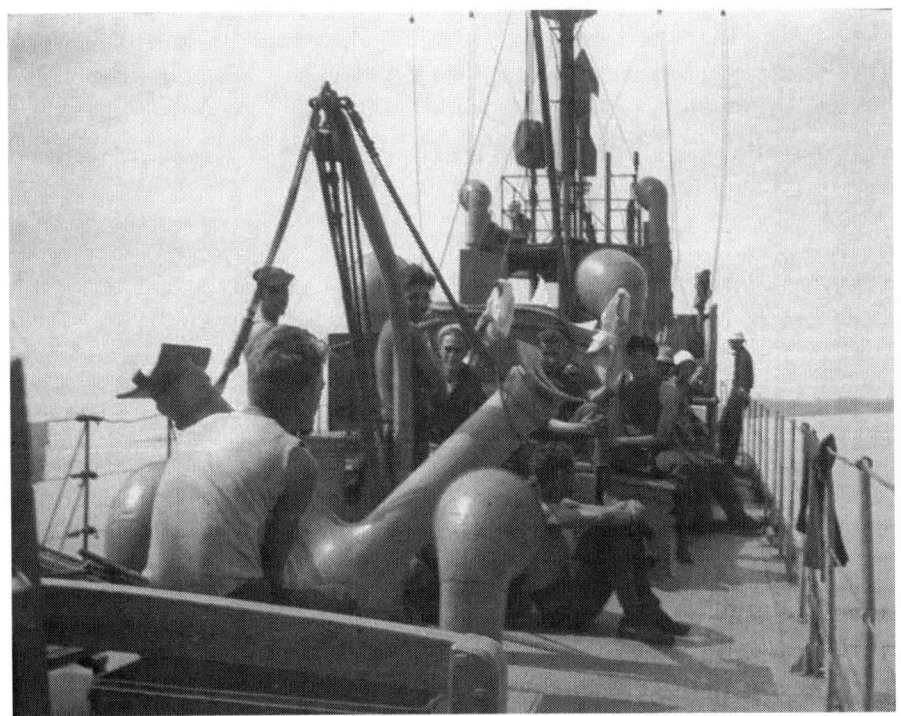

*Y-gun on a submarine chaser. Arbors are shown, inserted into the end of each arm of the Y-gun. To fire the gun, a depth charge is affixed to each arbor, and a blank round is detonated in the base of the Y-gun, propelling the arbors and depth charges over the sides of the chaser.*

eighteen-charge scenario, before the unit would be required to re-stock its supply of charges.

**After the Attack.** Once the pattern of charges had been dropped, the chasers were to be prepared to continue the attack, using the deck gun in the case of a surfaced sub, or re-grouping to engage in another depth charge attack if the situation warranted.

One of the tricks of submarine commanders was to "play dead." For a period of time if conditions allowed, the sub could sit quietly on the bottom with its motors off, in hopes that the chasers would assume they had achieved a kill and move on. Thus another post-attack procedure was to run the trailing wires back and forth across the attack zone to try and detect the hull of a sub on the bottom. If they should detect a metal object with the trailing wires, they would mark the spot with buoys, run the opposite direction and mark the spot again, indicating that the hull was somewhere between the two buoys, and

> From the foregoing we deduce the following:-
>
> S eek the Sub always.
> U tilize all information.
> B e ready for every contingency.
>
> C hase by sixty degree method.
> H unt according to visibility.
> A ttack en masse.
> S ecure some evidence.
> E xercise patience.
> R eport all useful information.
>
> D evelope initiative.
> O rganize for every contingency.
> C o-operate in all things.
> T hink alike and signal little.
> R emember your guns.
> I dentify suspicious sounds.
> N ever assume the defensive.
> E xcell in Sub Chaser spirit.

*Perhaps thinking it an unfinished work without a memory device, Capt. Cotten appended this one to a tactical document. There is no record of the chaser men actually committing this to memory.*[13]

drop a pattern of depth charges over the area.

Naturally, they were advised to return with proof of the kill whenever possible, but this proved nearly impossible since the expected result of a kill would be for the target sub to sink to the bottom of the ocean.

## Duties of the Officers and Crew during a Chase

Time was a critical element in the chase. In Unit E, Ens. Dole and Ens. Mundy were integral parts of Lt. Borgeson's attack unit, and their crews had to be prepared to respond immediately to orders and signals from Lt. Borgeson, and to man their stations efficiently so that they could transmit sound bearings back to the unit leader accurately and without delay. The key roles during a chase were as follows:

**Commanding Officer.** Ens. Dole and Ens. Mundy, commanding officers of the wing boats, were stationed in the pilot house of SC 93 and SC 92, respectively. They issued orders to their engineers for running ahead or stopping, issued orders to the listeners to raise or lower tubes, and orchestrated all maneuvers. On SC 90, as commanding officer of the unit leader, Lt. Borgeson had additional duties, including operation of the position plotter to fix the location of the sub, and issuing orders to the wing boats with the bearing, distance and speed for the chase. When within attack range, Lt. Borgeson would order the attack. Ens. Dole and Ens. Mundy would then track the timing of the attack and issue "fire" orders at the correct intervals.

**Executive Officer.** The executive officer's station was below the pilot house in the officer's cabin. He took the role of Plotting Officer, plotting each run of the vessel's course on paper, and issuing the "stop" instruction to the commanding officer at the correct moment, based on his calculations. For each step of the chase he would record the bearing, distance and speed orders transmitted by the listeners on the unit leader, tracking each course change and computing the correct remaining distance at each interval. When the correct location for the attack was reached, he would issue the "fire" directive to the commanding officer.

**Listeners.** The listeners were stationed in the listening room (the forward magazine). They were responsible for operating the hydrophones, lowering and raising them as directed, and reporting detected sounds at specified intervals. standby listeners were on hand to help raise and lower the tubes, and to signal the correct timing for reporting detected sounds. If no sound were detected, the listener would report "no bearing" at the specified moment.

**Radio Operator.** The radio operator, located in the radio room, was responsible for transmitting and receiving radio messages and recording the time each message was sent or received. He communicated with the commanding officer through a voice tube running from the radio room to the pilot house.

**Recorder.** The recorder, stationed in the pilot house, recorded the time that the engines started or stopped, and when a "mark" command was given. Twenty seconds after full stop, he would give the commanding officer the "down tubes" signal.

**Signalmen.** The signalmen were stationed on the bridge aft of the pilot house. Their role was to send and receive ship-to-ship signals and report them to the commanding officer. They also were to keep ammunition ready for the machine guns, and man the guns if so ordered.

**Arrow Men.** The arrow men were stationed on top of the pilot house, and operated the bearing indicator and reported received bearing signals from other chasers in the unit.[14]

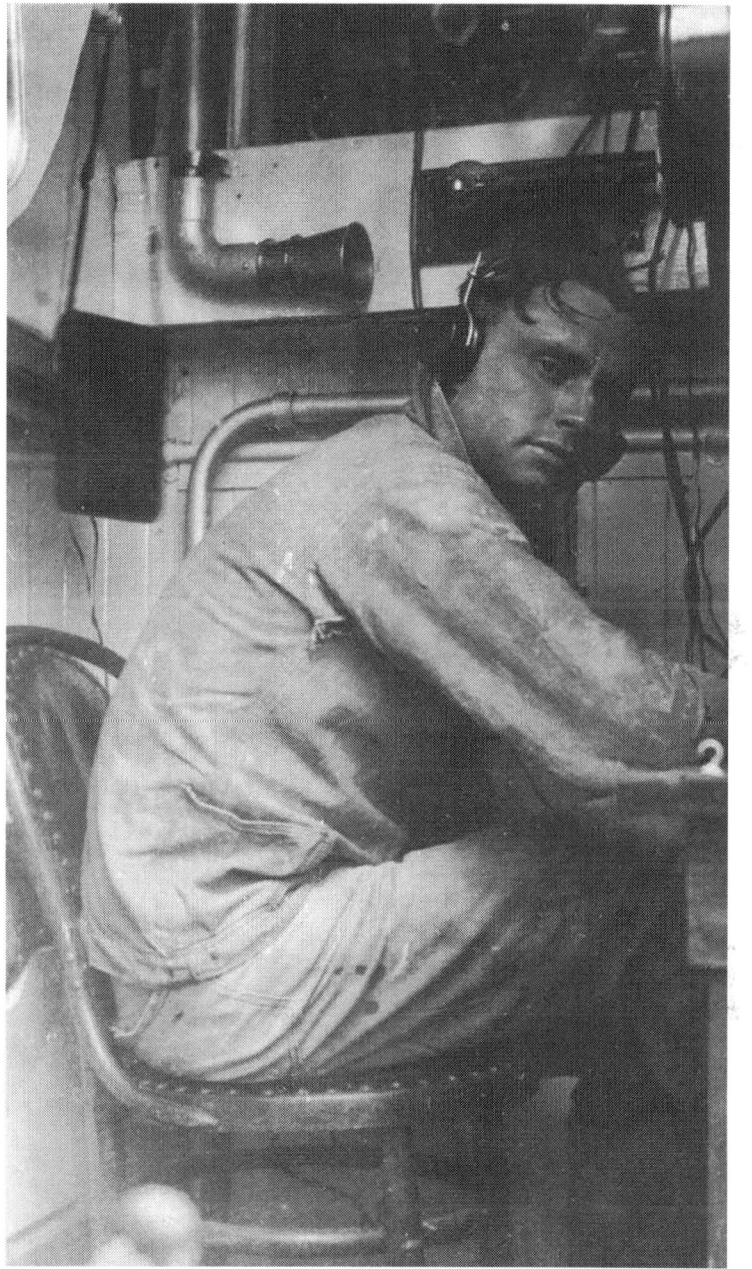

*Radio operator on subchaser SC 354. Note the speaking tube in the upper left, used for communication with the officer on duty in the pilot house. Mounted to the right of it is a microphone for the radio telephone set. The transmitter for the radio telephone is mounted above, partly visible.*

The array of equipment and armament on the chasers that allowed them to engage in these tactics, all packed neatly into such a small space, was an impressive engineering achievement. Rear Admiral Robert S. Griffin, Engineer in Chief of the Bureau of Steam Engineering, writes:

> It was extremely interesting to note the effect produced upon naval officers of all nationalities when inspecting these craft for the first time. As one feature after another was exhibited and explained – the very complete main-engine equipment with its auxiliaries; the three or four types of detection apparatus; the special signaling lights and other signaling equipment; the radio telegraph for distant communication and the radio telephone for tactical work; the novel armament and navigational devices; the arrangement for messing, berthing and heating – it became quickly apparent that these were no ordinary motor launches, but miniature ships, comparable in the intricacy and completeness of their equipment to imposing men-of-war on the line.[15]

In their new duties overseas, the men of the subchasers would put these new, "miniature ships" to the test. By the time he reached his destination, Ens. Dole would be prepared to lead SC 93 into the first subchaser hunt on the Otranto Barrage, where these tactics and the readiness of his crew would be brought to bear, this time against the U-boats in the live arena of war.

# Chapter 3 – Crossing the Atlantic

*"Thermometer 80° in the shade. Have discarded winter clothing and feel fine, and not overloaded with winter garments. It seems hardly credible that we were bucking ice such a short time ago."*[1]

Ens. Dole, on arrival in Bermuda

On 24 February 1918, the first convoy of chasers set out for Bermuda, the first of several stops along the way to their classified destination on the Otranto Barrage. This leg of the journey would be another test of the men and the vessels, a violent storm at sea stretching their capabilities nearly to the breaking point.

## The Passage to Bermuda

To cross the Atlantic in a 110' motorboat was an audacious undertaking. The chasers were not built for crossing the ocean. They were too small and held too little fuel for long runs. To make the crossing feasible, it was broken into several smaller runs. The first step, from New London to Bermuda, would prove to be the most challenging part of the journey. It was a remarkably dangerous trip that would test the "sea legs" of the men. Several days out, the sky darkened, the sea rose, and the convoy found itself in a fierce winter storm that would last for two days. It was a vicious beating for the little single-hull chasers that would open seams, swamp the galley fires, drive the convoy apart and blow some of the vessels days off course.

Many of the officers came to their duties with no experience whatever in sailing or navigating a ship, a point not lost on those critical of the chaser fleet, particularly when it came to the matter of depending on chasers to make their own way through rough seas. But two accounts by different chaser commanding officers of this passage to Bermuda illustrate the unequal capabilities and experience of the subchaser commanding officers. Some of the officers, including Ens. Dole, came to their duties on the chasers with considerable skills in seamanship.

"Had great passage to _____," writes Ens. Dole, duty-bound not to write the name of their location in a personal letter, since it was still classified even after the landing had been achieved. "If you noticed the weather reports," he continues, assuming that his family knows where he is regardless of the secrecy order, "you may have had a faint idea of what we were up against. The storm lasted two days. The sea sure looked majestic and grand. It was a beautiful sight and the boat did all that could be asked of it. The engines were right on the job in pinches. For a few minutes the sun appeared through a rift in the clouds and I do not ever recollect a more inspiring sight. The sea was white as snow at times with big combers. The velocity of the wind was as high as 85 to 90 miles per hour at times. On the whole the boat was fairly comfortable and the pilot house is still on deck. I think it will stay there from my recent experience."[2]

*Chaser in rough seas.*

In his book *Maverick Navy*, Ens. Alexander Moffat, commanding officer of SC 143 in the same convoy, offers a much different account. Moffat explains that he came to the job with no knowledge of navigation. "I had no more idea how to use a sextant than a saxophone," he writes.[3] He had to rely on others, staying close by the other vessels and trusting that their commanding officers knew what they were doing. To Ens. Moffat, it was a grueling and terrifying passage to Bermuda:

Fear for my ship and for my own life lay like a quivering lump in my belly. Never had I seen anything like these racing seas, backs streaked with foam, tumbling crests that folded like breakers on a beach... No. 143 staggered up the face of each wave to be cuffed viciously and buried in a smother of white water that cast the hull broadside into the trough, there to fetch it up with a shattering jolt. I did not see how any structure built of wood could survive the wrenching onslaught of these great marching seas that lifted, battered, and dropped their victim in an endless succession of dizzying falls while the decks shouldered off tons of churning water...[4]

Ens. Dole corroborates the story of the high seas. "I should estimate the waves in between 25 and 30 ft. for the biggest ones, about 20 ft. on the average," he writes. "One of the sailors thought they were 200 feet high." Two days of this kind of storm was an intensive test not only of the capability of the officers and crew, but of the chaser design. Remarkably, all eleven chasers reached their destination, battered but intact. However most of the chasers completed the journey in tow behind the larger vessels in the convoy.

Ens. Moffat, boasting of his chaser's successful landing on its own, writes, "Only one other chaser in our New London contingent made Bermuda under her own power." The other chaser arrived "in a rather unorthodox route the night of the day we arrived," Ens. Moffat comments. "The skipper had a chart of the North Atlantic showing the location of Bermuda, but had neglected to obtain a large scale chart of the island. He was a good navigator and his landfall was perfect. He saw the lights of the dockyard and headed directly for them, not knowing that he was going over a barrier reef that extends the length of the north coast of Bermuda. By some miracle the ocean swell lifted his chaser over several coral formations. He came into port without touching bottom blissfully unaware of a narrow escape from being wrecked."

That navigator, the only one in Ens. Moffat's account other than himself to bring his vessel across to Bermuda on its own power, was Ens. Dole – but Ens. Dole's account of the landing lacks the expressions of terror and pending doom. "We hit some young storm on the way over," he tells his brother in a letter. "Drove us two days off our course. Engines were on the job. ... We made a good landfall." Of his narrow escape from shipwreck on the reefs he writes, "The channels around this place are quite difficult and at times require close work. The water is however so clear that with ordinary vigilance there is hardly any excuse for grounding the ship."

On 3 March 1918, Ens. Dole reported on the passage to the Senior Officer Present at H.M. Dockyards, Bermuda: The chaser's engines had consumed 1,240 gallons of gas on the trip, and 105 gallons of lubricating oil. The auxiliary engine, they found, was installed with the exhaust pipe placed too low – below the water line – resulting in excessive back-pressure and overheating. The main engines had operated satisfactorily, although the center engine's exhaust pipe, also installed below the water line, had caused similar problems. Seawater had come into the cylinders through the exhaust pipe when the vessel was moving slowly, shorting out the igniters. This, he felt confident, could be remedied easily by raising the exhaust pipes. "At no time," he reported, "were we unable to use an engine, but due to the above faults of construction on installation it was necessary to shift from one engine to another, and keep most of the engine force working on the motors temporarily out of commission."

*Subchasers docked in Bermuda.*[6]

The storm at sea resulted in significant losses of food stores. Ens. Dole reported that on SC 93 they had lost 100 lbs. of sugar, 100 lbs. of beans and 4 bushels of potatoes, because the lazaret could not be closed tightly enough to keep out water.

His official account of the storm conforms with his remarks in letters home and furthers the contrast with Ens. Moffat's account of swamping seas and water flooding the vessel:

The boat did not make bad weather of the gale at any time. The strain when the wing engines were used caused the seams to open a little in the engine room, and we took in a little water due to that cause. The amount of water was so slight that it was practically inconsiderable. We took considerable spray on board but no green water at any time during the gale. The boat handled easily and was comparatively dry, considering the conditions.

His men also had performed satisfactorily, under the circumstances. "The crew stood the trip fairly well," he reports. "Several were seasick most of the time but not in such condition as to greatly reduce the efficiency of the vessel. In most instances they were able to stand their watch in regular order."[7]

A curious component of long-range travel for chasers was the need to refuel at sea. During the trip across, USS *Leonidas* (AD 7), the ship assigned to serve as mother ship to the chasers in the Otranto Barrage, performed early trials of this procedure with SC 90. The greatest challenge was to hold the

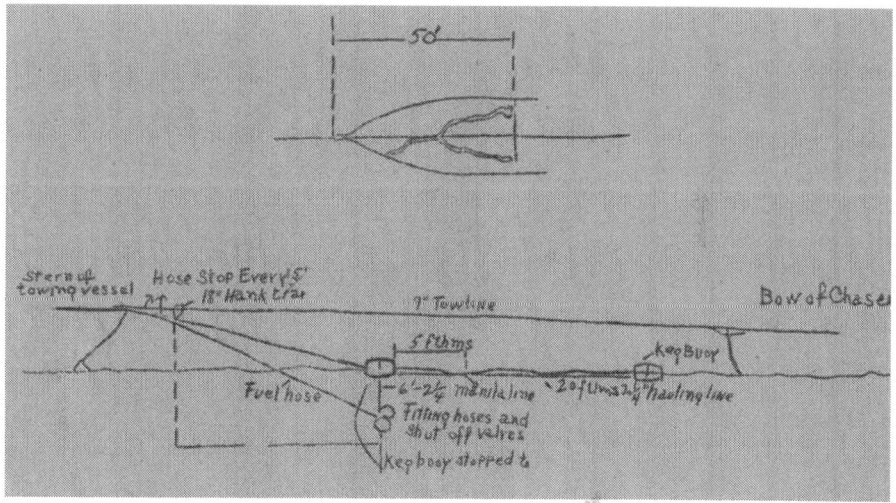

Sketch of early fueling arrangement from official report, USS Leonidas and SC 90, April 1918.[8]

chaser steady. The chaser was secured to a towing bridle with a 6" line, but even in clear weather and relatively smooth seas, they found that SC 90 rolled as much as 20 degrees. This created such a strain that the use of 7" or 8" line for this purpose was recommended. Further, the yaw of the chaser caused it to be towed by one leg or the other of the bridle at a time rather than each side carrying half the strain. This created a concern that in a heavier sea the process would rip the clips off the sides of the chaser. It was recommended that the chasers be fitted with a steel band instead of the wire bridle.

At first they assumed that the best method would be for the chaser to run slow ahead, to reduce strain on the tow line. But the tendency of the chaser was to overshoot the line a bit, and then come back under tow with a jerk, posing the risk of snapping the line. Moreover, they determined that towing the chaser with its engines off only reduced the speed of the mother ship by about one knot, and didn't have a negative effect on steering.

Next was the matter of extending the fuel line from the mother ship to the chaser. The fuel hose was ribbed with a spiral of metal wire, which if bent or over-stressed could cause it to become kinked or broken. Thus the hawser used to carry the fuel line to the chaser could be allowed only the absolute minimum of slack. After several experiments, the arrangement settled upon was for one or more chasers to run alongside the tanker and refuel while underway, and the chasers were fitted with appropriate towing gear for this process.

With the convoy safely docked in Bermuda, a routine was quickly established, the chasers put into a rotation for guard duty and shore leave. This was more what we might call "gofer" duty (as in "go fer this; now go fer that"). Each day the chaser on guard duty would fetch and deliver the mail, bring men with liberty leave ashore, and perform whatever other errands the Patrol Force Commander directed.[9]

Shore leave in the city of Hamilton was granted, with the caveat from Lt. Comdr. Falconer, Commanding Officer of the flagship, USS *Wadena*, that "Commanding Officers are warned to inform their crews that they must be particularly careful of their conduct while ashore in a foreign port, as the local authorities have intimated that serious cases of misconduct may make it necessary to prevent enlisted men from American ships visiting Hamilton."[10]

Yet the chaser men started early in making a name for themselves as unpolished members of the navy fleet. Two days after their arrival, a memo from USS *Wadena* to the commanding officers of the chasers admonished them that, "Difficulty has heretofore been encountered when in formation, in obtaining the attention of S.C. boats to calls and signals. You will please direct your signalman to be ever alert for calls and signals from the flagship and to answer them in the prescribed manner, by hoisting an answering pennant or flag hoist, as the case may require."[11] A similar memo from an officer on USS *Yacona* (SP 617) noted, "Attention of all Commanding Officers is called to the violation by men of the fleet, of dockyard regulations, in that men have been seen tossing a baseball back and forth in the yard. Men are permitted to play baseball at the athletic field outside Dockyard gate and will not be allowed to play in any other place."[12] The chaser men might not be commanded by regular navy men, but they would follow protocol.

Notes from the flagship notwithstanding, the mood in Bermuda was high. They had sailed from the icy harbors of New London through a monster storm, to the clear, clean, blue waters of a tropical paradise. Life, for the time being, was good. The men packed away the long johns and heavy coats and attended a dance on the Isle of White, enjoyed the sun in Hamilton and visited local tourist spots.

"Have been on shore twice," Ens. Dole writes to his father, about a week after arriving. "Hired a rig and drove through palm and coconut groves. This is a quaint place. Expect to gather a coconut before I leave this place and make an ash tray out of it. If I can get some of the native candy will send you some of it. It consists of brown sugar and coconut as far as I can discover."[13]

Taking advantage of the warm weather, the men performed much-needed repairs. They had been without a working wireless telephone for a couple of weeks, and the boat needed painting. This was work not only for the enlisted men, but for the officers as well. The captain picked up a brush and helped with the painting. "We are in the midst of painting ship at present, and I spend most of my time with a bucket of gasoline cleaning my clothes," Ens. Dole writes.

His Executive, Ens. Frank A. Snow, took up the task of repairing the wireless. In the space of a few weeks things were in good shape. "The ship looks fine now," Ens. Dole writes, "and is ready for the long leg of the journey. It will be some trip. Am looking forward to completion of the trip and real service."[14]

But while anxious to get into active duty chasing submarines, Ens. Dole recognized the value of a little time in Bermuda. When compared to duty in the frigid waters of the north Atlantic, duty in Bermuda was indeed a vacation. Food was plentiful, and the men spent free time at saltwater swimming instead of chopping ice off the decks. "Will think of you in camp soon," he writes. "You will have nothing on me. This trip has been more like a pleasure cruise than war so far, though there is considerable work attached to the job. Am gaining weight but the next sea trip will get me back to normal. Have got to quit eating or have the hatches enlarged." To his brother he writes, "Wish you could get a taste of the salt air and breezes fresh from the open sea."

While stationed in Bermuda, the subchaser men engaged in drills at sea, to further prepare them for action against the enemy. A typical drill technique was for one chaser to act as a target, the "noise maker," and a unit of chasers to practice listening and plotting the location of the target chaser, as in this example from 21 March 1918. In this case, on orders issued from USS *Yacona*, Ens. Dole's chaser, SC 93, is the "noise maker," and SC 178, SC 255 and SC 244 are on the hunt:

> When signal is made to form for "K" tube exercises, #93 will proceed on course 120° (true) and run for about five (5) miles. She will then stop and zig-zag at slow speed on reverse course. No. 93 must not get completely out of sight and keep a strict watch on the flagship. All other chasers will open

*"Repairing the wireless. Mr. Snow and seaman aloft."*

out their distance to 800 yards, stop, and put over "K" tube. Exercises and drill will then be carried on by each ship, individually, using the "K" tube in an endeavor to locate #93. Flagship will ask for bearings of noise maker, both by telephone and bearing indicator.[15]

To test the accuracy of the listening and plotting process, the chasers in the unit operated in a triangle formation with established distances between vessels, so that their locations relative to one another were set. (Later, the standard procedure during hunt operations would be to operate line-abreast rather than in a triangle formation.)

In April, as the chaser men were continuing preparations for the next leg of the journey, the Naval Base in New London issued orders for "Prevention of Submarine Devices falling into the hands of the enemy." The listening and plotting devices and procedures were considered top secret. Should a chaser be in a position to be captured, the commanding officer was to implement a process of destroying all sensitive materials, in which each man was responsible for specific items:

The **Commanding Officer** would destroy all sensitive books and papers, sinking them in a weighted bag if the safe-keeping locker itself could not be thrown overboard.

The **Executive Officer**, with the assistance of the **Quartermaster**, would remove and throw overboard the position plotter, radio telephone gear and loud speaker.

The **Gunner's Mate**, assisted by the **3" Gun Pointer**, would cut the cables of the K Tube buoy and throw the K Tube overboard, for which potential purpose a pair of cutters was to be secured to the K Tube reel at all times. If possible, he would then detach the reel itself, and throw that over.

The **Ship's Cook** and **Mess Attendant** were to destroy the brush contacts of the trailing wire and remove and throw over the trailing wire reel.

The **Y-Gun Captain** would remove and discard the breech block of the Y-Gun, and the **Arrow Reader** was to break off the point and feather of the bearing indicator.

The **Radio Operator** would destroy all wiring diagrams, log books, and instructions pertaining to any electronic equipment on board. For this reason he was to store all such documents in a weighted folder at all times.

The **Listeners** would loosen the mounting hardware of the S.C. Tube and allow it to drop out of the boat.

The **M.B. Tube Operator** would destroy the K Tube compensator box and throw the tubes overboard.

The **3" Gun Captain** would remove the breech block of the gun and throw it overboard.[16]

Nothing of any possible naval intelligence value was to be left on board to be seized by the enemy. Moreover, before they reached the war zone, the commanding officers were to instruct the crew thoroughly, and to question them frequently to be sure each man understood his role.

## The Azores

Early in April 1918, the departure from Bermuda was under way. On 8 April, USS *Leonidas* left Bermuda with seventeen chasers, among them the unit leader of Ens. Dole's unit, SC 90. Ens. Dole's vessel was in the second group, which left on 15 April with eighteen other chasers, convoyed by USS *Salem* (CS 3).[17]

The twelve-day trip to the Azores, a group of Portuguese islands in the Atlantic about 900 miles west of Lisbon, was notably less dramatic than the passage from New London to Bermuda. Ens. Dole writes, "We had a fine trip. The sea was like a mill pond for all except two days when a southwester kicked up a nasty chop, and saved us the trouble of washing the decks. Had the most beautiful moonlight nights." Once again he experienced the seaworthiness, if not comfort, of the submarine chaser design. "The boat is a great sea boat," he writes. "We have experienced all kinds of weather during the winter and spring, from long heavy seas, combers, and all kinds of choppy seas to short, heavy seas, and the boat seems to treat all as a joke. During the chop on this last trip the boat rolled her beam ends under every 3 seconds as an average. I took time on a split second stop watch used for chronometer sights and the period varied from 2¼ to 3½ seconds. It was impossible to stay in bed or get any sleep. You had to hang on and rest a little."[18]

The trip provided the crew with some well-needed experience at sea. "The crew is 'seagoing' now," Ens. Dole says. "This last trip put them on their feet, although some have not acquired 'sea-legs.' The long roll of the first two days put some under but they gradually came through and were in good shape the rest of the trip."[19]

To elude any enemy submarines that might be lurking in their path, the convoy cruised with the running lights off through a sub zone, and, as Ens. Dole notes, "In fact we cruised without lights most of the nights to get in practice" for duty on the barrage line, where lights would not be used.

*Chasers at Ponta Delgada, San Miguel Island, Azores.*

They made good landfall on 27 April, and joined the other chasers at Ponta Delgada, a busy port on the island of San Miguel. Both the landscape and the food in the Azores were to Ens. Dole's liking. Local vendors sold fresh produce to the navy men, and when on leave, the men enjoyed the local cuisine.

Ens. Dole writes home, "Went ashore last night and looked the place over. Started by getting a good feed, roast chicken, steak and eggs, French fried potatoes, wine and pineapple. It sure was good. They grow everything here that can be grown, and the pineapples were great, fresh and dead ripe. The feed cost 1500 reis ($.70). Am going to get another feed tonight. It sure is a change from salt horse, canned willie and bacon... This is the most beautiful place I was ever in, that is the landscape. High mountains and wonderful stretches of gardens and fields on the sides of the mountains."

When shore leave allowed, Ens. Dole enjoyed sightseeing in the countryside. "Went ashore yesterday," he writes, "and took an auto ride through the

*Produce vendors.*

country. Went out to a pineapple farm and got eight big pineapples for $.10. They are grown under glass. It was very interesting." On the return trip he picked up a fellow New Englander, a young man from Fall River, Massachusetts, who came in handy as an interpreter. But mostly Ens. Dole was on his own. "Am getting pretty good at making myself understood," he explains, "can order a meal from soup to nuts and get all the tools with it, though mostly by monosyllables and gestures."

But with a note of longing for his summer days at the family's camp in Maine, Ens. Dole adds that, "The sea has a fascination all its own, and after I get through with this outfit, I do believe I can stay away from the sea."

For the time being, though, these were mere longings. The steel sharks had yet to be defeated, a reality not lost on Ens. Dole. "Read your sermon this morning," Ens. Dole writes to his father, remarking on a sermon in support of the Allied cause against the enemy. "It was fine. One of your best. Two of the crew have read it already, and found it very profitable and helpful. I do not think Germany will be permitted to gain the ascendancy by the methods she has been using. Provided that her cause was just, which it is not, her methods would defeat her in the end. Germany must be defeated on the field of battle, as you say, and I believe she will be."

Ens. Dole was anxious to get to it. "Will be out of here long before you

*Leaving Gibraltar with the tanker British Light en route to Malta and Corfu, May 1918.*

get this letter," he writes on 30 April, shortly before their departure from the idyllic islands. "Expect to go Hun-hunting very soon. ... Am looking forward to some interesting times, and believe we have the goods and will get them."[20]

## Malta

Early in May 1918, secret orders were issued by Capt. Nelson from USS *Leonidas*, establishing rendezvous points for the convoy, leading them to the coast of Portugal and then through the Strait of Gibraltar into the Mediterranean.

The rhetoric of the sea war was making the news at home, with stories of German reports of sinking two or three ships out of each convoy. While Ens. Dole described these reports as untrue, the convoy of chasers nonetheless proceeded along their route prepared to engage with enemy subs at any time. So far, as he notes in a letter home, the subs "have given us a wide berth."[21]

During each leg of the journey, Ens. Dole had been practicing the use of a sextant to determine the precise position of the boat. He found the clear weather and bright stars in the Mediterranean especially well suited for this, and took regular readings, honing his skills. "Am beginning to find that work easy," he tells his father. "Hope I can keep the charts as they give some interesting data about the time sights."

Arriving in Malta in late May, Ens. Dole found it an interesting but odd place. The weather was very hot and the landscape remarkably foreign. He went ashore to visit notable spots, including the Cathedral of Saint John in

Valetta, which he found impressive. "The cathedral is very beautiful," he tells his brother, "the mural paintings especially, and also paintings by Michelangelo representing the beheading of John the Baptist." But he found the pomp of the service to be excessive. "After the service the clergy paraded through the streets. The street was strewn with leaves and purple flowers. As the priest passed the common herd groveled in the dust." Too much show for a New England Swedenborgian.

Their stay in Malta offered an opportunity for repairs, inspection of the listening apparatus and painting in a large dry dock accommodating ten chasers at a time.

*Ten submarine chasers in dry dock, Malta. SC 93 is the foremost vessel. In the second row, left to right, are SC 327, SC 255 and SC 92.*

On 2 June 1918, as the chasers were setting out on the final leg of their journey, the reality of their upcoming job became clearer. Ens. Dole writes home about a ship sunk by an enemy submarine. Near Malta a merchant ship had been sunk, and several chasers were sent to the scene of the wreckage, where crates of produce had floated to the surface. "Picked up a deck load of lemons the other day," he writes. "They did not start coming up till 5 hours after the ship went down. Am anxious to get a look at a sub. They arrived on the above scene about 2 hours after the ship went down." German submarine commanders, eager to receive credit for their kills, would lurk in the area for some time after a sinking, to identify the ship and to mark the time of its sinking.

Gerard Fernandez, a crewman on SC 81, wrote lightheartedly about this incident in an article published in the newsletter of the Submarine Chaser Club of America:

> Sub-Chaser Detachment Two, en route to Corfu, arrived at Malta about May 27, 1918. The town was filled with all kinds of stories about the activities of pesky U boats in the vicinity of the island. One story had it that a U boat took on stores about a mile and a half off shore from an old schooner, and another had it that a U boat tried to make a sea nymph out of Jesse James by popping out from behind a lamp post (they meant a lighthouse) and holding up a British freighter. And so, with one story following another, we were beginning to believe that the Subs were a lively proposition in the Mediterranean. ...
>
> A few days after our arrival we were hailed alongside the *Leonidas* for what we found out later to be "secret orders." Of course, old Dame Rumor started to fly around as to what was involved in the secret orders. The story that had most effect on many minds was that a ship was torpedoed about 100 miles south of the island and that we were to rush to the rescue and recover any survivors or bodies from the wreck.

Fernandez tells of their race out to the location of the sinking and subsequent hunt for the sub. By the time they arrived, a destroyer had already reached the spot, and they slowed down as they entered the field of wreckage:

> Glancing over the surface of the water we seemed to be floating in an immense punch bowl. Lemons covered the surface and cases of lemons, big and bulky, bobbed up and down. Running a short distance from the lemon field we soon discovered that soap was part of the cargo of this ill-fated steamer. After searching the area for about an hour we decided to prove to our worthy brethren that ours was a lemon of a trip. Putting over the wherry, we started combing the surface for as many cases of lemons and soap as we could carry. After stuffing the forepeak with a good supply of soap and the deck with an oversupply of lemons we started our run back to Malta, not showing the least resemblance to the war terrier. We looked more like an East River "lighter."[22]

The chasers performed listening periods en route back to Malta, but the submarine was not detected, no doubt long since having documented the kill and left the scene. Trading crates of lemons for other goods provided some entertainment that day. But seeing the wake of destruction left by an unseen enemy must also have magnified the chaser men's sense of proximity to danger, and underscored the need for the service they were about to render.

## Chapter 4 – American Bay

*"There will be something doing from now on. Some of us will not come back, but those that do will have the experience of their lives."*[1]

Ens. George S. Dole

**Base 25, Corfu**

In establishing a navy base for the subchasers of the Otranto Barrage, the Americans looked to the Greek island Corfu, near the mouth of the Adriatic. Corfu was a strategic location, close enough to the barrage line to be practical for short-range vessels, but sheltered from open ocean. A small, unimproved bay below Comeni Head on the east side of the island several miles northwest of the city of Corfu was chosen for the construction of Base 25, which would become the new home for the American submarine chaser contingent.

Fustipidima Point, a narrow tip of land at Comeni Head, curved into the water creating a bay roughly a quarter mile across, an adequate harbor for the chasers and their mother ship, USS *Leonidas*. Northeast of this little bay a narrow channel formed a natural gateway to the Adriatic, a relatively short distance from the location of the barrage line between the coasts of Italy and Albania.

The bay had the added advantage of being far enough from settled regions to keep the Americans safely distant from malaria outbreaks that were plaguing the island. In his monograph on the subchasers, Lewis Clephane points out that at the French base on Corfu at Govino, up to 70 percent of the men had contracted malaria.[2] The little cove at Fustipidima Point was adequately remote, but also close enough to the city of Corfu to take advantage of some of the island's resources.

Prior to the construction of Base 25, this region around Comeni Head was undeveloped. Ens. Hilary R. Chambers, commanding officer of SC 128, describes the setting:

> Beautiful green grass ran to the edge of an embankment which was about ten feet high, of rocky formation and almost perpendicular, which insured sufficient depth of water. Olive trees grew on this embankment all the way up to the hills in the background. There were no buildings except a sheep herder's hut a few yards from shore.[3]

Ens. Dole and his fellow subchaser sailors arrived to discover a pristine bay in a picturesque setting of rocky terrain and ancient olive groves. "We

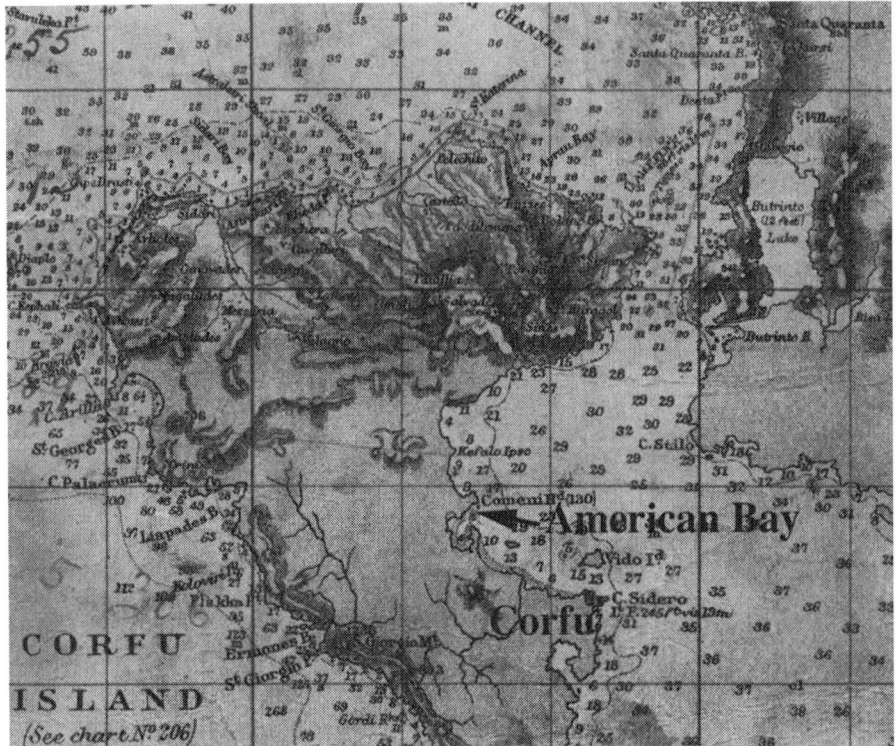

*Section of nautical chart from subchaser SC 93, showing the location of American Bay on the eastern side of Corfu Island, northwest of the city of Corfu.[4] The chart is pencil-marked in a grid pattern for use in the Otranto Barrage. Labels for American Bay and Corfu added for emphasis.*

have a location that is full of promise," he writes home, describing the remote spot. "The place we are at had no name, so it has been named after this bunch."[5] Thus was coined the name American Bay, which was to be home to thirty-six chasers.

Because the island lacked adequate stores of construction materials, there were no completed buildings when the first group of chasers arrived, only the shell of a new communications station. Completion would have to wait until American forces acquired and delivered building materials.

The navy leased storehouse space in Mandukio, a suburb northwest of the city, a few miles by sea from Fustipidima Point, and telephone cables were installed to connect the storehouse with the communications office at American Bay.[6]

Base 25 was rapidly built into a functioning navy base, designed for the express purpose of servicing the American chaser fleet of the Otranto Barrage.

*Chart detail of the small bay formed by Comeni Head and Fustipidima Point, location of Base 25, American Bay.*[7]

A set of large fuel tanks was installed high on the point, so that vessels in the bay could pull up to the pier and refuel. The communications station was built with masts for radio equipment, and a small city of tents was set up overlooking the harbor.

The chasers tied off in groups to mooring buoys in the bay, an arrangement that lent itself to social interaction. But Alfred F. Loomis, a crewman on SC 78, notes that there was a cost in comfort due to the hot weather of the Mediterranean.

> In harbor the lack of air was not so marked, because it was possible to open the ports and fit in them the wind scoops provided for the purpose of arresting every vagrant breath of air that might be stirring. But it was the chaser custom

*Base 25 under construction. Note the fuel tanks on the small island, and the pier extending into American Bay.*

*Base camp, American Bay.*

to moor to a wharf in clusters of five or six (or a dozen if no one called a halt) whence it followed that none but the outboard boat received more than half the benefit of natural ventilation. The quarters aft were particularly insufferable because of the heat which billowed forth from the galley long after the fire had been extinguished following the evening meal, but nobody objected strenuously to harbor conditions, because all who were not gifted with the physique of a salamander took their mattresses topside and slept in the open air.[8]

*USS Leonidas and subchasers moored in American Bay.*

## Arrival of the Chasers

Ens. Dole's chaser and the chaser on which Alfred Loomis served were in the first group to arrive in Corfu, on 4 June 1918, a day before USS *Leonidas* arrived, and barely a week from the time that the orders were received to establish the base. The electricians and telegraphers who would build the communications infrastructure had arrived the day before. In this first group were nine chasers:

| | | | | |
|---|---|---|---|---|
| SC 78 | SC 93 | SC 244 | SC 327 | SC 349 |
| SC 92 | SC 147 | SC 255 | SC 337 | |

Summing up the voyage from New London to Corfu, Ens. Dole writes, "We crossed the ocean to this place about 5,000 miles without the use of lights except when on the trail of subs. Used 10,000 gallons of gasoline in going from New London to this place. Had no accidents, only trouble was one night already mentioned when we had trouble with water in the gasoline. We are now ready for the real work and am looking forward to being of some use."

Ens. Dole went ashore, sat in the shade of an olive tree, and smoked the last of his cache of cigars. "This is a fine base. Very beautiful scenery," he tells his father in a letter home. "We are anchored in a cove and have the point all to ourselves, i.e., the chaser fleet. Have fine swimming here and we sure make use of it. We are pioneers in this field and will have to make our own base and [when] the picks and shovels come will 'dig ourselves in' on shore."

The enemy wasted no time in scouting out this new base. "Hostile aeroplanes have already paid us a visit," Ens. Dole reports, just a few days after his arrival. "No damage done to either side. Expect the Hun got the photos he was after & departed."[9]

The next group, including Ens. Chambers' chaser, arrived the following day, in the convoy led by USS *Leonidas*. There were twenty-one chasers in the convoy:

| | | | | |
|---|---|---|---|---|
| SC 77 | SC 94 | SC 127 | SC 215 | SC 338 |
| SC 79 | SC 95 | SC 128 | SC 225 | |
| SC 80 | SC 96 | SC 129 | SC 227 | |
| SC 81 | SC 124 | SC 151 | SC 256 | |
| SC 90 | SC 125 | SC 179 | SC 324 | |

And on 19 June, supply vessel USS *Carib* arrived with six more chasers:

| | | |
|---|---|---|
| SC 82 | SC 131 | SC 217 |
| SC 130 | SC 216 | SC 248 |

This put the full subchaser fleet at Base 25, Otranto Barrage, at thirty-six:[10]

| | | | | |
|---|---|---|---|---|
| SC 77 | SC 93 | SC 129 | SC 217 | SC 327 |
| SC 78 | SC 94 | SC 130 | SC 225 | SC 337 |
| SC 79 | SC 95 | SC 131 | SC 227 | SC 338 |
| SC 80 | SC 96 | SC 147 | SC 244 | SC 349 |
| SC 81 | SC 124 | SC 151 | SC 248 | |
| SC 82 | SC 125 | SC 179 | SC 255 | |
| SC 90 | SC 127 | SC 215 | SC 256 | |
| SC 92 | SC 128 | SC 216 | SC 324 | |

The chasers at Corfu were arranged in two squadrons of six units, with three chasers to a unit, as follows, the unit leader of each unit listed first.[11]

**Squadron 1:**
Unit A: SC 124, SC 125, SC 127
Unit B: SC 215, SC 128, SC 129
Unit C: SC 349, SC 255, SC 256
Unit D: SC 225, SC 327, SC 244
Unit E: SC 90, SC 92, SC 93
Unit F: SC 94, SC 227, SC 151

**Squadron 2:**
Unit G: SC 95, SC 179, SC 338
Unit H: SC 147, SC 324, SC 337
Unit I: SC 77, SC 78, SC 79
Unit J: SC 96, SC 80, SC 81
Unit K: SC 130, SC 131, SC 216
Unit L: SC 248, SC 217, SC 82

*Unit E, moored in American Bay, Corfu.*

## Joining the Barrage Line

On 12 June 1918, the American submarine chasers engaged in the first hunt on the Otranto Barrage. Ens. Dole's chaser was in the first group to serve on the barrage line, which included Unit C , Unit D and Unit E.[12]

Each chaser was assigned to a specific starting location on the barrage line. A classified document circulated to the commanding officers of the chasers, *No. 1: - Routes to Stations*, provided precise instructions to their assigned locations, including the bearings and runs that would bring each chaser to its spot on the line, and a graphical depiction of the routes on a rough nautical chart marked in a numbered gridwork. The full-sized nautical chart used for navigation was marked in a corresponding gridwork, divided into numbered sections or "squares," each encompassing 5' of longitude and latitude, roughly 4½ miles x 5¾ miles. These numbered squares would be referenced frequently in official reports of chaser activity.

The officers on the flagship were anxious to receive details of the hunt. On the day prior to this first assignment of U.S. subchasers to the barrage line, a memorandum was issued from USS *Leonidas*, instructing the listeners to maintain a log, two copies of which were to be submitted to the operations office immediately upon their return to base after a patrol. Official forms were issued for this purpose, and a set of conventions was adopted for listener log entries, with abbreviations for various types and strengths of sounds, water noises and sea conditions.

The expectation was that the listeners would be fully capable of distinguishing not merely the sound of a vessel, but the type of engine sound and the type of vessel. They were to note if the sound was of a reciprocating nature or that of a turbine; whether it was fast or slow; whether it was from a submarine or a motor launch.[13] This was not merely a hunt for submarines, but an investigation into the new tactics of antisubmarine warfare, and no detail was to be lost. The nine chasers in the inaugural hunt headed through the North Channel and into the Strait of Otranto, eager to put their training to the test.

# AMERICAN BAY

```
S E C R E T
No.1:- ROUTES to STATIONS
                UNITS
From Gate steer 20°
From outer Barrage Gate steer 20° until St.Gorgio
Monastery bears 140° then steer 320° until north
extreme of Cape Kiephali bears 90 then steer 304°
for 9-1/2 miles when north extreme of Merlera I.
should bear 289° which is point "P" - from point
"P" steer as follows:-

S.C._____ steer P to A -- 311°  (true) 16       ms.
S.C._____ steer P to B -- 305°  (true) 17-3/4 ms.
S.C._____ steer P to C -- 300°  (true) 20-1/2 ms.
S.C._____ steer P to D -- 294°  (true) 24-3/4 ms.
S.C._____ steer P to E -- 292°  (true) 27-3/4 ms.
S.C._____ steer P to F -- 290°  (true) 30       ms.
S.C._____ steer P to G -- 287°  (true) 35-1/4 ms.
S.C._____ steer P to H -- 286°  (true) 38       ms.
S.C._____ steer P to I -- 285°  (true) 41-1/4 ms.
```

*Section of "No. 1 Routes to Stations" orders document. The chart is rotated 90° clockwise from the north-south orientation. At the bottom left is the top of Corfu. The barrage line runs westerly from point A to point I.*

85

## Chapter 5 – On the Otranto Barrage

*"I expect to come back very much alive. However if the Huns get me my last moments will be the happiest and proudest of my life."*[1]

Ens. George S. Dole

Ens. Dole and his fellow chaser commanders would spend the next five and a half months stationed at Base 25, Corfu, Greece. Periodically, units were sent for tactical training off the coast of Italy, and occasionally a few chasers were sent on various missions that called them away from the barrage line temporarily. But for the most part, this period of the chasers' service was spent in a rotation of several days on the barrage line then several days in American Bay. The typical rotation at Otranto was four days on and four days off.

*An Italian submarine, probably Nautilus*[2], *and American subchasers. The submarine served as a tracking target for subchasers during training exercises in the use of the hydrophone listening equipment and coordination of reporting sound bearings. (T. Woofenden Collection.)*

### Service in American Bay

The crews had plenty to do while in port in American Bay, particularly in the early days. The vessels and equipment required regular maintenance, and tactical training continued. Moreover, they had to be ready for new dangers. It was no secret that this new American force had arrived, so in addition to their regular regimen of signal drills and other tactical training, the chasers at Base 25 engaged in airplane attack drills.[3]

There was also more work to be done in fitting the boats, to improve their effectiveness in delivering lethal depth charges into the paths of enemy subs. On 11 June 1918, Ens. Dole brought his chaser alongside USS *Leonidas* to have depth charge racks built on the stern.[4] On the larger warships, charges were secured on long racks, so that during an attack these "ash cans" could be rolled off the stern of the ship. SC 93 was fitted with abbreviated versions of the same type of device, three short angle-iron racks, the open end resting on the stern and the other end elevated. Two or three depth charges could be lashed to each rack, allowing the crew to keep half a dozen or more charges at the ready, to be let go simply by releasing the lashing.

*Depth charge racks on stern of SC 244 (left) and SC 93 (right).*

Ens. Dole would have occasion to make use of this new equipment in short order. On 15 June 1918, Unit E engaged in the first depth charge attack by a chaser in the Otranto Barrage. At 5:57 p.m., the attack flag was hoisted, and Ens. Dole ordered his men to drop a charge in the target zone, set to explode at a depth of 150'. Chasers SC 90 and SC 92 also let charges go.[5] After half a year of preparation, Ens. Dole and his crew were finally "in the game."

Back in American Bay, Ens. Dole was in high spirits. "Returned from duty and am resting for the next tour of duty," he writes home. "Had great time. This ship was the first to make an attack." He knew he had not sunk a sub, but to cause the enemy some trouble was a good start. While sinking submarines was the expressed purpose of the chasers, a critical tactical advantage could be achieved by keeping the pressure up, helping to break the spirit of the enemy. "Without the human failings of those that operate them they are practically invulnerable," he tells his brother of the U-boats. And "like every other invention of the devil they can be beaten by the force of courage alone."[6]

Force of will would also be useful. At the onset of summer at Otranto, the crews faced the challenge of blistering heat. "Today is the first day of summer," Ens. Dole writes, "but nothing like the Maine summer. Have to wear tropical helmet for protection. It sure is hot here. When there is no breeze it is a considerable strain to stay on deck, as when we are on the line no awnings can be up. ... It sure is fascinating to see the planes go racing by overhead. You sort of envy the cool breeze they must be enjoying, while we stand dripping with perspiration most of the day. At night the decks are often so hot that you can hardly bear your hand on the under side."[7]

The heat would persist, sometimes making high seas seem like a blessing because of the wind. "Had 4 days of bad sea and the rest dead calm," he tells his father in mid-July, "with not a ripple or wave on the surface and the thermometer 112° in the shade. Could not sleep and just get up every few minutes and take a rubdown with a towel. Tried sea water but that did not help any."[8]

During certain stretches, especially in the stifling heat of summer, chaser service at Base 25 might have seemed a bit monotonous. For weeks at a time the units rotated on and off of the barrage line, performed guard duty in American Bay and in Mandukio where the warehouse was located, took on stores from USS *Leonidas*, ate, slept and tried to stay cool.

Periodic shore leave allowed Ens. Dole to visit the Kaiser's Palace, the city of Corfu and other locations around the island. These visits, even if brief, were a welcome change of pace, and in addition to having a rejuvenating effect, offered the men an opportunity for some social interaction with Allied forces on the island. As the summer progressed the concerns about malaria outbreaks at the French base apparently diminished, for in July Ens. Dole speaks of a visit to the French aviation base, located in a cove south of American Bay.

In addition to touring the base, he enjoyed a fine meal. "Had a great time and some dinner, one of the best I ever demolished. Started with cocktails, soup, omelet cooked only as the French can cook, also fried chicken and French fried potatoes, and beans. I never ate beans like them."[9]

A visit to a Serb camp left him feeling grateful for the rather modest

*The French aviation base on the bay at Govino. In the foreground is a church on a tiny island across the bay.*

*In a hangar at the French aviation base.*

*Serb encampment, Corfu.*

accommodations of his cabin on the chaser. "The Serbs present a pathetic sight. They live in small tents made of canvas, burlap or tarred paper, pitched under the trees."

A favorite pastime was swimming. The pristine waters of American Bay (now enjoyed by tourists staying in Greek luxury resort hotels) offered a temporary respite from the heat, and an enjoyable sport. "Just returned from the beach and had a fine swim," Ens. Dole writes home. "The one thing that is superb about this place is the swimming. After I completed my swim I had a smoke under the olive trees and ate a couple of peaches that I purchased from a vendor who has a stand on the beach."[10]

*Italian soldiers in Gallipoli, Italy.*

In mid-August 1918, Ens. Dole's chaser was selected for a special mission, to be part of a convoy running with the Belgian tanker *Matzouk* to Gallipoli, Italy, then to Sicily and back to American Bay. The convoy consisted of four chasers – SC 90 (flagship), SC 92, SC 93 and SC 327 – and the tanker.[11] Not only would this trip provide some relief from barrage duty, but it would afford Ens. Dole a chance to see the sights, including a smoking Mt. Aetna.

On one of these expeditions, Ens. Dole found himself in a mini-adventure that would require a bit of clever strategy, caught by officials for failing to provide identification.

> Had a RR ride for the first time since I left the U.S. Got pinched for traveling in uniform without pass or identification papers. Had all the officers on the train from a Lt. General down laboring to explain what was wanted. It seemed to me it would be foolish to let them get the idea that I knew what was wanted, and they gave it up as a bad job. Was to be turned in to the military police at the destination I was headed to, but managed to lose the guard in the crowd.

> Stayed in the city that night and went to the station in the morning and demanded a pass back to \_\_\_\_\_ where my ship was. After about an hour I managed to get about everything I wanted except the pass. The military officials said that they had to have the signature of \_\_\_\_\_ and he could not be located, so I told them to notify the conductor to pass me on. One of the officials was a Lt. Colonel. He seemed very excited and had just reached the conductor when the train pulled out and the conductor and I jumped aboard.

> Had an amusing time telling the conductor to explain it to the military inspector of the train. First they wanted my ticket and then they wanted my passport, and as I had neither it was not policy for me to understand what they wanted, as I feigned I would have too much trouble to explain. I intimated I was going to the next station beyond my stop. I had to point it out on the map, and they did not notice when I left the train as it was pulling out of the station. Got back to the ship o.k.[12]

## Service on the Barrage Line

While time in American Bay meant escaping now and then for short adventures, when on the barrage line Ens. Dole and his crew were engaged in serious business, never to be taken lightly. Before the end of their first month at Base 25, SC 93 would see action three times against enemy subs, the first attack on 15 June 1918, followed by another on 27 June and a third on the return trip to base the following day. By mid-July, a mere five weeks after their arrival, the chasers at Corfu had engaged in half a dozen submarine attacks, making their presence known both to enemies and allies.

On 13 July 1918, Unit E was on patrol on the barrage line when at 11:10 a.m., two explosions were heard. Lt. Borgeson, Ens. Dole and Ens. Mundy raced to the location, where they came upon an English ship hit by enemy torpedo fire on the starboard bow.[13] The ship was able to make way – and one might speculate that the British captain felt a sense of good luck that these three little "terriers of the sea" had shown up to drive off the sub before it could circle around for the kill.

In the early engagements the subchaser men lacked experience. This was the first employment of these tactics in a live theater of battle, and it would take time for the men to develop the art of ASW and to sharpen their skills. Within a couple of months, however, the crews were becoming more proficient in the use of the equipment and in the employment of chase tactics, and Ens. Dole was able to look back on the first days on the barrage line with a sense of accomplishment but also with good humor. "The crew is in good shape and can deliver the goods," he writes home, in early September. "We are getting better every minute and the first attack would seem like a nightmare to us now. We often have a good laugh over it."[14]

A stable factor throughout, however, was the physically and mentally challenging nature of the work. Describing his duty on the barrage line, Ens. Dole remarks, "It is a strain from the time we hit the barrage till we are through the mine fields and back in port."[15] But the men had a sense that the barrage line was proving effective. Contacts with submarines became less frequent, a fact that Ens. Dole attributes to the overwhelming force of mines and warships assembled in the Strait of Otranto.

Overall, Ens. Dole's unit, Unit E, would prove to be among the most active units on the barrage line, although true to form, Ens. Dole declined the temptation to spin yarns of submarine kills. "There are quite a few subs missing from the Kaiser's Navy," he tells his parents, mid-September 1918. "We have traveled many thousands of miles looking for them. ... We have been in three attacks and several contacts but that is all I can say at present. We have no definite evidence as to the success of the attacks."

On 17 October 1918, Ens. Dole received notice of a half-stripe promotion, giving him the rank of lieutenant (junior grade). In the same mail delivery he received a fresh package of cigars from his father, and enjoyed one in celebration of his advancement in rank.

**Pursuits and Attacks**

Before the signing of the armistice, the chasers at Corfu would engage in a total of thirty-seven hunts.

The success of the chasers (which is treated in the Epilogue) has been a matter of much discussion. On all types of warships serving in the submarine zones, tales of submarine hunts and kills proliferated. It seemed that every ship had its "kill" story. Ens. John Langdon Leighton, an intelligence officer under Adm. Sims, remarked, "If as many submarines had been sunk as were claimed, Germany would have had to have built about five thousand of them."[16] As the tales of sunken subs far exceeded the evidence, the men of the warships found themselves faced with demands for irrefutable proof of a kill before any credit would be awarded. Gathering proof, however, was often nearly impossible, as a sunken sub in the deep waters of the Strait of Otranto generally couldn't even be located, let alone parts of it salvaged. Proof sank with the enemy.

Lt. Dole points this out in a letter home. "It is very difficult to tell when you have damaged a sub, in fact often impossible to get any direct evidence as the water is deep and we can not trail for them. Very seldom any evidence appears after an attack that is conclusive. We are sure however that it is a considerable risk for a sub to attempt to get through our line."[17]

Official accounts of submarine kills by American submarine chasers varied, some sources claiming none, and others listing specific kills. Ens. Leighton credits the chasers with two kills: the first on 18 June 1918 by chasers stationed in Corfu, and the second on 2 October 1918, during the bombardment of Durazzo.[18] Both of these claims are questionable however, and even Leighton's own account is murky. His work includes two lists of U-boat sinkings[19] that not only don't include the alleged kill on 18 June (presumably the attack by Unit G listed below), but don't even match up with each other. Moreover, even after more that eighty years have passed, divers and historians are discovering new evidence that helps support some claims and contradicts others. It is a messy study.

Nonetheless, we can gain insight into the exploits of the American chasers from several sources. One is the first-hand, official accounts of the chaser officers serving at Corfu. Each attack was recorded and reported to naval authorities, and we can see in the record the stories of many notable events on the barrage line, including submarine detections, pursuits and attacks. The notations of "squares" in reports of pursuits and attacks refer to the numbered segments on the nautical chart.

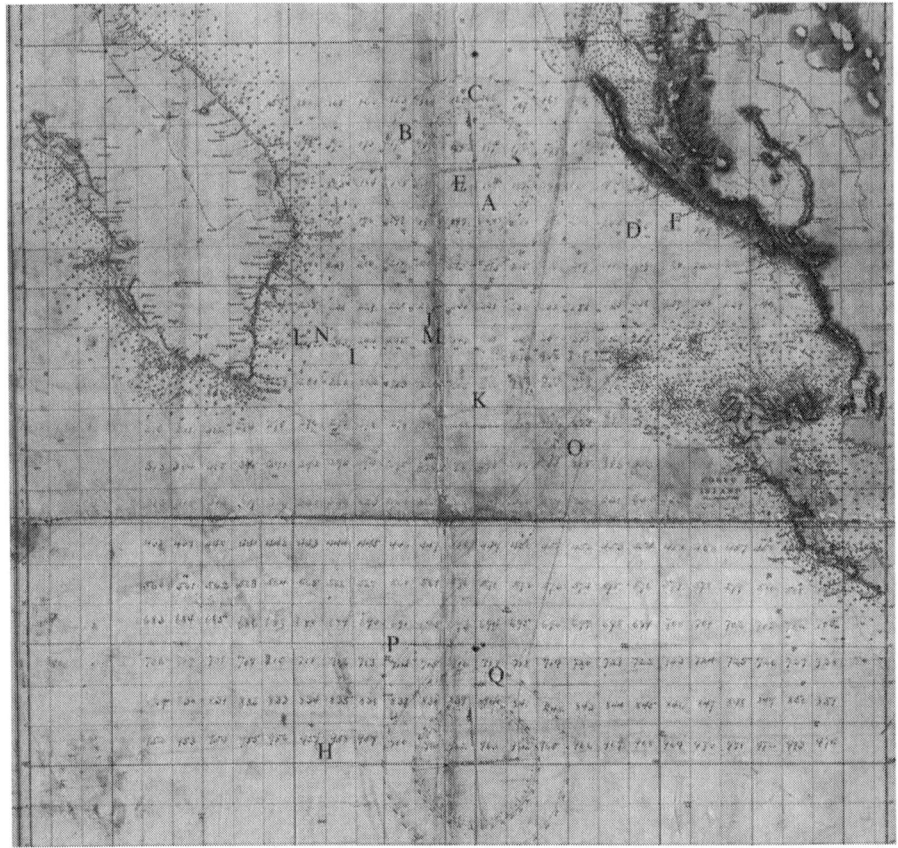

*Section of nautical chart used on SC 93 on the Otranto Barrage. Letters have been added to show the rough locations of pursuits/attacks.*

## Otranto Barrage: Submarine Chaser Hunt Incident Reports

**15 June 1918**

Unit E (SC 90, SC 92, SC 93) was on duty on the barrage line in the vicinity of square 188. SC 93 dropped the first depth charge by an American subchaser on the Otranto Barrage. SC 90 and SC 92 also dropped charges. There was no evidence observed of damage to a sub.[20] *Chart: point A*

**18 June 1918, 5:29 p.m.**

Unit G (SC 95, SC 179, SC 338) made sound contact with an enemy submarine, and followed it northeastward, attacking at Lat. N 40° 19', Long. E 18° 49' with a spread of 17 depth charges. A joint British-

American inquiry on USS *Leonidas* several days later concluded that while there was no confirmed kill, it was probable that an enemy submarine was damaged or destroyed.[21] *Chart: point B*

**19 June 1918, 11:30 a.m.**

Unit G (SC 95, SC 179, SC 338) and Unit F (SC 94, SC 227, SC 151) made sound contact with an enemy submarine. After losing and regaining contact several times, Unit G attacked with a spread of 16 depth charges at Lat. N 40° 24', Long. E 19°. Based on subsequent sound contact of the sub heading northward the attack was assumed to have been unsuccessful; but the supply of depth charges on board had been expended, so no further attack was made.[22] *Chart: point C*

**27 June 1918, 6:45 p.m.**

Unit E (SC 90, SC 92, SC 93) was located at Lat. N 40° 07', Long. E 19° 26', and detected several sound bearings, leading Lt. Borgeson, in command of unit leader SC 90, to believe that there could be two submarines in the vicinity. At 9:00 p.m., a sound was centered, and the unit waged an attack with no conclusive result, although the sound ceased. The second sound was detected at a distance, and the unit spent the night patrolling the hunting ground, but discovered no evidence of damage to a sub.[23] *Chart: point D*

**27 June 1918, 7:50 p.m. GMT**

SC 78 of Unit I (SC 77, SC 78, SC 79), on patrol in square 187, detected a sound at close range, at a bearing dead ahead. Five depth charges were dropped 30 seconds later. The chaser turned and stopped to listen with the K Tube, detecting a propeller noise and a rumbling sound for ten seconds. No further sounds were detected, and there was no evidence of damage to a sub.[24] *Chart: point E*

**28 June 1918, 2:30 p.m. and 8:45 p.m.**

While en route to relieve units on the barrage line, Unit H (SC 147, SC 324, SC 337) detected and tracked an enemy submarine for about two hours, then turned the hunt over to Unit E (SC 90, SC 92, SC 93), which continued the hunt, launching an attack in square 206, at Lat. N 40° 9', Long. E 19° 33', expending all but two of the unit's depth charges. The noise ceased, and the listener on SC 92 detected what he judged might be the sound of unsuccessful attempts to re-start a motor. At 8:45 p.m., Unit H detected the sound of a submarine close to its location and dropped a pattern of depth charges. There was no conclusive evidence of damage to a sub.[25] *Chart: point F*

**19 July 1918, 3:40 p.m.**
Unit A (SC 124, SC 125, SC 127) sighted a submarine on the surface with sails set, disguised as a trawler. The submarine submerged, and two depth charges were dropped. There was no evidence of damage to the sub.[26]

**30 July 1918, 4:40 a.m.**
Unit L (SC 248, SC 217, SC 82), positioned on Lat. N 39° 02', Long. E 18° 35', sighted a submarine heading southward. Unit L pursued, and the submarine was detected changing course to westward, about five miles away. At a distance of about three miles from the suspected location, the unit lost contact. No attack was waged.[27] *Chart: point H*

**19 August 1918, 4:00 a.m.**
Unit C (SC 349, SC 255, SC 256) received a report of a submarine, but was unable to make sound contact because a convoy was running engines during the listening period. After an Allied seaplane dropped a marker buoy on the spot of a sub heading northwesterly, Unit C dropped a pattern of 15 depth charges over the location, at Lat. N 39° 52', Long. E 18° 40'. There was no evidence of damage to a sub.[28] *Chart: point I*

**19 August 1918, 6:50 p.m.**
Unit L (SC 248, SC 217, SC 82) detected a submarine. A spread of 16 depth charges was dropped in square 229, Lat. N 39° 55', Long. E 18° 53' at 9:05 p.m. The sound ceased, but there was no evidence of damage to a sub.[29] *Chart: point J*

**22 August 1918, 2:00 p.m.**
Unit K (SC 130, SC 131, SC 216) detected the sound of a submarine on the surface, and engaged in a chase. At 4:35 a.m. the sound of a sub was detected, and an oil slick was sighted. SC 216 dropped two depth charges at Lat. N 39° 46', Long. E 19° 01'. A heavy wooden door was observed on the surface, and air bubbles and oil were observed for 90 minutes following the attack. No further sounds were detected.[30] *Chart: point K*

**1 September 1918, 8:00 p.m.**

SC 79 of Unit I (SC 77, SC 78, SC 79) intercepted a report from a British Motor Launch of a submarine in the vicinity, and proceeded to the location, detecting the submarine at Lat. N 39° 53', Long. E 18° 32'. SC 79 followed the sound to the west and joined the Motor Launches in the hunt. At 2:00 a.m. on 2 September contact was lost and the chase was discontinued.[31] *Chart: point L*

**8 September 1918, 2:25 GMT**

Unit A (SC 124, SC 125, SC 127), after a five-hour chase during which the unit leader had difficulty receiving good sound readings from the wing boats, dropped a pattern of 18 depth charges at Lat. N 39° 54', Long. E 18° 54'. Italian sea planes searched the hunt area, but detected no evidence of damage to a sub.[32] *Chart: point M*

**22 September 1918**

Unit H (SC 147, SC 324, SC 337), while hunting for the source of suspected underwater signaling near Cape St. Maria di Leuca, Italy, detected a slow engine sound, and engaged in a chase. At 8:29 p.m. a pattern of 18 depth charges was dropped on Lat. N 39° 54', Long. E 18° 35'. No further sounds were detected, and it was too dark to see anything on the surface. At daylight oil was detected on the surface of the attack location.[33] *Chart: point N*

**27 September 1918 3:55 p.m.**

Unit H (SC 147, SC 324, SC 337) detected a sound at Lat. N 39° 43', Long. E 19° 17', and engaged in a chase. At 4:15 p.m. air bubbles were seen on the surface, and two depth charges were dropped on Lat. N 39° 40', Long. E 19°16'. No further sound was detected. There as no evidence of damage to a sub.[34] *Chart: point O*

**2 October 1918**

Durazzo bombardment.
(Details in the next section.)

**19 October 1918, 1:08 a.m.**

Unit B (SC 215, SC 128, SC 129) detected a submarine at Lat. N 39° 15', Long. E 18° 47', heading southward. The unit conducted a 40-mile search, but was unable to locate the sub.[35] *Chart: point P*

**24 October 1918, 2:16 p.m.**
Unit E (SC 90, SC 92, SC 93) sighted a submarine on the surface near Lat. N 39° 08', Long. E 18° 45', believed to be an Austrian No. IV type, and engaged in a pursuit. A depth charge attack was mounted near Lat. N 39° 12', Long. E 19° 03', and crew members witnessed the form of a submarine lifted up from the sea, leaving a large oil slick and debris on the surface. The unit engaged in subsequent listening periods and detected a faint submarine sound. Contact was lost, and it is unknown if the attack was successful.[36] (See details of this attack in the Prologue.) *Chart: point Q*

## The Bombardment of Durazzo Harbor

Among the most discussed and publicized exploits involving American subchasers in WWI was the bombardment of the enemy naval base at Durazzo, Albania (later Durres), on 2 October 1918.

Units B, D, G and H, were called to Brindisi, Italy, on a special, top-secret mission. On 21 August 1918 the unit leaders of units H and K had been exchanged[37], so SC 130 led unit H in this mission; and SC 244 of Unit D was among those called for the assignment, but had mechanical problems[38] and remained in Brindisi. This left a force of eleven chasers to participate in the bombardment:

Unit B (SC 215, SC 128, SC 129)
Unit D (SC 225, SC 327)
Unit G (SC 95, SC 179, SC 338)
Unit H (SC 130, SC 337, SC 324)

The mission was the obliteration of an enemy naval base located in Durazzo harbor on the coast of Albania. Three Italian light cruisers and three British light scout cruisers were to bombard the base while the chasers provided a screen and kept any enemy subs occupied, and small Italian motor craft would speed into the harbor to launch missiles at short range.

Adm. Sims's account sets the stage: "Two subchaser units, six boats, were assigned to screen the Italian cruisers while the bombardment was underway. One unit, three boats, was stationed at Cape Pali, to the north, to prevent any submarines leaving Durazzo from attacking the British cruisers..."[39]

Crewman Stephen Crane West of SC 215 describes the activities of the morning of 2 October, as the crews of the chasers prepared to leave Brindisi harbor and head for Durazzo.

Preparations were immediately made for the destruction of all confidential information in the event of capture and orders for the destruction of the chaser itself, rather than allow it in the hands of the enemy. The life rail removed and a thin rope substituted forward to give the gun free action, ammunition passed up, depth charges set, and, for the first time in our experience, the officers and petty officers wore automatics and the crew life jackets.[40]

As the vessels approached the enemy base, they fell into formation. West continues the story:

Following Commander Nelson our line described a complete square to permit the battleships now coming up rapidly from the west to take their positions. One division of the larger ships went to the north and the other to the south of the harbor entrance. The chasers followed suit, the leading six going to the south with Commander Nelson and the remaining five under Lieutenant Commander Bastedo followed the 215 to the northward and nearer the shore, maneuvering for a position where we might maintain a course opposite to the battleships and between them and the shore.

*Italian destroyers steaming toward Durazzo.*

Shore batteries began firing, but the early shots fell far short of the chasers, which were safely out of range for the moment. Following the plan, the big guns began firing from the rear, first the Italian cruisers and then the British cruisers.

As the enemy batteries continued firing, subchaser Unit B was called to intercept a hospital ship attempting to leave the harbor. This required moving closer to the shore and within range of the enemy guns. "We were startled by a scream and crash, all involuntarily ducking our heads as an enemy shell

*Warships firing on Durazzo.*

passed close over, striking the water one hundred yards beyond us. This was almost immediately followed by another as close but short of us, and we commenced zigzagging or zagzigging as the excited flags insisted upon spelling it," West writes.[41]

But reports of submarine sightings cut short the pursuit. The interception of the hospital ship was left to other vessels. In rapid succession, two separate

*HMS Weymouth, torpedoed at Durazzo.*

attacks were made by the chasers on enemy subs. Even so, by the time the engagement had come to its conclusion – the shore batteries silenced, the shipping in the harbor sunk and the town in flames – the enemy submarines had managed to find a target. British cruiser HMS *Weymouth* suffered a torpedo hit to the stern, and four men were killed. On the return trip the ship limped back into Brindisi harbor, escorted by the chasers.

*Subchasers returning to Brindisi harbor after the attack on Durazzo. SC 179 in foreground.*

Yet on the whole, damages seemed relatively light. No Allied ships were lost, and HMS *Weymouth* was the only Allied ship to suffer crew fatalities.

The men on the chasers would return with tales of the kill, claiming the sinking of two submarines. Ens. Hilary Ranald Chambers, commander of SC 128, includes this account of a submarine kill at Durazzo:

> The 129 was the last boat in our unit and set off after the submarine she saw, just as our leader the 215 and we saw another. These subs, when the light cruisers had started north had evidently set out after them, and when they turned back to the southward they had stuck their periscopes up to see what was going on. They did not seem to pay the least attention to us, but had their eyes on the bigger game.
>
> The second shot from the 215's three-inch gun hit the periscope of the second submarine about 750 yards away and a big column of water and compressed air shot up six feet from the surface. The submarine kept going, however, as such a shot does not put them out of business. The escaping air from the periscope left a trail on the water and 128, maneuvering to the starboard

side of the 215, got him right between us (we were now one hundred yards apart), and we let go fourteen bombs with the result that up came pieces of the underwater craft. We did not stop to pick up evidence, however, as a third submarine was then reported by 129.

Meanwhile 129 had set off to intercept the sub she saw 1,600 yards distant. The periscope had not been seen for about a minute, which is a long time under such circumstances, when the executive officer stepped on the whistle, which is a signal to drop a depth charge. At the explosion of this charge, up came both periscopes of the submarine to see what had so jarred its peaceful progress. This gave the submarine's exact bearing to the chaser, and although the bomb had crippled the chaser's engine, in this condition she kept going and was able to intercept the course of the U boat, where she let go enough depth charges to entirely destroy the submarine.[42]

West picks up the story of SC 215's attack:

A little hummock of white water moving rapidly in the direction of the battleships indicated a submarine close under the surface and only a few hundred yards away. We swung about at once heading directly for it, leaving the 128 on our left in regular "hunt" formation, but with an interval of only one hundred yards. At first the "A" frame in the bow prevented a shot from our gun, but we swung two points to the left and Gundy let her have it. The first shot was too close, breaking our temporary life line and splitting the spray board. The second followed quickly and with wonderful results. The white hummock was converted for a moment into a fountain of spray as if forced up by compressed air, indicating a crushed periscope, and then disappeared. This was not sufficient and we ran directly over the spot where the spray disappeared and with the 128 dropped charges set for fifty feet. Ten seconds on the same course and then another from each boat; another ten seconds and both turned at right angles oppositely, firing the "Y" guns and at the same time letting one go from the stern. Six charges went off together, each containing more than four hundred pounds of TNT. There was a terrific detonation and in the pillar of water that rose there were discernible black parts of the submarine that sank back again and forever from view.

We had no sooner completed this evolution than our attention was called to the 129 now under way and dropping charges. She reported that while laying to, a submarine had appeared almost beneath her and through the quick action of one of her machinist's mates, she had been able to get under way, let go her bombs and bring home evidence of a submarine destroyed.[43]

In another account of the raid, Ray Millholland of SC 225 underscores the strategic value of the target:

> Durazzo was the most dangerous of the Austrian naval bases because it was closest to the Otranto Barrage. Allied naval experts classed its defenses against sea-attack with Gibraltar and the Dardanelles. It was considered impregnable.[44]

Millholland describes a situation in which Italy's very survival depended on the success of the mission, and he delivers an edge-of-your-seat account of the battle.

> Hour after hour the Austrian shore batteries fought a hopeless duel with the Allied Battle Fleet. But their mine fields had proved ineffective; their reliance on their submarine defense against bombarding battleships vanished under a barrage of depth mines...[45]

These contemporaneous accounts by men who served in the offensive portray the battle of Durazzo as a glorious affair, a showcase of the strategy of the navy and an example of the prowess of the subchaser men: It was a testament to the essential value of these small craft in the war, punctuated by the claim of sinking two enemy subs.

Recent historians have viewed the event in a significantly different light. One notable naval historian, Paul G. Halpern, states that, "The bombardment of Durazzo on 2 October 1918 can be compared to using a hammer to swat a fly."[46] Halpern points out that the Austrians evacuated Durazzo on 11 October, just over a week after the attack, a fact that he attributes to the military situation in the Balkans rather than to the bombardment of 2 October, and which he believes suggests that the attack on 2 October may have been pointless. Moreover, he notes that, "The Americans for many years cherished the erroneous belief that their submarine chasers had sunk two submarines that day. They had not."

Lt. Dole's visit to Durazzo would be in the second mission, on 18 October, when another team of chasers arrived and found nothing to attack, as the base had by then been abandoned. Instead they combed the harbor looking for mines, something Lt. Dole considered to be make-work, useful mainly as preparation for post-war mine clearing duties. One might suggest that since SC 93 was not in one of the units engaged in the more glamorous events of 2 October, Lt. Dole may have had motive to understate the Durazzo bombardment. Maybe so, but he was not one for talking big, even with regard to those events that directly involved his own chaser. His tendency to maintain a level-headed calm in his discourse might render his account worthy of note.

His view on the 2 October bombardment seems to support the less flattering position voiced by Halpern, at least with respect to what he viewed as exaggerated news accounts of the chasers' role. Apparently within weeks of the bombardment, stories had already begun to fly concerning the impact of the chasers in this event, and letters from home touched on the notion that chasers were being credited for assisting in the sinking of enemy warships in Durazzo harbor. This was an idea that Lt. Dole found ridiculous. "In one of my letters I mentioned activities at Durazzo," he writes. "Am not at liberty to state any particulars etc. The newspaper statements are not correct showing that they do not come through official channels. All was accomplished that has been in the papers but not in the manner indicated." This, evidently was especially true of the chasers' role. "The part that the chasers played is not that given in the account of the papers in most respects," he continues. "It is folly to think of these chasers sinking shipping in harbors when battleships & cruisers are at hand any one of which could sink the whole fleet of ships at D\_\_\_\_ before an S.C. could make much of an impression on one of them."[47]

Even after these comments, letters from home continued to touch on reports of the heroism of the men on the subchasers at Durazzo, and how perhaps in telling the story of the chasers a couple of exciting chapters might be devoted to the bombardment. "In regard to the Durazzo affair," Lt. Dole responded, "I am afraid that when you hear the true story the 'two chapters' will dwindle to a few lines... It was a very interesting but tame affair and the second episode still more so."[48]

On the matter of sinking submarines and other enemy warships at Durazzo, Lt. Dole doesn't directly comment, but his account is consistent with the more modern interpretation of the events. "Can not write of operations, but no chaser fired a shot at Durazzo engagement except 2 at a periscope and one shot at a floating mine that sunk without exploding."[49]

A rather curious account of the Durazzo bombardment appears in an issue of the Submarine Chaser Club of America newsletter. In the June 1921 issue, a transcript was posted of a letter purporting to be from Rear Admiral A. Catinelli of the Austrian navy, who was present during the bombardment of Durazzo. The letter is addressed to Mr. Blumenthal, probably Ens. Hugo W. Blumenthal, commanding officer of SC 80, who, according to the letter, had claimed the sinking of a sub by an American subchaser at Durazzo. As SC 80 was among the subchasers that performed diplomatic missions along the Albanian coast after the war, it is certainly plausible that a conversation between Adm. Catinelli and Ens. Blumenthal on the topic of the Durazzo bombardment took place.

The letter, a portion of which follows, is titled *Durazzo – The Other Side of the Story*, and is dated Vienna, 5 March 1921.

> You told me when you were in Cattaro that on October 2 you had sunk one of our submarines. If I denied this at the time my statement was entirely in accord with the facts. I had under my command at that time three destroyers in the harbor and two submarines ten miles seaward from Durazzo. One of these U boats, according to the report of its commander, torpedoed a small English cruiser (type Glasgow). Besides these U boats there was a German submarine, possibly two, still further seaward from Durazzo. Now a German U boat was missing at the end of October and I therefore assume that this might possibly be the one which was sunk by you.

The letter, if it is authentic, calls into question the claim that two enemy subs were sunk, but leaves open the possibility that one may have been. Lt. Comdr. E.E. Spafford, in his report on post-war duties on the Dalmatian coast notes a similar report concerning the Austrian submarines at Durazzo. "I was also informed by Lieutenant Commander Loftin that he had seen the officers in command of the Austrian submarines off Durazzo and that they denied having been sunk or of having had their periscopes shot away."[50]

But even if we were to dismiss the notion of the sinking of submarines at Durazzo by the chasers, two questions remain. First, did the chasers contribute to the outcome? And second, did the bombardment have a strategic value? The answer to the first question is almost certainly yes. Even Halpern notes that the screening function of the chasers thwarted an Austrian sub in its effort to get into position to attack the Allied warships.[51] And if the account by Adm. Catinelli is authentic and accurate, and two, possibly four subs were present in the vicinity during the raid, then considering the plethora of Allied warships to target, the single shot to HMS *Weymouth* by enemy submarine fire would suggest that the chasers did indeed perform their intended function rather effectively.

The strategic value of the bombardment is a matter that may never be settled, for the answer depends on one's point of view concerning the purpose of the raid. If the purpose was to eliminate a dangerous enemy naval base, as Millholland suggests, then Halpern's view is probably correct, and we may chalk it up as an example of military overkill. But as the Armistice neared, the sense of the need to demonstrate the absolute domination of the Allied forces over the enemy may have been, if not the ostensible reason for the raid, at least a strong factor leading to its approval. The symbolic value of destroying a strategic enemy base as the prospects for victory grew brighter shouldn't be overlooked. The bombardment of Durazzo, involving the navies of Italy, England and the United States, was an assertion of the inevitable victory of the Allies in the sea war.

**The Armistice**

By mid-October 1918, Lt. Dole felt confident that the war would be won, and soon. "Everything is going nicely, and it looks as if the real scrapping was over, at least on the sea. The chasers have accomplished the purpose for which they were sent in a satisfactory manner. ... Am satisfied that the Hun is on his last legs and will not again become seriously threatening."[52]

A few weeks later, at 9:58 a.m. on 11 November, USS *Leonidas* sent signals to the chasers that the Armistice had been signed by Allied staff. Hostilities were to cease; no more sinking of enemy vessels.[53] The war was over.

In Corfu, USS *Leonidas* and the chasers fired celebratory salutes. "News of the signing of the Armistice by Germany came over the wire this a.m.," Lt. Dole writes home. "This gang sure did send up a shout, and toot whistles. ... For all practical purposes the murderer is chained and modern Babylon fallen."

Life would now become considerably simpler. "It will seem strange to pass through mine fields that are buoyed and cruise with running lights and navigational aids, to be able to light a cigar or pipe at night and smoke it on deck," Lt. Dole writes. "It will be a picnic."[54]

The celebration lasted into the following day, when, as Lt. Dole reports, "Representatives of the Allied fleets fired 21 guns at morning colors. The SCs circled through the fleet and also saluted. Moving pictures were taken, and perhaps you may be able to see them in the U.S. before I get back."[55]

*The celebration at Corfu, 11 November 1918.*

*Subchaser firing a salute at Corfu, 11 November 1918.*

It seemed that before long the chasers would be headed back to the United States, and there was nothing left to do but wile away the hours. "This war is over for all practical purposes and we will soon start from here on a pleasure cruise about the Mediterranean killing time while awaiting favorable weather for crossing the Atlantic, unless we unexpectedly get word to return immediately to the U.S., which is improbable," Dole writes to his brother.[56]

But soon the notion of a quick trip home would seem equally improbable. Some of the chasers, including SC 93, would be called upon to perform diplomatic missions along the eastern Adriatic coast. These small vessels might have seemed a curious choice as vehicles of diplomacy, but tensions between Italy and Albania made it a prudent matter to call on American service men for the task. Both the pleasure cruise and the trip home would have to wait: Lt. Dole and his fellow chaser commanders were ordered to sail for Cattaro.

## Chapter 6 – Post-War Diplomacy and Travels

*"The great guns that made the harbor practically impregnable we saw dismantled and their foundations destroyed."*[1]

Lt. George S. Dole

For the chaser crews, the signing of the Armistice lifted an immense burden. The tireless search for enemies lurking below came to an end, and travel on the seas became much less perilous – in no small measure due to the new freedom to operate with running lights on. "Going through a storm now is easier than a sub search in calm weather," Lt. Dole writes.[2] Moreover, during the war it had been necessary to keep six men stationed on deck with binoculars, in addition to the lookouts and signalmen, to search the surface of the sea for evidence of mines. Now, with most mined areas buoyed, navigation was considerably simpler.

But although the Otranto Barrage had been discontinued, military matters in the Adriatic were far from settled. The rumors that subchasers might be assigned to trips to China or to the mine sweeping operations in the North Sea would be set aside for the time being.

The practical component of the U.S. Navy's post-war mission in the region was to assist with the transfer of Austrian warships in the Adriatic Sea according to the terms of the Armistice with Austria. But a greater challenge confronted them: the tense, often violent relations between people on the eastern coast of the Adriatic Sea who were attempting to form a new government with political autonomy and control of the region, and the government of Italy, seeking a settlement that would include Italian control of this strategic coastal territory. The value of an American naval presence in the region to help maintain order quickly became apparent, and the subchaser divisions at Corfu were in the right place at the right time to take part in the early phase of this service. Therefore, on orders from Rear Adm. W.H. Bullard, Commander of U.S. Naval Forces in the Eastern Mediterranean, the chaser force at Base 25 embarked on another tour of duty.

The movement from Base 25 started on 10 November 1918, when subchaser Unit J, under the command of Lt. Comdr. Frank Loftin, proceeded to Cattaro, a seaport town north of Durazzo, about a quarter of the way up the coast. Then on 15 November, Lt. Comdr. Spafford received orders to take command of six units of chasers, and to assign them to Lissa (Unit F), Meleda (Unit I), Spalato (Unit C), Pola (Unit G) and Fiume (Unit A and Unit L). The primary mission of these chaser units was to report developments in these ports to Adm. Bullard. But they were also advised to "get in touch with Jugo-Slav representatives and do everything in your power to convince them of the sympathy of the United States," and to be prepared for the takeover of ships, a likely scenario. "In case of the surrender of ships now under the flag of the Jugo-Slavs according to the terms of the Armistice," they were advised, "hoist colors of the United States together with flags of co-operating associate powers. Give receipt in the name of the United States and take all precautions to safeguard material, ships to be treated as held in trust by the Allies and the United States until their final disposition by peace negotiations."[3]

Operating from SC 248, Lt. Comdr. Spafford carried out his orders, visiting locations along the Adriatic coast, assigning chaser units to each of the specified ports, and reporting on the ships present in each port, the flags currently flown, and the disposition of the people toward the U.S.

Reporting on his arrival at Spalato (Split) on 17 November, he remarks, "People on shore came running down waving and cheering. The impression made upon me was that the number of small chasers were symbolic of the United States in that separately they had little strength, but united were formidable."[4] As he entered the harbor at Spalato, he found two Austrian battleships, *Radetzky* and *Zriski*, complying with orders concerning the pending transfer of authority to the U.S. Navy by flying both the American flag and the new flag of the provisional government.

The people on shore received him warmly, the three men that comprised the local provisional Jugoslav government at Spalato eager to curry favor and to complain to him of their treatment by the Italians. (This new government would be known until the late 1920s as the Kingdom of Serbs, Croats and Slovenes, but for the sake of brevity, the terms Jugoslav and Jugoslavia are used in this text.)

The first intrigue occurred on the morning of 18 November 1918, when Lt. Comdr. Spafford discovered evidence that the commanding officer of *Radetzky* was engaged in trafficking in provisions, using the steamer *Fram*, a formerly Austrian vessel, to pick up local provisions on the pretense of distributing them to local populations in need. Instead *Radetzky* appeared to be handing over the goods to a government official at Spalato, who was selling them and turning the money over to the provisional government.

Lt. Comdr. Spafford ordered a stop to the transfer, "taking the stand that the Jugo-Slavs not having been recognized, that I could do absolutely nothing to aid them in raising revenue."[5] This created an uproar on the vessel, resulting in Lt. Comdr. Spafford's decision to take command of *Radetzky* promptly, before the incident was allowed to escalate. He took command of the ship that afternoon, and issued a receipt in the name of the United States. Arrangements were also made to place two torpedo boats in the harbor under U.S. protection, and Lt. Comdr. Spafford assigned a subchaser for that duty.

Soon all the units of subchasers from Base 25 were engaged in post-war duties along the Adriatic coast. On 18 November, Unit B, and SC 225 and SC 244 of Unit D, were sent with Belgian tanker *Matzouk* to provide fuel for the chasers stationed in the Adriatic; and on 19 November, Unit H was sent to Cattaro. Units A, C and G returned to Corfu on 21 November, and left the following day with units E and K, carrying a draft of six officers and one hundred twenty-five men bound for duty on the Adriatic coast. "One year from the date the 93 left Bayonne, NJ, almost to the hour," Lt. Dole reports, "we weighed anchor and eased out of our base at Corfu."[6]

**Cattaro**

The passage to Cattaro on 22 November was difficult, just one day in duration, but the seas were among the roughest Lt. Dole had seen while stationed in the Mediterranean. In a letter home, he reports:

> When it came my turn to go below I spent about five minutes trying to get into my bunk and finally succeeded only to be thrown out and wreck all the furniture in the cabin. It took me about ten minutes to get clear of the wreckage. I tried to take a nap on my mattress which I put on the deck but had no luck in staying on it so decided to go topside and get the fresh air of which there was plenty. Our course was directly in the trough of the sea and we caught all the combers in the Adriatic. The boat stood it finely but was pretty wet most of the time.[7]

They arrived safely in spite of the weather, and Lt. Dole was impressed with the port. "Cattaro is the finest harbor I have ever seen, one of the finest in the world, and was one of the great sub bases the Austrians had," he writes. Ens. Hilary Chambers, commanding officer of SC 128, was equally enamored of the harbors of Cattaro. "This is a very beautiful harbor half way up the east side of the Adriatic," he writes. "There are three immense harbors one behind the other and protected from the sea by high mountains that leave but a narrow entrance to the first of these."[8] He describes the large submarine base located at Cattaro, and the acquisition by the chaser men of all types of tools, equipment and supplies from the base. While stationed in Cattaro, Lt. Dole and his colleagues saw this strategic and well defended submarine base disarmed, the large guns removed and their bases destroyed.[9]

Their mission at Cattaro at this early stage of diplomacy was primarily to show an American presence, but small vessels also proved useful. The chasers

*U.S. sailors patrol a road at Cattaro.*

performed transport duties, carrying American troops between stations. Lt. Dole enjoyed the work and had high praise for the American soldiers, finding them to be in good health, enthusiastic and "willing to go back into the trenches if necessary."

Here, too, tensions were high between the Jugoslavs and the Italians. A report from SC 77, ordered to Cattaro on 25 November, describes the situation at this port:

> At 0900 went alongside U.S.S.C. 80 and conferred with Lieutenant Commander F. Loftin, U.S. Navy. It appeared that at any time there might be bloodshed between the Italians and the Jugo-Slavs, and that the situation is extremely critical. ... We went aboard the Jugo-Slav flagship and paid a call on Rear Admiral Catinelli, who received us most courteously. Apparently he has the best of good feelings for the Americans.[10]

Adm. Catinelli, now commander of the Jugoslav navy, had met earlier with Lt. Comdr. Spafford, and had shown the same favorable feelings toward the U.S., not only supporting the hand-over of ships to the Americans, but recommending to Lt. Comdr. Spafford that the vessels taken over by the U.S. be assembled at Cattaro, a port he considered to be superior to all others in the region.[11]

*An ammunition dump at Cattaro.*

Lt. Dole likewise reported that the Jugoslavs at Cattaro were friendly toward the Americans, and that they hoped that a U.S. presence would be maintained there. He writes, "The Jugo-slavs welcome us with great enthusiasm. They want the Americans to handle their affairs till the peace is settled. They do not trust the other nations. The Jugo-slavs look upon Wilson as a second Christ, come to redeem them from slavery."[12]

This characterization was less an exaggeration than one might think. As the political tensions between Italy and the provisional government worsened, the United States assumed the peculiar role of protector of the emerging Jugoslav government – largely comprised of Serbs, an Allied power – against the aggression of Italy, another Allied power. A Navy Department report describes American efforts "to check Italian expansion in the Adriatic at the expense of the then amorphous Jugoslavia, and to support the new state in conformity with Wilson's principles of national self-determination."[13]

The chasers continued to operate at Cattaro until the movement of U.S. troops was complete and the French had arrived to take charge of that region.[14] SC 93 and the other chasers receive orders to sail for Spalato on 27 November.

**Spalato**

While Lt. Comdr. Spafford's initial assessment of Spalato had been that conditions there were acceptable, the availability of food and other provisions among the local populations had rapidly diminished. When SC 93 arrived, Lt. Dole found what he considered a wrecked society, noting that the local people's food stores were so badly depleted that his men generally declined to eat ashore, not wishing to take what little the local people had.

When he did go ashore, Lt. Dole found the Jugoslavs there as friendly toward the Americans as they had been at Cattaro, but that there was considerable tension in the region, not all due to anti-Italian sentiment. "There are a few Huns here and they practically control all the restaurants," he writes. "They do not admit that they are Huns tho."[15] On the streets as well, Lt. Dole came across people whom he suspected of being "Hun sympathizers," who showed him none of the warmth that he felt from the Jugoslav population.

By this time, talk of the next tour of duty for the chasers had already started. "We get rumors hourly," Lt. Dole remarks.[16] The rumor of the chasers heading to China resurfaced, a voyage that Lt. Dole estimated as requiring ninety days at sea, requiring a tanker to allow for refueling, and calling into question the very practicality of such a venture. Even upon receiving orders to prepare for such a trip, he remained convinced that the trip would never actually take place.

But regardless of the destination, Lt. Dole was anxious to be on the move again. The choppy, short seas of the inland waters meant that the boat was constantly wet. The men brought their bedding up on deck to dry whenever

*Harbor at Spalato.*

*Street in Spalato.*

there was sun, but November was a rainy month, and much of the time their quarters were soaking wet. "I have slept with oilskins and rubber boots," Dole notes, "and an oilskin hat for a pillow. There have been times of a week at a stretch that the bunks have been soaked and if you get any sleep at all you had to put on oilskins and lie on top of the bunk."[17] The prospects for open ocean travel, where longer seas meant a smoother and drier ride for the chasers, seemed attractive.

Lt. Dole's crew spent Thanksgiving Day, 1918, on board the chaser, and remained in the region into mid-December. But as the days passed, the likelihood of a China trip grew fainter, and rumors began to crop up that the chasers would be sold to the Italians. This was a possibility that seemed more to Lt. Dole's liking, as it would mean a much more rapid return to the United States. In the meantime, they continued their duties, which included assisting in the transport of civilians and the officers and crews displaced by the takeover of vessels by the U.S. Navy to ports up and down the coast near their homes.

While operating in this region, the officers of the chasers enjoyed relatively warm relationships with commanders of Austrian submarines. From his discussions with these men, Lt. Dole found insight into the nature of the submarine chasers' work at Corfu:

Since arriving at the Austrian sub bases we have been able to get a line on our work. The Austrians say that prior to the coming of the SC boats the subs had everything their own way and rarely submerged when passing through the straits. The chasers here have accounted for several U boats according to their own (the Austrian sub commanders') statements and the SCs were the only boats they feared. They had to put crews on subs at the point of the bayonet after the SCs got their barrage established and frequently the subs would refuse to pass our line. They would return to port. The commander said it was very difficult to shake off the SCs and they never took a chance of passing through the line on the surface even at night. They would escape on the surface from British and Italian craft but would dive when sighting an SC whether the SC sighted them or not. Often they would attack a British or Italian boat but they never took a chance with the SC boats. They had orders to dive immediately and make every effort to escape.[18]

But in spite of the good relations enjoyed with most of the people on shore, Lt. Dole was unimpressed with Spalato, and took only a few shore leaves. Shortly before leaving this port, he took a day trip into the country, passing through the villages of Krlis and Salona, and visiting the ruins of a palace of Diocletian and "a couple of ancient cities." Perhaps anxious to be finished with his tour of duty in this region, he remarks, "They are interesting only to an archeologist."[19]

As the work progressed, additional French and American forces arrived, and the full force of chasers was no longer required. The U.S. Navy would maintain a presence in the region for more than two years, the final withdrawal not taking place until Italy's renunciation of its claim to the region put the matter to rest; and some chasers would play a role in this protracted U.S. presence. But most were sent back to Corfu in December 1918. SC 93 was among nine units of chasers that received orders to return to Corfu in mid-December and were soon ordered to proceed to Malta for repairs in dry-dock. The possibility of a trip to China now seemed remote, and Lt. Dole looked forward to fair weather for a return trip to the U.S.

## Malta

After the brief stop in Corfu and yet another stormy passage, SC 93 made landfall at Malta on Christmas Eve, 1918. There were many ships waiting for dry-dock services, and it would be almost two weeks before SC 93 would have its turn. As the Americans at Malta celebrated New Year's Eve, Lt. Dole reported that while he was on guard duty and thus couldn't participate in the festivities, the other chasers made enough noise to give the Americans a high

*The harbor at Malta.*

average for celebration.[20]

The weather at Malta was pleasant, the rainy season over, and temperatures warm enough to allow the men to sit on deck in shirtsleeves, or spend an afternoon in the countryside. Food stores were starting to become more readily available, adding to the sense that things were getting better. The hotels,

*Pleasant memories of the Maltese People. Lt. Dole, center.*

however, were under ration conditions, and Lt. Dole found, "I could get a better meal aboard my own ship."

He found the people of Malta to be friendly, and his stay there enjoyable. In summing up the visit, he writes, "Suffice it to say that up to the present my most pleasant recollections of the Great War will center about Malta and its people."[21]

## Italy

On 17 January 1919, SC 93 reached Messina, Sicily. Here Lt. Dole witnessed the still-evident destruction of a devastating earthquake that had taken place about ten years before. "The loss was so terrific that the city and its people have never recovered from the shock," he writes. "The streets are filthy, evil smelling, the people poorly clad, ill fed and seemingly without energy."[22]

In part as a form of recognition for their duty on the Barrage line, but also because logistics of the return trip allowed some leeway, the chaser men were allowed some free time to see the countryside. Lt. Dole spent two days in Rome, touring the Forum, the Baths of Colcara, St. Paul's Cathedral and St. Peter's Cathedral, and the Vatican. Italian officers treated him to dinner at Civita Vecchia, and he enjoyed his time moored in the port at La Spezia, a

*La Spezia, Italy.*

beautiful Italian harbor.

Receiving letters from home discussing post-war reconstruction, Lt. Dole conveyed a sense of the tenuousness of the peace, and the gravity of the political situation: "All Germany wants is a 'breather' and time to form coalition with

Russia to again take up arms. This may seem far fetched but such would be the case if opportunity were granted. ... Have seen quite a few of the prisoners both Austrian and German, and they do not make delightful company, and seem to live with the idea of turning the tables."[23]

Skeptical of the Germans' commitment to the terms of the Armistice, Lt. Dole believed that the Germans had not disarmed as agreed, and that in short order they could re-equip armies. The appropriate response would become a topic of continuing debate lasting to this day. In Lt. Dole's mind, the Germans needed to be made to pay dearly for crimes committed in the war, and given very little leeway in the process.

**France**

At the end of January, several units of chasers, SC 93 among them, arrived in picturesque Villefranche harbor, near Nice, France. Here they made plans for a tour of French cities.

*The unit at Villefranche, France.*

Lt. Dole toured Villefranche, Nice and Marseilles, and a side-trip to the casinos at Monte Carlo offered good entertainment. In Nice he attended a dance hosted by the Y.M.C.A., and "had a fine time," but found the dance steps to be over-complicated, and chose to spend time at the refreshment table.

SC 93 received orders to sail for Gibraltar on 14 February, and from there, if plans to sell the chasers to the Italians didn't materialize, he anticipated retracing the route they had taken from New London. Once again, the prospects for going home seemed to be good. "We feel as if we were within a reasonable distance from the U.S. as we can see the Atlantic, and have just put 1,800 miles behind us," Dole writes from Gibraltar.[24]

In Gibraltar the chasers were placed in quarantine because of reports of cases of the flu aboard some chasers. SC 93 remained quarantined for three days, after which time the crew were allowed to come ashore, and Lt. Dole enjoyed walks on the mainland.

Here Lt. Dole and his crew would begin to dismantle and remove the armament on the chasers in anticipation of sale of the vessels. Orders issued from the U.S. Naval Base in Plymouth, England (Base 27) were distributed to all chasers, calling for the removal of the K Tube, trailing wire, Y-gun, deck gun, radio telephone, shape signals, machine guns, rifles, small arms and all ammunition. The chasers were to be completely disarmed.[25] Additionally, secret code and signal publications were to be destroyed and reports of their destruction filed with naval authorities.[26]

First to go were the depth charges, removal of which meant the removal of a major source of problems for the chaser men. "We have trouble with these carried on deck every time we hit a rough sea," Dole explains, "and we have had some lively times trying to secure them when they go adrift on the deck. Will say farewell to them with a great deal of pleasure."[27]

Before they were able to remove the charges, the crew saw some excitement in the form of a fire in the engine room, caused by one of the main engines backfiring into the bilges. They used pyrene to put out the fire, and another chaser stood by with a pressure hose, but it wasn't needed. Lt. Dole writes, "No damage was done to the vessel outside of giving the crew a sizeable paint scraping job in the engine room."[28]

In Gibraltar Lt. Dole would part company with Mr. Snow, his Executive Officer, who was re-assigned as commanding officer of SC 256. Lt. Dole had found Mr. Snow to be a good executive officer, but was pleased to see him receive a command of his own.

During his leave from the boat, Lt. Dole visited two German U-boats – one of the type UC III boats and one of the large Type UE 2 submarines – that had just been brought into the harbor by the British. He was impressed with the equipment on these submarines, and remarked on the power of the smaller U-boat's periscopes.

## Portugal

Lt. Dole received orders to sail from Gibraltar to Lisbon, Portugal, and set out on 13 March 1919. He still had no idea of what lay ahead. A large-scale sale of chasers overseas didn't seem to be taking place. Of the thirty-six chasers that had served on the Otranto Barrage, only eight were sold to Italy, SC 78, SC 82, SC 94, SC 128, SC 179, SC 215, SC 248 and SC 327. Had his chaser been sold, he would have expected to be on his way home on a transport ship; and if not, he would have anticipated sailing for the Azores, Bermuda, and then to somewhere on the east coast of the U.S. Being ordered to Lisbon was an indication that another tour of duty lay ahead. "Everything is going nicely," he writes home, "but all dope about getting back this summer may be badly upset. Am willing to spend what time is necessary to clear things up in good shape, and will not ask for release till it is all over."[29]

*Chasers in Lisbon, Portugal.*

Late in March, rumors began to develop of an assignment to Archangel, Russia, to assist American troops there. "Do not believe this will materialize," Lt. Dole writes, "but anything may happen. The situation in Russia is acute, but can't see what use these chasers would be there. We might run up a few rivers and distribute supplies but barges could do better and more efficient work. ... Have an idea that the scheme of sending us to Russia will be abandoned."[30] But in this case, the rumor would prove to be true. Soon Lt. Dole would be heading for Inverness, Scotland, to prepare for a trip over the Arctic Circle and into the White Sea.

# Chapter 7 – The Northern Russia Expedition

*"We are some gunboats now. In fact have more powerful guns than the old gunboats of the Spanish war. ... The batteries of these boats are equal to eight complete field batteries, or more than the complement of a small army."*[1]

Lt. George S. Dole

## Military Situation, White Sea

The primary ostensible reason for the U.S. participation in the Allied intervention in northern Russia near the end of the war and into mid-1919 was the protection of trading ports such as Murmansk and Archangel, which were considered strategic military targets. A Department of State memo dated 3 August 1918 presents the official U.S. war time position:

> The only present objective for which American troops will be employed will be to guard military stores which may be subsequently needed by Russian forces and to render such aid as may be acceptable to the Russians. With such objects in view the Government of the United States is now co-operating with the Governments of France and Great Britain in the neighbourhood of Murmansk and Archangel.[2]

The prospect of these supplies falling into the hands of the Germans, or worse yet of German sub bases being constructed in northern Russia, had to be prevented. Leonid Strakhovsky, author of several works on the history of this region, would later describe this component of the military objective in northern Russia as "eminently successful, since it checked German designs to use the Northern Russian ports as submarine bases and prevented a large amount of war supplies, which the Bolsheviks had no time to evacuate, from falling into German hands."[3]

But the political and military situation created by the presence of Allied troops in northern Russia was complicated. In July 1918, as President Wilson prepared to send American troops to the region, the Russian Revolution was fully under way, and as author Ernest Halliday notes in his work on the role of American troops in northern Russia, "...many prominent Allied leaders regarded the demise of the Soviet regime, in the midsummer of 1918, as not only highly desirable, but in all probability easy to bring about, since the Communist leaders were plagued by the most formidable economic, political, and military problems imaginable."[4] Moreover, the Russian people present in the areas of Murmansk and Archangel were mostly "White Russians," Tzarists, so as the Allies entered the region to protect trading ports, they naturally began working alongside the enemies of the Bolshevik movement.

It is perhaps unsurprising, then, that regardless of the official position of the Wilson administration, U.S. troops joining British and French forces in the region became involved in active warfare against the Bolsheviks.

In late October 1918, Rear Admiral Newton A. McCully assumed command of U.S. Naval Forces in Northern Russia, with the patrol yacht USS *Yankton* as temporary flagship. A guidance statement for Adm. McCully described the U.S. policy with respect to Russia, which was more or less the same as it had been in August:

> ... This government regards Russia and the Russian people as Allies and as cobelligerents and that the Bolsheviki movement has not modified the purpose of the United States wherever it may be able to do so to assist the Russian people in maintaining the liberties they have gained by the Revolution, and becoming masters of their own affairs.[5]

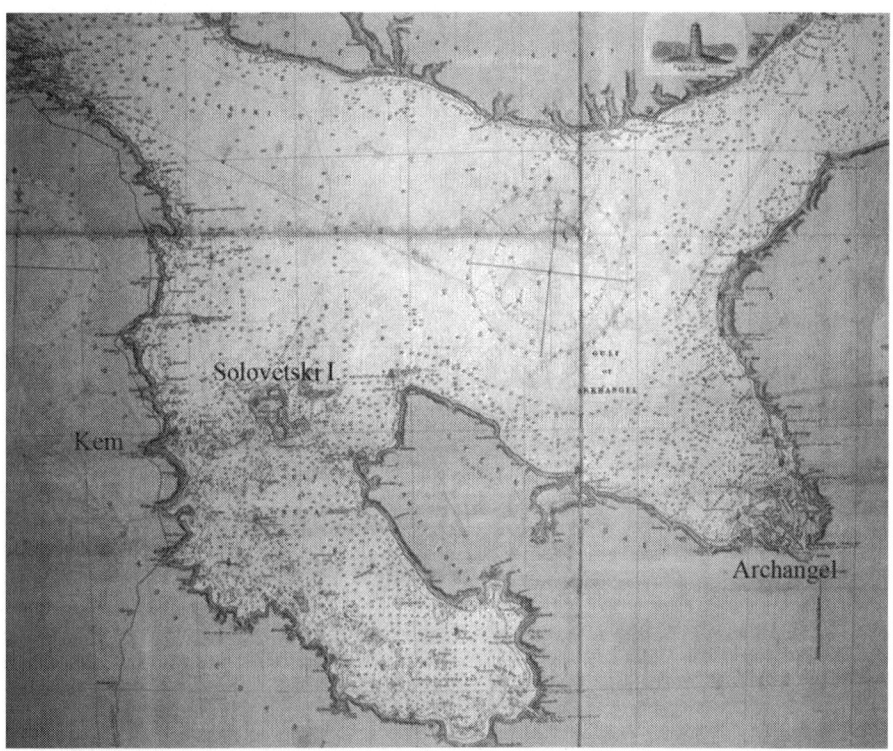

*Section of original nautical chart from SC 354: 2278 White Sea. (Place name labels added)*

U.S. troops in the region, according to this statement, were not there for the purpose of engaging in the Bolshevik turmoil, but rather for the purpose of helping local Russians. But this was an increasingly fine and delicate line to draw. The Bolsheviks considered northern Russia to be under their sovereign control and had called for the withdrawal of the Allied forces from the region. By stressing this need to "assist the Russian people," the Wilson administration could ignore the demands for withdrawal without taking any position with regard to the political subtext of seeking the "demise of the Soviet regime."

With the signing of the Armistice, the threat of German invasion had passed. While no immediate plans were made for withdrawal of U.S. troops from northern Russia, the war was over, and ideological objections to communism notwithstanding, the administration found it increasingly difficult to justify keeping U.S. troops there. Yet the onset of winter and the blockage by ice of key northern waterways made it impossible to effect a hasty withdrawal, even had the administration chosen to do so.

In this context of the annual winter ice conditions at Archangel and the potential for further belligerence involving American forces, Adm. McCully and Adm. Sims began to make preparations for the coming spring, when the melting of the ice would allow passage of heavily armed Bolshevik vessels. Adm. McCully reported that when the waters opened up, if the enemy "makes a determined effort we will meet with disaster." He requested that two more warships be sent, a Denver-class cruiser to replace USS *Yankton* as flagship and the gunboat USS *Sacramento* (AG 19) to engage in patrol duties. Additionally, he noted that small war vessels with adequately shallow draft to allow them to run up the Dvina River and other waterways as soon as the ice melted would be highly strategic, providing mobile firepower to destroy enemy communications and mount a defense against hostile vessels on the river. "Only heavy reinforcements of reliable troops can make situation secure," he reported. "For subsequent operations on the Dvina recommend twelve subchasers with tender be sent, as vessels drawing seven feet cannot operate in this river. Vessels of subchaser type can operate in all interior waters of Russia from White Sea to Caspian."[6]

Adm. Sims confirmed this recommendation in a cablegram message to Adm. William S. Benson:

> You have message from McCully requesting chasers. In a subsequent cable after conference with senior Allied Naval Officer, Murmansk, he states that the vessels likely to be most useful for active operations are chasers. He is thoroughly familiar with capabilities of these vessels. Am of the opinion they will be most useful assistance in same withdrawal of Army and consider

situation such that we should take no chance lack of vessels. Recommend chasers be sent.[7]

Plans were made to send twelve chasers to Inverness, Scotland, to prepare for duty in the White Sea. Denver-class light cruiser USS *Des Moines* (C 15) was detached from service in the South Pacific and ordered to proceed to Archangel. USS *Sacramento* was also assigned to this service; as were three Eagle boats, a new type of ASW vessel larger than the chasers, produced on assembly lines by Ford Motor Company.[8]

**Submarine Chasers Assigned to Northern Russia Service**

In the third week of March 1919, Capt. Nelson began soliciting chaser commanders for northern Russia service, issuing from USS *Leonidas* a call for volunteers:

> Preparations will be made here to fit out 12 chasers for service in Russian waters. These chasers will be fitted with two 3" guns and rapid fire guns. Here the Bolsheviki have, especially on the Dwina, armed vessels, and the Allies, in addition to the chasers, have monitors. When the river opens up in the spring the Allied land forces, which are badly outnumbered by the Bolsheviki will be in a dangerous position. The chasers are expected to be of great service to them in protecting their communications on the Dwina and raiding the Bolsheviki communications.[9]

Lt. Dole was among three officers chosen from his detachment for this service. "I am transferred and will tomorrow assume command of the SC 354, bound for Arkhangel Russia," he tells his brother. "The Bolsheviki are getting gay and it looks as if I would have to pay my respects to Trotsky and Lenin."[10] He looked forward to the trip, although he knew it meant putting off his return to the states, perhaps for a year or two. "Do not wait to get married till I get back," he tells his brother, whose engagement was imminent. "If you do you are likely to get baldheaded first. Will be with you in spirit."

His preference was to take SC 93, but the authorities believed that SC 93 had seen too much service, and decided to give him the command of SC 354, a newer chaser which had served in Plymouth, England. SC 256 was also slated to be among the chasers headed for Russia, but Ens. Snow, Lt. Dole's former executive officer and current commander of SC 256, was not chosen for this service. Instead Ens. Snow was re-assigned as commander of SC 93 for its homeward journey. At the end of March, Lt. Dole assumed command

*Subchaser SC 93 flying homeward bound pennant from the main truck.*

of SC 354. SC 93, under Ens. Snow's command, left for the Azores on 6 April 1919.

Lt. Dole was unimpressed with the condition of his new chaser, and his crew would spend considerable time in the near future cleaning and sprucing up the boat. "Wish I had the 93 instead of this crate," he writes home. "The 93 has it all over this boat. Have some hopes of getting this ship clean in a few weeks. It is some louse-house. Have a two weeks' job to clean the bilges alone, outside of scraping all paint work. The paint peels off like cheese. It was put on over grease and all kinds of dirt."[11]

*"My new command, the louse-house 354." SC 354 moored next to another chaser and a sailing vessel.*

Nonetheless he was enthusiastic about his new crew, many of whom were sailors who had served on SC 354 and had volunteered with the provision that they remain assigned to the same chaser.

The local hull markings for SC 354 would undergo several rapid changes. When Lt. Dole took command, the hull was marked "CX." This was changed to "AU" while they were in Lisbon, and soon would be changed to "BT," the local designation of the chaser while stationed at Inverness.

*Subchaser SC 354 with "AU" hull marking.*

Twelve chasers were selected for service in northern Russia and sent to Inverness:[12]

| | | | |
|---|---|---|---|
| SC 1 | SC 98 | SC 257 | SC 271 |
| SC 90 | SC 137 | SC 258 | SC 321 |
| SC 95 | SC 256 | SC 262 | SC 354 |

Of these, three had served at Corfu, Greece (Base 25), SC 90, SC 95 and SC 256; nine had served at Plymouth, England (Base 27), SC 1, SC 98,

SC 137, SC 257, SC 258, SC 262, SC 271, SC 321 and SC 354; and two had later served at Queenstown, Ireland (Base 6), SC 1 and SC 271.

In Lisbon, two 3"/23-caliber deck guns were installed on SC 354, one in the standard location on the forward deck and one amidships where the Y-gun had been mounted. On 10 April 1919, Lt. Dole sailed for Brest, France, where the arming of the boat was completed.[13] SC 354 left Brest on 19 April, a heavily armed gunboat. In addition to the two deck guns, the vessel was equipped with 30-caliber Mk. VI Lewis machine guns, Browning automatic rifles, Springfield rifles and Colt automatic pistols, along with mounting hardware, tripods, holsters and belts, bayonets, hundreds of ammunition clips and other gear.[14]

"Have 9 machine guns on board now capable of shooting 4,500 shots per minute besides the two 3" guns using shrapnel. This does not include ship rifles, automatic pistols, etc.," Lt. Dole notes. "We are loaded down with ammunition. The engine exhausts are 6" under water now. Every square inch of the ship is stowed to capacity."[15]

The first stop was Milford Haven, Wales. As they headed north, Lt. Dole started to notice the lengthening of the day, the sun setting late in the evening in this region. He found Milford Haven a cordial and pleasant town. His stay there was short, however, and they soon set off for Belfast, Ireland, with orders to proceed to Inverness via the Caledonian Canal system across Scotland, a two-day journey through the locks.

The weather was good, and the chasers made good time, choosing to skip the stop at Belfast and proceed directly to Inverness. They traveled through locks all day, and stopped at Fort Williams for the night.

On 24 April 1919, SC 354 proceeded through the final set of locks and reached Base 18, Inverness. "Inverness is a beautiful place," Lt. Dole writes home, "expect to enjoy what spare time I have here which will be very little. Will be very busy as we go into dry dock for extensive overhaul for the long trip north. Will probably have 10,000 miles of running before we get another chance at docking, and it is important to get everything in the best shape possible."[16]

"There is a chance that the Russian trip may prove a fizzle," Lt. Dole added, "but things look interesting now." Plans for the withdrawal of American troops from northern Russia were already taking shape, but Adm. McCully remained convinced that to have chasers on hand would still be advisable. "If only to assist in evacuation of troops they probably will not be needed," he states in a message to Adm. Sims, "but think best to hold them in readiness if special emergency should arrive."[17]

Thus at Inverness the crews and Base staff would complete the mounting of guns and other preparations for the chasers, readying them for the trip to the White Sea. Stanchions were installed on the bridge for the Lewis machine

*"Working the locks. Caledonian Canal."*

*Two subchasers in the locks, Caledonian Canal.*

guns, canvas covers were made for the two 3"/23-caliber deck guns, the coal bunkers were filled, racks and storage areas were prepared for the small arms

*SC 354 crew members at Inverness.*

and ammunition, and food storage space was increased.[18] If sent up the Dvina, the chasers would be separated from the large vessels, so they needed to have enough supplies on board to be self-sufficient for long periods.

In early May, military authorities were continuing to assess the situation in northern Russia. Adm. Benson sent a letter to President Wilson requesting further clarification of the Administration's policy with respect to Russia. He listed the additional ships being sent to the region, and indicated that he was holding twelve chasers on the Scottish coast. In addition to the support of Adm. Sims and Adm. McCully, the British had indicated that they favored sending the chasers; but Adm. Benson remained skeptical of the need, if the objective were simply to withdraw our troops and not to engage.[19]

Wilson responded, "There are no plans whatever for active operations, and what is intended is merely to insure a safe withdrawal of our land forces."[20] Nevertheless, on 7 May, possibly because the ice melt had taken longer than anticipated, hampering troop withdrawal, Adm. Harry S. Knapp issued an order, "Dispatch subchaser expedition as soon as it is ready."[21]

The chasers had orders to proceed, but their departure was hampered by setbacks. Lt. Dole received word that the flagship, USS *Des Moines*, had reached Brest but was disabled and in need of considerable repairs. Although anxious to be under way, he chose to make the best of it. "They say the salmon fishing in the river Ness is very good, and I hope to take a shot at it," he writes.

A more critical problem occurred the following week, when the tanker HMS *Elerol*, assigned to the expedition, suffered a collision en route. The chasers might have proceeded without the flagship, but they couldn't possibly make the trip without re-fueling along the way. They would have to wait for another tanker to be assigned, and USS *Des Moines* would head for Archangel without them.

Adding to the frustration of the chaser men, the supply ship hadn't arrived at the base, so the men hadn't received their pay. Taking it in stride, Lt. Dole scraped together enough money to spend some of his leave time on the golf courses at Inverness; and eventually the supply ship arrived safely with the payroll.

On 10 May, USS *Sacramento* and Eagle boats 1, 2 and 3 arrived at Base 18, but there was still no tanker for the chasers, so once again they were left behind.

Amid fears that the trip would be scrapped altogether if a tanker couldn't be secured soon, preparations continued on the chasers. SC 354 went into dry dock at Thornbush Dockyard, Inverness, on 20 May. The remaining listening tubes, still attached to the keel, were removed, bent propellers repaired, and the seams caulked. Sheet iron was installed from 1½ ft. above the water line to 2½ ft. below, from amidships to the exhaust outlets, as protection against ice.

*Subchaser in dry dock at Thornbush Dockyard.*

## Unit Command

Near the end of May, plans changed for the chasers waiting at Inverness. Instead of twelve boats, only one unit would proceed to Archangel: SC 354 (flagship), SC 256 and SC 95. Lt. Dole writes to his brother of the plan. "Many things have happened, the principal thing of which is that only one unit of chasers will be sent to Russia and I have been placed in command of that unit. I will have the 354 as flagship and carry a flag officer to Russia." He jokes, "Met him a few days ago, and gave him an awful trimming at golf. That may be the reason he picked me to go up there. He probably wanted to get even with me."

*The unit at Inverness. Left to right: SC 354 (BT), SC 95 (AS), SC 256 (AR).*

The chasers would leave in the first week of June, and as unit commander, Lt. Dole had a job ahead of him, plotting their route. "Have enough charts and have been busy plotting the minefields from Comarty Firth to Holmengraa, Norway. Expect to be able to keep clear of them," he writes home.[22] The more challenging leg of the trip would be rounding the North Cape to Murmansk. "Have ice fields of 26 May charted about North Cape. The land is covered with ice at this time of the year and will be hard to pick up," he writes.

The newly-assigned British tanker HMS *Birchol*, commanded by Lt. W.G. Clay, RNR, arrived safely at Inverness, and on 5 June 1919 Lt. Dole received

Operations Order No. 1 of the Northern Russia Expedition. The chasers were to depart, and HMS *Birchol* was to fall into formation 300 yards to the rear of the chaser unit.[23] The convoy was to make the greatest speed possible, as determined by the maximum speed the tanker could make, ideally over 8 knots.

## The Coast of Norway

Lt. Dole departed on the morning of 6 June carrying on board flag officer Lt. Comdr. R. M. Griffin, Dvina Detachment Commander. The three chasers and HMS *Birchol* headed for Lerwick, Shetland Islands, Scotland, arriving at 6:15 a.m. the following day. After the tanker took on fuel and performed engine repairs, and the chasers refueled, the convoy headed across the North Sea for Norway. Notorious for its high seas and spectacular storms, the North Sea delivered a rough passage. This caused consternation among the members of the convoy, because in addition to its cargo of fuel, HMS *Birchol* carried 2,000 rounds of live ammunition for the deck guns. "If the ammunition had ever started to shift," notes Lt. Dole, "well, the expedition would have been off."[24]

On 8 June, the convoy reached Holmengraa, Norway,[25] and from there proceeded to Bergen, Norway, where the officers of the chasers and the tanker gathered for group photos. Present were flag officer Lt. Comdr. Griffin, a USN paymaster, the six officers of the submarine chasers and three British officers from HMS *Birchol*.

The next leg of the journey would take them along the coast of Norway, where a series of fjords and islands created a natural inland waterway up the coast. Lt. Dole plotted a course through these inner passages, avoiding open-ocean travel as much as possible in order to protect the chasers from the hazards of high seas and keep them close to shore to accommodate frequent stops.

This route also afforded them the opportunity to experience the stunning natural beauty of Norway. "Maps give no conception of the nature of this country," Lt. Dole writes. "Navigational charts give only an approximate idea. The whole scheme of nature is on such a grand scale that photographs fail to show the impressive grandeur of the scenery. This country must be seen to be appreciated. New vistas of snow-capped mountains rising abruptly from the sea with the picturesque Norwegian villages at their bases were continually opening up."[26]

What the nautical charts do show is the intricate nature of the route through the fjords. Lt. Dole's route would carry them through a maze of hundreds of islands and along fjords that sometimes provided only a narrow passage,

Northern Russia Detachment officers at Bergen, Norway. Left to right: Ens. C. Read Richardson, executive officer of SC 95; Lt. (jg) P.W. Boness, CO of SC 256; the executive officer of SC 256; Lt. H.R. Clay, RNR, commanding officer of the tanker HMS Birchol; Ens. Lawrence E. Williams, executive officer of SC 354; Lt. Comdr. R. M. Griffin, commander of the Dvina detachment; Lt. G.F. Aldrich, USN paymaster; Lt. (jg) George S. Dole, commanding officer of subchaser unit leader SC 354; the first and second officers of HMS Birchol; and Lt. (jg) George J. Leovy, Jr., commanding officer of SC 95.

SC 95, SC 256 and HMS Birchol getting under way from Bergen.

requiring careful navigation even for vessels as small as the chasers.

Even in the relative safety of the inland waterways, they encountered some days of rough weather, forcing a stop at Fuglo Island, Norway, so that the tanker could repair its pumps.[27] Lt. Dole took advantage of the down time to go ashore for a few hours.

Conspicuously absent in their journey was a repair vessel. Until they reached Murmansk and joined USS *Yankton*, the chasers and the tanker would have to make their own repairs, and try to see that nothing major went wrong.

Fuglo Island, Norway.

Thus in addition to their scheduled stops at planned intervals, brief stops were made along the way to facilitate repairs to the steering apparatus on SC 95 and several minor repairs to the tanker's engines.

While traveling the inland waterways, the chasers conserved fuel by taking advantage of one of the more peculiar components of chaser travel, sailing the boats. A spar and a boom off the main mast supported a large canvas sail,

*Sail rigging on SC 354.*

converting the boat temporarily from gas-powered motorboat to sailboat. As they moved along the fjords of Norway, Lt. Dole put up the sail, and his crew enjoyed the pristine scenery of mountains and sheltered waterways.

The practicality of using wind power on this journey may have been in part a function of the tanker's top speed of under 10 knots. Moreover, some of the fjords were too narrow for the tanker to navigate, requiring HMS *Birchol* to part company at times and travel by more circuitous routes. Under engine power, the chasers found themselves stopping periodically to allow the tanker to catch up.

SC 95 Under sail, fjords of Norway.

Capable of much higher speed when necessary, the chasers presumably could raise sails and relax their pace now and then without any danger of being left behind.

Even so, they couldn't possibly complete the trip without several stops alongside the tanker to re-fuel, so while their routes diverged now and then, the chasers never ventured too far ahead.

Progressing along the Norwegian waterways, they crossed the Arctic Circle, and at midnight on 12 June, seven days after leaving Inverness, Lt. Dole reached Tromso, Norway, the midnight sun shining brightly. They moored alongside the tanker, and at 6:00 a.m. spruced up the boat, scraping and washing the deck, adjusting the equipment and painting the flag lockers. Early afternoon the men received £2 English currency on account, and liberty parties went ashore.[28] "Tromso is the metropolis of the Arctic Circle," Lt. Dole writes, "and presents a thriving appearance."[29]

*Lt. Dole taking a sextant reading, midnight sun, 14 June 1919.*

Ahead of them lay the Arctic Sea, where they would leave the protection of the inland waterways and travel in open ocean, made all the more hazardous by the presence of ice. A short 18 hours after arriving at Tromso they set off through Soro Sound into waters northeast of the North Cape. Lt. Dole led the convoy on a route several miles offshore to allow for navigation around ice floes.

On 15 June, near the Kola Inlet leading to Murmansk, the chasers met USS *Yankton*, which would escort them to Archangel. They came within hailing distance and stopped, and the wherry on SC 354 was lowered. Lt. Comdr. Griffin made a brief visit to USS *Yankton* and returned with their orders. They were to proceed directly to Archangel, and not to stop at Murmansk as originally planned.

The convoy made a stop at Vardo, Norway, to refuel, and with USS *Yankton* leading, headed for the White Sea. As they proceeded along the Murman coast they encountered not only ice, but fog. On the night of 16 June, the flagship signaled to the chasers and the tanker to reduce speed and follow on course as they navigated the ice fields. The next day the fog grew denser, and they crawled along the coast of the Kola peninsula at one third normal speed.

*USS Yankton leading the convoy.*

## The White Sea

Finally, on 18 June, the convoy entered the White Sea, and at the mouth of the Dvina River picked up local pilots to guide them through the delta to Archangel. At 10:45 a.m. they reached Archangel and the three chasers dropped anchor abeam of USS *Des Moines*, the cruiser that would take over as flagship of the detachment.

*Looking across the bow of SC 95 at USS Des Moines, Archangel.*

Eagles 1, 2 and 3 had also arrived, and two other ships, the British depot ship HMS *Cyclops* and the French cruiser *Conde*, shared the harbor with the American detachment. Ens. Lawrence E. Williams, executive officer of SC 354, describes the city of Archangel.

> The city has about 40,000 inhabitants but is so spread out that the downtown section looks like a country town. Most of the houses are of wood and not a few are of logs with neatly dove-tailed corners. The space between the logs is plugged up with mud and moss. Many of the roofs are nothing but heavy moss. Then too there are a number of fine buildings here. The government buildings including the American Embassy are beautiful large brick and stone structures.[30]

Adm. McCully's directive for the Naval forces now present at Archangel, in keeping with the directives of the Navy Department, was to engage in

"Observation, Communication and Report." By this time, most of the American troops had withdrawn, sailing for Brest, France. The remaining troops would be withdrawn soon.[31] In orders circulated by Adm. McCully to the chasers and other navy vessels in the region, commanding officers were advised, based on State Department directives, as follows:

> We shall insist, so far as our operation is concerned, that all Military efforts in Northern Russia be given up except the guarding of the ports themselves, and as much of the country around them as may develop threatening conditions. We will of course do our utmost to send supplies, but cannot undertake General Relief.[32]

However Adm. McCully indicated, "It is not considered advisable that the Naval Forces should be withdrawn altogether, and there should still remain sufficient Forces in the Region to carry out the Duties mentioned ... particularly as in the near future there will undoubtedly be important operations by Allied Military and Naval Forces."[33]

The American naval forces were to represent the U.S. as a neutral, friendly nation, in the face of deep mistrust of the Allied forces by the Russians – and to be prepared for any contingency.

The vessels of the Northern Russia Detachment were to be split up and sent on missions at different stations on the White Sea. The two main bases of operation were at Archangel, in the southeast corner of the White Sea, and at Kem, on the western shore. Because they were the smallest vessels of the expedition, the chasers were generally assigned to duty on the rivers, while the larger Eagle boats were responsible for communications between the bases. The large vessels would act as depot ships, supporting the effort.

On 19 June, SC 354 sailed for Popov Island and then to Kem; SC 256 sailed for Keret Bay; and SC 95 remained at anchor in Archangel.

The destination of SC 354 in the Kem region was Solovetski Island. "The U.S.S.C. No. 354 has the distinction of being the first vessel flying the American flag to visit this port," Lt. Dole remarks. At Solovetski they toured the massive and ornate Solovetski monastery, where Lt. Dole was impressed with the grim nature of the murals. "Everywhere you turn you are greeted with representations of men and women undergoing various forms of torture. The slaughter of the innocent, various tortures by hell fire, devils with spears, and the whipping post seemed to be the most favored designs."[34]

The priests, however, were quite friendly, inviting the men in for tea and showing them around the monastery and grounds, where Lt. Dole discovered that in addition to their religious work, the residents engaged in various business

*Solovetski Monastery.*

enterprises, operating a shipbuilding plant, a dry dock, passenger service, and traditional farming and fishing.

Adm. McCully's assignment of "Observation, Communication and Report" manifested itself for the chasers in the form of ferrying passengers around the White Sea and sometimes visiting with the local residents. At times this meant many high-ranking officers aboard the chasers. While docked at Solovetski, for instance, Adm. McCully, Lt. Comdr. Griffin, British officers, a French officer and a representative of the monastery took a white-tablecloth meal on the bridge of SC 354.

This also meant that the chasers didn't stay for very long in any one place. The day after sailing to Kem, Lt. Dole headed back across the White Sea to Archangel, then a few days later made another trip to Kem.

Their duties in the White Sea were not limited to ferry service, diplomatic visits and sightseeing. There was still a distinct possibility of an outbreak of hostilities, and the vessels of the detachment were expected to be prepared. A week after arriving, the detachment engaged in a six-day, controlled regimen of target practice drills in Keret Bay, north of Kem. This involved at various times the three chasers, the Eagle boats, USS *Yankton* and USS *Sacramento*.

On 27-28 July, SC 354 took part, engaging in short-range and long-range battle practice, under the watch of a team of Navy Observers. The results of the

*Officers' meal on board SC 354, Solovetski Island.*

drills were charted, and complete reports filed, showing the percentage of hits for each vessel.

For the men on the chasers to hit the targets required considerable concentration and skill, as even in the relatively placid waters of the White Sea, the boat at rest would roll, so that effectively the stationary floating targets were moving targets. Nevertheless, Lt. Dole was satisfied with his performance. "I shot the Officer's string and got 2 hits out of six shots, which was good considering the roll and pitch factor, which amounted to 4. Had 1 minute to get the shots off." Illustrating the difficulty of the task, he remarks, "The S.C. #354 had high score of the S.C.'s with 6 hits in 40 shots, actually 31 shots as the after gun was disabled after the first shot."[35]

*Target rafts, White Sea.*

For the remainder of the month of June, the chasers performed ferry service between ports.

By early July, the evacuation of the American ground troops was almost completed, leaving little reason for a U.S. Naval presence in the area. On 4 July, the Northern Russia Detachment participated in a showcase celebration of the American Independence Day, on Kego Island, one of the islands in the Dvina River delta.

*SC 354 ferrying citizens of Archangel to Kego Island, 4 July 1919.*

"Today we will act as ferry for the city of Arkhangel carrying all who care to go to Kego Is., where the U.S. Naval and Land forces will celebrate and show the young Bolsheviks in this region how to play baseball, box, etc.," Lt. Dole writes.[36] A crowded SC 354 brought officers, enlisted men and residents of all ages to the celebration.

*Fourth of July celebration on Kego Island.*

On 5 July 1919, the three chasers of the Northern Russia Detachment were ordered to cast off, and started their journey back to England. The first stop would be Murmansk, then regular stops along the route for refueling and repairs.

This time, however, the chaser men were hoping for delays. The prevalent rumor was that they would be assigned to service in the mine sweeping operations in the North Sea, perhaps the most perilous service that any chaser had been involved in. "The longer we delay," Lt. Dole writes, "the more mines will be swept before we get there, and the authorities may change their minds about using chasers as mine sweepers." Lt. Dole was not interested in avoiding service in the North Sea so much as he was skeptical of the chasers' value in that work. "Would be willing to take a mine sweeper," he writes. "It would be interesting work, but do not have any faith in chasers being of any use in sweeping mines."[37]

Possibly out of a sense that the chaser crews deserved a short break after navigating the coast of Norway and serving in northern Russia, Adm. McCully requested permission to allow the men to spend a week in Christiana (later Oslo), Norway, before heading back across the North Sea for service in mine sweeping operations.[38]

While the visit was cast as diplomatic, to the chaser men a week at Christiana was a vacation. For Lt. Dole it included a "peace dinner" at a restaurant, about which he remarked, "I do not know when I enjoyed a meal more or one that was better cooked."[39]

*Frognesvettern Inn, Christiana (Oslo), Norway – site of the "peace dinner."*

Unlike the plain, rural communities of the White Sea, Christiana offered plenty of leisure-time opportunities. The sailors spent their shore leave in the city.

Lt. Dole welcomed the opportunity to spend some time on shore. "Have been ashore only a couple of hours," he writes on his second day at Christiana, "long enough to engage a room at the Grand hotel for next Tuesday. Am looking forward to sleeping in a real bed, and getting off the ship for a couple of days." The northern Russia expedition had taken its toll on Lt. Dole, his men and the chaser. "We have cruised over 5,000 miles without a mother-ship, at either end of the line, and we are about at the end of our rope until we can secure some spare parts for motors. This trip is very near a record for S.C. boats or gas powered boats of any kind, carrying no machine shops."[40]

Lt. Dole couldn't see how the chasers could be of use in mine sweeping operations. In their experiments with that work back in October 1918, when they had worked the abandoned mine fields around Durazzo harbor, he had concluded that the chasers were too small and too light for cutting mine tethers. What he had not counted on was the problem faced by minesweepers when attempting work at the enormous scale presented by the prospect of

*Beer garden, Christiana (Oslo).*

clearing the North Sea mine barrage. Ordinarily the sweepers worked on small, local seedings of mines, clearing channels mined surreptitiously by enemy submarines. Now they faced over 50,000 mines in a concentrated band across the North Sea, which presented a new problem: how to deal with live mines cut from their tethers that floated to the surface without detonating. The solution, as Lt. Dole was soon to learn, was for subchasers to run behind the sweepers and shoot and sink the strays.

# Chapter 8 – Mine Sweeping in the North Sea

*"This work is easily the most spectacular of any we have yet been in, also the most interesting, though hard on the personnel. Am looking forward to getting home to see you all before the close of the year."*[1]

Lt. George S. Dole

On 28 July 1919, SC 354 arrived at Kirkwall, Orkney Islands. Lt. Dole's unit of chasers, returning from the White Sea, would now join the ranks of chasers already serving in the minesweeping division.

Work commenced immediately to fit the boats for duties on the mine fields. The deck guns, not needed for duty on the mine fields, were removed along with all 3" ammunition on board. Gas drums were removed from the deck and transferred to repair ship USS *Panther*. A critical job was the removal of the iron sheeting that had protected the chaser hulls from ice in the Arctic Sea. The mine fields were sown with Mark VI mines, which were fired by a magnetic field created when the metal hull of a vessel came into contact with the mine's antenna wire. The three newly-arrived chasers were beached in turn for the removal of the iron.[2]

Pulling alongside USS *Panther*, Lt. Dole was provided with a complete set of charts of the mine fields and organizational documents on the minesweeping division. The sweep operations required the use of small vessels to run behind the sweepers and use rifle fire to sink cut mines that floated to the surface. This was the assignment given to the chasers. The target practice operations in the White Sea might come in handy, after all.

## The Mine Barrage and the Mark VI Mine

The North Sea Mine Barrage was a set of mine fields stretching from Norway to the Orkney Islands, blockading the entire northern exposure of the North Sea. Its purpose was to contain the enemy, preventing the U-boat commanders from reaching open ocean and attacking Allied shipping. In all, over 70,000 mines were laid, more than 50,000 of them American-made.

The mines were anchored to the ocean floor, fixed in place by mooring cables that held the mines at specified depths below the surface. The navy had documentation of the mine-laying operations, a careful accounting of the location of each mine field. Nonetheless, the prospect of removing the mines was fantastically dangerous. Not only was it a complicated matter to deal with tens of thousands of metal containers of TNT rigged to explode on contact, but tides, storms and shifting of the ocean bed could have caused the

*Transport of mines by train. (T. Woofenden Collection).*

*Unloading mines, Base 18, Inverness. (T. Woofenden Collection.)*

mines to move from their original location.

The design of the American Mark VI mine made the task of sweeping the mine fields particularly challenging. It had been an essential component of the barrage strategy, and now posed a technological dilemma that had to be solved in order to remove the barrage.

The idea of blocking the North Sea by means of a mine barrage had been discussed by military tacticians, but was deemed impractical due to the sheer number of mines that would be required. The type of mine then in use covered a limited area, as it ignited only when horn-like triggers on the body of the mine were struck by a passing vessel. The new American Mark VI design solved this problem, with its vastly expanded coverage area. By using this new type of mine, the navy could reduce by magnitudes of scale the number of mines required.

The Mark VI mine consisted of standard-looking metal casing containing 300 lbs. of TNT, but its internal firing mechanism and triggering design were new. In addition to four horn triggers it had a long, copper antenna held upright by a float. These five trigger devices were connected to a coil inside the mine, and when a metal object – the hull of a vessel – came in contact with any part of the antenna or any one of the horns, a magnetic field was produced, which activated the detonation mechanism.

Now, with the war over, the navy was faced with not merely clearing a channel through the mine field, but clearing the entire barrage, including over 50,000 of the most technologically advanced and lethal mines ever produced.

**Sweeping the Mark VI Mine**

The American Mark VI mines in the North Sea mine barrage were laid at four depths below the surface, 45 feet, 80 feet, 160 feet and 240 feet, creating, in effect, a curtain of mines and antennae.

To sweep this kind of mine field involved several new considerations. How could the danger of damage to the minesweepers be minimized, given the presence of this kind of mine? What tactics should be used to remove the mines? And how could the work be completed in a timely fashion, given the enormous scope of the task?

To help protect the minesweepers from accidentally triggering the mines, each sweeper was equipped with an *electric protective device* to generate an electromagnetic field around the vessel that was intended to neutralize the effect of inadvertent contact with a mine trigger. The mechanism consisted of a trailing wire with a metallic plate at the end and a generator to produce the current. It was a simple design, but it had to be installed properly and set accurately to create a field of the right polarity and intensity to counteract the mine circuit design. If the polarity were reversed it would actually cause mines below the vessel to detonate; and if it weren't operating in the proper range, it

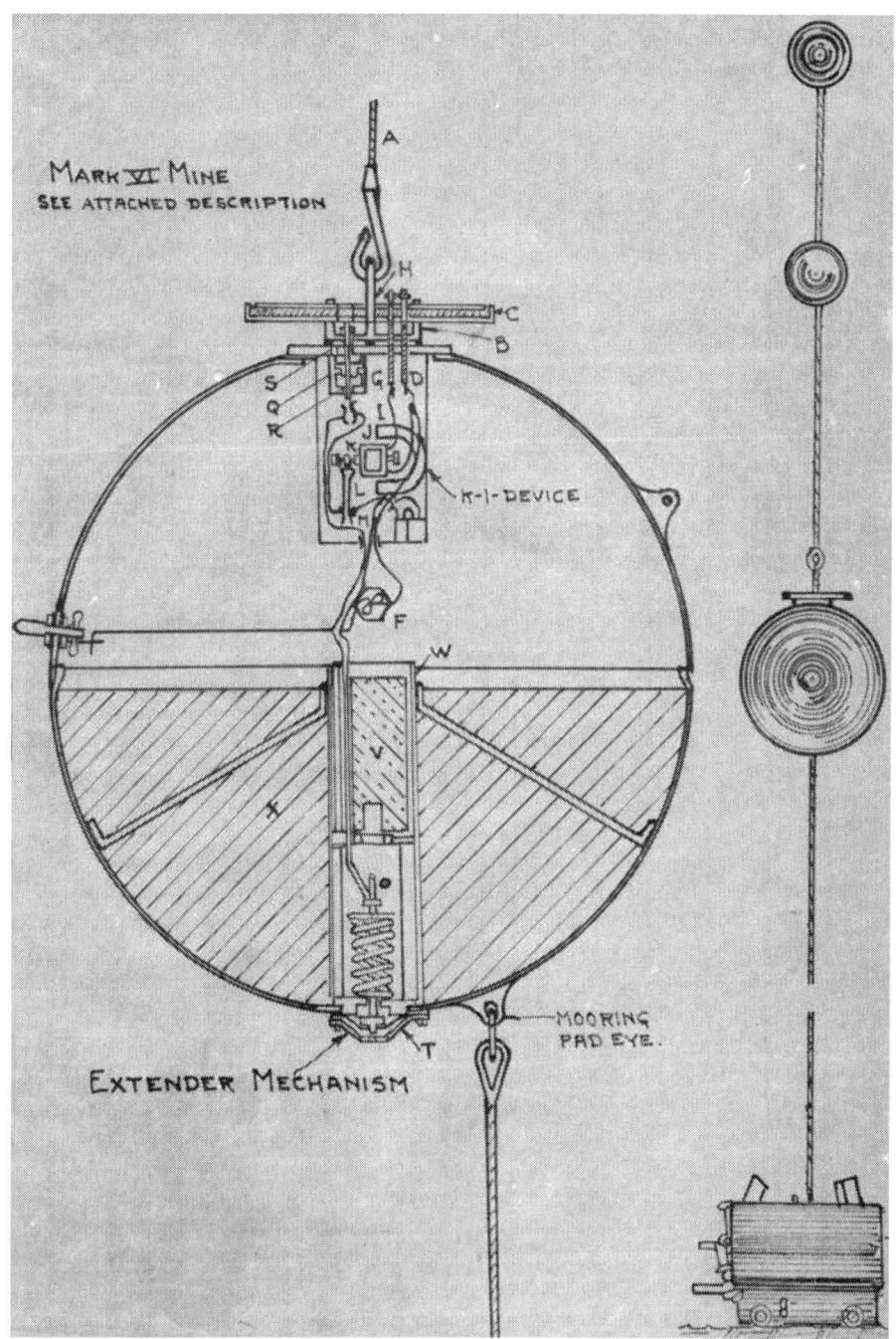

*Cross-section of the Mark VI mine, from the Minesweeping Orders for the Minesweeping Detachment, May 1919.*

*The Copper antenna (A) which is held upright in the water by the floats above, is connected through the tripod (B) to the lower copper plate (C). This plate is connected by wire (D) with one end of the pivoted coil. The four horns (F), two of which are shown, are also connected to this side of the coil. The other side of the movable coil is connected through (G) to the upper copper plate (H). When a steel vessel in salt water comes into contact with the antenna or a horn, the pivoted coil is thus connected to a salt water cell, the plates of which are the steel hull and the copper top plate (H). The coil being in the field of the magnet, tends to turn 90 degs. from that shown. When the coil turns, cup (K) attached to the coil shaft tips and spills out a gold ball from the cup. The ball drops through the fall tube (L) to the contact fingers (M) bridging the gap in the circuit from battery (N). This circuit is the detonator firing circuit.*[3]

wouldn't create an adequate field to protect the vessel. The apparatus was thus constantly monitored whenever a vessel was in the mine fields.[4]

The standard process of sweeping mines involved extending a serrated metallic sweep cable between two minesweepers, holding the cable at a set depth using metal kites, and passing through the mine fields, with the objective of detonating the mines and cutting the tethers of mines that didn't detonate, so that they would float to the surface, where they could be sunk with rifle fire. But with this new type of mine, some new thinking would be required.

*Minesweeper USS Lapwing. (T. Woofenden Collection.)*

Several ingenious ideas were tested. For instance, at the outset of the sweeping operations, military tacticians attempted to take advantage of the magnetic detonation mechanism in the Mark VI mine, by passing an electrical current through the sweep cable, so that when the sweep cable came into contact with the steel mooring cables of the mines, the electrical current would travel up the mooring cable and cause the mine to detonate. This idea was tested in the first sweep operation on 30 April 1919, but didn't work as planned. The electric charge administered to the mooring cable was evidently insufficient to trigger detonation; moreover, it created an electromagnetic field that disrupted the ship's compass, making it difficult to stay on course.

*Transverse sweeping* – running through the fields at right angles – was also initially employed. But by the fourth mine sweeping operation, they had found that *longitudinal sweeping*, running parallel to the mine field, was faster, more efficient and safer for the mine sweeping vessels.

A persistent problem was entanglement of mines in the sweeping gear, and parting of the sweep line caused by detonations. An enormous quantity of mine sweeping gear was being lost because of these problems, and mines fouled in the sweep lines posed a serious threat to the men and the vessels when hauling in the lines. These problems appeared to be related. Both were largely a function of the sweep lines sliding up the mooring cable. In some cases, the cable became entangled in the hardware of the sweep line, often where the kite was attached; and in other cases the sweep line would slide up and contact the body of the mine, so that detonation would occur with the mine in direct contact with the sweep line, parting it. These problems led to a change in tactics. Instead of attempting to run the sweep wires through the mooring cables, the lines were raised so that they would come into contact with the copper antennae, a tactic called *antenna sweeping*. In all cases, multiple passes were made across each mine field, to make sure the mines had been successfully removed.[5]

Regardless of the specific tactic in use – transverse sweeping, longitudinal sweeping, antenna sweeping, or holding the sweep line at different depths – the result of a pass through the field inevitably was that some mines were detonated, some were detonated by countermining (a mine detonating and causing the detonation of a nearby mine, sometimes resulting in a string of detonations), and a number were cut free and floated to the surface without detonating.

This is where the subchasers came into play, their role being to follow the sweepers and sink all the floating mines with rifle fire.

The deployment design of the Mark VI mine included two pressure-sensitive safety devices incorporated into the electrical circuit, which prevented the detonator from activating until the mine reached a certain depth. This allowed

*Looking off the stern of a minesweeper at a surfaced mine caught in the sweeping gear.*

the mine layers to deploy the mines with less danger of accidental detonation. For the submarine chasers engaged in the mine sweeping operations, this design had another benefit, at least in theory. When the tethers were cut, the mines would float to the surface, and these pressure-sensitive devices would theoretically once again deactivate the mine. It could then safely be pierced by rifle fire and sunk, without undue danger of detonation.

Theoretically, a mine of this type fouled in sweeping gear also was relatively safe, and could be manually deactivated. This procedure involved turning it upside-down and placing a short-circuiting clip across the metallic plates. Then the entire detonation mechanism would be removed from the mine, rendering it safe.

But in practice, the mines were unstable. Detonations occurred regularly, both under water and on the surface; and as the navy had no interest in saving the mines or in putting the sailors in jeopardy unnecessarily, the directive was to destroy the mines, not to attempt to deactivate or recover them except as a last resort, such as when a mine was entangled in sweep gear in close proximity to a minesweeper.

## The Minesweeping Detachment

When the Armistice was signed on 11 November 1918, ending hostilities, the work of the mine layers came to an abrupt close, and USS *Black Hawk*, flagship of the Mine Laying Division, turned to the task of clearing the newly-blocked waterways. Minesweepers were fitted and assigned to the new division, and the division became fully operational in early May 1919. Adding to the enormity of the task was the need to complete the work quickly. Since sweep operations were impossible in winter, if they didn't finish in time, the region would face another entire winter season of blocked trade lanes.

By the time Lt. Dole's unit reached Kirkwall, mine sweeping operations were well underway, and twenty-one chasers were already part of the division:[6]

| SC 37 | SC 45 | SC 110 | SC 182 | SC 254 |
| SC 38 | SC 46 | SC 164 | SC 206 | SC 259 |
| SC 40 | SC 47 | SC 178 | SC 207 | SC 272 |
| SC 44 | SC 48 | SC 181 | SC 208 | SC 329 |
|       |       |        |        | SC 356 |

The addition of SC 354, SC 95 and SC 256 would bring the total count of chasers to twenty-four. USS *Black Hawk* served as flagship of the minesweeping detachment, with USS *Panther* as repair ship.

*USS Black Hawk and a minesweeper.*

During the course of the operation, thirty-four minesweepers served in the division. These were bird class minesweepers, 157' 10" long and 35' 6" abeam, with a displacement of 1,009 tons and a full-load draft of 15':[7]

| | | | |
|---|---|---|---|
| USS *Auk* | USS *Flamingo* | USS *Pelican* | USS *Tanager* |
| USS *Avocet* | USS *Grebe* | USS *Penguin* | USS *Teal* |
| USS *Bobolink* | USS *Heron* | USS *Quail* | USS *Thrush* |
| USS *Chewink* | USS *Kingfisher* | USS *Rail* | USS *Turkey* |
| USS *Cormorant* | USS *Lapwing* | USS *Robin* | USS *Whippoorwill* |
| USS *Curlew* | USS *Lark* | USS *Sanderling* | USS *Widgeon* |
| USS *Eider* | USS *Mallard* | USS *Seagull* | USS *Woodcock* |
| USS *Falcon* | USS *Oriole* | USS *Swallow* | |
| USS *Finch* | USS *Osprey* | USS *Swan* | |

Also on mine sweeping duty were USS *Patepsco* and USS *Patuxent*, which had previously served with USS *Black Hawk* in the mine laying operation, seven repair and auxiliary vessels and 20 trawlers, including the ill-fated USS *Richard Bulkeley*, sunk on 12 July 1919 by a mine explosion.[8]

Crewman Charles Post of SC 40 describes a day on a chaser in the minefields during the second mine sweeping operation in May 1919, when a mine exploded close by:

May 18th, better weather, and started sweeping across the two miles of mines, as they thought that was the safest way, as the boats wouldn't be over the mines all the time, but that put the chasers in a bad spot. May 20th we got a terrific jolt, right under my boat. I had just gone down to the engine room to write my log. Someone shouted down, "Hang on! She's going to break starboard!" and slammed the hatch down. We rolled to port and it felt like a ton of water came down on us. Skipper dropped into the engine room. I had kicked a deck plate aside and was checking to see if water was coming in the bilge. He asked if we were all right and if those two engines were out of commission. I hadn't noticed they weren't running. The men said they had stopped them. Told them to start up and see if they were OK. They were. Told the Skipper, "No water coming in the bilge. He said, "No wonder. It all came down on top of us" and left the room. No radio as our antenna was down. The Quartermaster semaphored the sweeper, "No serious damage to 40. Just kicked our butt and kissed us." They signaled back, "Ha, ha, ha." Well, that's the Navy![9]

*USS Panther.*

## SC 354 in the Minesweeping Division

On 28 July 1919, Lt. Dole entered Kirkwall harbor, and moored SC 354 alongside of USS *Panther*. The weather was generally rainy, but on occasion the sun came out, and on 30 July, the sailors were on deck enjoying the music of a band playing on the deck of USS *Panther*. "It is the first time we have heard a band in a long time," Dole remarks, "and it sure sounds good!"[10] Soon liberty would become scarce, and the work more dangerous than ever.

Service in mine sweeping operations didn't require as big a crew aboard the chasers as their previous work had, and a number of men were reassigned, including Lt. Dole's executive officer. Lt. Dole was now the sole officer on the vessel, with nineteen crewmen. He might have requested a transfer himself, but chose, instead to stay with his crew. "I will apply for release when my present crew is detached," he writes, "which will probably be in October. Feel that I ought to stay with the crew till the finish of the minesweeping operations this fall."[11] SC 354 spent sixteen days at Kirkwall in preparation for service on the mine fields.

Lt. Dole joined a detachment plagued with accidents and fatalities. By the time he arrived, many incidents had already occurred:[12]

**May 10**

A middle-level mine was countermined under USS *Turkey*, opening seams, shearing rivets off of the hull, damaging the bilge keel and damaging the rudder.

**May 12**

A mine exploded on the surface near USS *Patuxent*, washing several men overboard. The Commanding Officer lost a thumb, and other minor injuries were sustained. The ship's steering gear, electrical plant, bulkheads and store rooms were damaged, and the hull opened up allowing 500 gallons of water per hour to enter.

**May 14**

Commanding Officer Lt. Frank Bruce of USS *Bobolink* was killed by a mine explosion while trying to clear a mine fouled in the ship's gear.

**June 8**

A mine sunk by rifle fire exploded beneath SC 208, opening seams.

**June 9**

A mine explosion caused a steam leak in USS *Teal*.

**June 17**

A mine explosion damaged USS *Pelican*, causing leaks. The chart house of SC 164 was damaged.

**June 21**

An explosion caused leaks in USS *Curlew*.

**July 7**

An explosion caused damage to USS *Oriole*, and USS *Rail*'s boilers were damaged.

**July 10**

USS *Flamingo*'s rudder was damaged by a mine explosion.

**July 11**

A mine explosion caused leaks in SC 46.

**July 12**

A mine fouled in USS *Richard Bulkeley*'s sweeping gear exploded, sinking the ship. Comdr. Frank King and several crewmen were lost. USS *Eider* was damaged by an explosion. The crew of SC 47 fired at a mine, which exploded, splitting the side of the pilot house and breaking windows.

**July 28**

In rough seas, a mine exploded near USS *Curlew*, and one man was lost at sea.

These incidents continued, occurring during every sweeping operation, including those in which Lt. Dole took part.

**August 2**

SC 38 was damaged by mine explosion.

**August 3**

SC 37 was damaged by mine explosion.

**August 14**

A mine fouled in the kite exploded near USS *Tanager*, bursting fuel tanks and breaking a main shaft.

**August 15**

A mine fouled in the kite exploded under the stern of USS *Penguin* and damaged both generators and the main engine.

**September 3**

Countermining damaged USS *Seagull*, opening hull seams and breaking fuel lines and pumps.

**September 4**

Countermining damaged USS *Sanderling*, opening hull seams. Mounts of all three engines on SC 38 were damaged, and the deck separated from the hull by an explosion directly beneath, requiring the chaser to be towed to Kirkwall.

**September 5**

USS *Kingfisher* was damaged by explosion.

*Stern of USS Bobolink, damaged by mine explosion. (T. Woofenden Collection.)*

On 13 August, USS *Panther* headed a convoy of the minesweeping detachment to a new, temporary base at Lerwick, Shetland Islands, nearer to the mine fields about to be swept. Lt. Dole was assigned to work with Sweeper Division No. 4, and on 16 August, SC 354 headed out to sea. The seas were high, and navigation was difficult. Their destination was a mine field ninety-one miles out, and Lt. Dole set a course first for a light buoy thirty-eight miles out. The gale was powerful enough to drive the chaser twelve miles off course on this first run, but after a series of radio communications and course

*Standing by for mines.*

corrections, Lt. Dole made his way to his assignment, and spent the day with Division 4, shooting mines.

That night SC 354 was assigned to deliver mail in spite of the rough weather, and Lt. Dole and his crew were put to the test navigating close to the other ships. The high seas twice drove the chaser into other vessels, ripping off fifteen feet of guard rail and bending stanchions, but the crew finished the detail without any major damage to the chaser.

During the night as they navigated through the continuing storm, the crew lost sight of the division, and at 5:00 a.m. Lt. Dole was awakened to find that they were lost. After several hours getting back on track, the chaser rejoined the division, and the crew spent the day at work on the mine fields. That night the crew once again lost the minesweeping division, having inadvertently followed the buoy division instead. When they realized the error, they stopped, losing the buoy division as well. Lt. Dole got on the radio telephone in the morning and contacted the buoy division to determine which field they were in, and made his way to them.

The work of the buoy division was to locate the mine fields by proceeding to the known coordinates where mines had been laid and performing sweeps to locate the actual perimeter of the field. On 19-20 August, Lt. Dole followed USS *Osprey*, and shot stray mines as the minesweepers located and marked the field. Lt. Dole's crew sank thirty-eight mines the first day and sixteen the second.

To sink a mine, they quickly learned, required hitting it with about ten shots – and this required moving in closer than the recommended 100-foot minimum in order to shoot all the mines quickly enough, with the roll of the ship working against them.

The work continued on the morning of 21 August, the men on SC 354 sinking another twenty-nine mines.[13]

Lt. Dole then brought the chaser to Lervig, Norway, for minor repairs, refueling, and a day's rest. He brought the chaser alongside HMS *Tyne* for routine engine repairs and to catch up on sleep. "I sure had a fine sleep that night," Lt. Dole writes. "Did not get up till 8:00 a.m. Had a good rest the following day and night. Had dinner aboard the H.M.S. *Tyne* and had a fine time."[14]

*Subchaser SC 354 alongside HMS Tyne, Lervig, Norway.*

The next morning SC 354 proceeded to Field 13 off of the coast of Norway, and continued the work of following in the path of sweepers in the buoy division, sinking another forty-six mines. In the next two days, the men on SC 354 shot and sank more than 200 mines.

During this sweep SC 354 would experience what so many other chasers already had, the explosion of a mine close enough to damage the vessel.

*Following the sweepers.*

"On one cut the sweepers cut 65 mines. Ten exploded," Dole writes. "We shot down one that exploded close aboard, throwing an engine off its base and opening up the seams underwater, so that we had to keep the bilge pump working all the time at full capacity to keep afloat."

Fortunately none of the crew were injured. To add to their troubles, a storm kicked up before the work on the field was completed, and they started on the 210-mile trip back to port with one motor out of commission. "Had hardly got started when the steering gear carried away and we had to rig relieving tackles," Dole writes, describing the ordeal. "We had no spare rope, and none was available. Unfortunately the sea was a stern sea and while we rode nicely could not keep within 45 degrees of the course. A sea would occasionally turn us through 180 degrees and the motor we most wanted was the one out of commission. The windward wheel was fanning the air most of the time."[15]

That night Lt. Dole decided not to rely on the crew to stay with the division, and instead stayed up all night to navigate the vessel himself. At midnight the center engine stopped and couldn't be restarted. SC 354 was down to one engine, and it was running hot.

He fell into a course behind tugs heading for Kirkwall, and radioed to them that he couldn't make over seven knots. The tugs slowed down to allow the chaser to stay with them. At dawn Lt. Dole turned in, but was awakened two hours later. The crew had once again lost their course. He got on the radio, set a course for Kirkwall and within an hour picked up the tugs, proceeding to Kirkwall in a full gale. "Waves were 40 ft. high and our clinometer showed a pitch of 45 degrees," he writes. "Our one remaining motor was so hot bucking the sea that we could not touch it."

Finally they reached Kirkwall, and tied up to a buoy by USS *Black Hawk*, relieved to be safely in port.

It would be the last tour of duty of SC 354 on the mine fields, for the operations were coming to a close and would be completed before SC 354 would be called on again. In the following days as the chaser was moored at Kirkwall for repairs, liberty parties were granted, and the men enjoyed some free time before embarking on the return journey.

There were no further engagements requiring the chasers. The war had been won, the evacuation from Russia completed and the trade routes cleared. After almost two years on the chasers, Lt. Dole would finally be heading home. His next stop would be Devonport, England, where SC 354 would receive extensive repairs in dry dock before crossing the Atlantic Ocean for home.

*Subchasers and other vessels in Kirkwall.*

MINE FORCE, U. S. ATLANTIC FLEET
U. S. S. BLACK HAWK, FLAGSHIP
Kirkwall, Orkney Islands,
26 September 1919

ORDER

Upon the completion of the minesweeping in the North Sea the Commander Mine Force desires to express his hearty appreciation of the hard work and sacrifice of the Officers and Men attached to the Sweepers and Sub-Chasers engaged in the task.

The removal of the minefield consisting of more than fifty thousand mines spread over an area of some six thousand square miles of the stormy North Sea presented a problem that could only be solved by the hardest kind of work and indifference to danger. That so difficult and prolonged an operation was performed cheerfully and without the stimulus of war or the incentive of the usual additional pay given for such work, is an evidence of the fine spirit existing in the Mine Force.

The Commander Mine Force takes pride in being able to pay this deserved tribute.

JOS. STRAUSS,
Rear Admiral, U. S. Navy
Commander Mine Force

*Mine sweeping appreciation note.*

## Chapter 9 – Homeward Bound

*"After this next leg is over we will be practically across the pond. Cape Razo fading in the distance sure looked good to me. Have seen all of Europe that I ever care to see. Expect to arrive at Hampton Roads the latter part of November."*[1]

Lt. George S. Dole

After the Armistice had been signed the navy had made efforts to sell the chasers stationed in Europe, but few were actually sold. The chasers of the minesweeping division, probably unlikely candidates for sale because of the rough condition of the vessels, were sent to Devonport, England for repairs in dry dock in preparation for a return trip to the east coast of the United States.

The chasers would return in two groups, the first convoyed by USS *Panther* and the second by USS *Black Hawk*. Lt. Dole's chaser was in the first group.

### Devonport

On 4 September 1919, Rear Admiral Joseph Strauss issued movement orders for six subchasers to sail for Devonport. The chasers were the three that had participated in the Northern Russia Detachment – SC 354, SC 95 and SC 256 – and SC 48, SC 208 and SC 259. USS *Panther* was to convoy the chasers to

*SC 354 and SC 95 at Granton, Scotland.*

Devonport to assist in repairs while the chasers were in dry dock and while they were moored in the harbor.[2] Orders were issued to the commanding officers of all seven vessels to turn over all signal books pertaining to operations in European waters before leaving, as these materials would no longer be needed.[3]

*Chasers in dry dock, Devonport. Front row, left to right: SC 259, SC 48, SC 256. Back row, left to right: SC 208, SC 95, SC 354.*

On 5 September, Lt. Dole took position at the head of the convoy, on the lookout for floating mines. 1,000 yards astern was USS *Panther*, and the remaining five chasers in column behind USS *Panther* at 400 yard intervals. The first step would be Granton, Scotland, a brief stop for re-fueling.[4]

The passage was uneventful, and at noon on 10 September the convoy reached Devonport. The following day all six chasers entered the dry dock. The chasers required extensive repairs. Working on SC 354, crews spent seven days caulking and repairing the hull alone. The propellers were removed so that new packing could be applied, and crews from USS *Panther* worked on the propellers and propeller shafts. The center propeller, damaged beyond repair, had to be replaced.

The plan for the return trip across the Atlantic was for the chasers to ride in tow behind the minesweepers. In anticipation of being towed much of the way home, the towing band on SC 354 was repaired, and a towing bitt was installed on the original forward gun base.

On 18 September the hull repairs were completed and the dry dock was

*Chaser in tow behind minesweeper, with towing bitt installed on gun base.*

flooded. The chasers exited and tied up alongside a jetty, where they would continue with the repair work, scraping pitch from the decks and adding caulking, fixing guard rail stanchions, painting out the numbers on the crow's nest canvas, and cleaning out the lazaret and magazines. Ten days of work brought the vessel into shape for painting topside and below decks, work that would continue into the first week of October.

In the second week of October, as minor repairs continued, the boat received provisions, filled the coal bunkers and fuel tanks, and prepared for departure. During this interval, six more chasers had arrived at Devonport, SC 37, SC 46, SC 110, SC 181, SC 207 and SC 329, bringing the full count of chasers for the first convoy to twelve:

| SC 37 | SC 95  | SC 207 | SC 259 |
| SC 46 | SC 110 | SC 208 | SC 329 |
| SC 48 | SC 181 | SC 256 | SC 354 |

Also present at Devonport were fourteen minesweepers, twelve of which would be assigned to tow the chasers on the first leg of the journey, to Brest, France.[5] On 10 October, the convoy departed Devonport, led by USS *Panther*, and had an easy passage to Brest. They spent five days at Brest, replenishing their supplies and awaiting orders to sail for Lisbon.

## Lisbon

With USS *Panther* again heading the convoy, the minesweepers and chasers set out for Lisbon on 15 October, the chasers once again under tow by the minesweepers. USS *Quail*, towing Lt. Dole's chaser, took up position behind USS *Panther*, the other vessels following in column formation.[6]

The advantage of towing the chasers back to the U.S. was that it would reduce the need for refueling, and allow the convoy to move along more quickly. Moreover, the minesweepers took on the role of supply vessels for the chasers, carrying enough extra parts and provisions to supply the chasers between ports as needed.

But towing the chasers wasn't without its difficulties, broken tow cables being a recurring problem. Twice en route to Lisbon the cables between USS *Quail* and SC 354 parted. The first time, Lt. Dole cut the broken cable and came alongside USS *Quail* to receive another cable; the next day the towing cable parted again, requiring another stop to re-attach it.[7]

The convoy reached Lisbon on 19 October, once again replenishing stores, and left four days later for San Miguel Island, Azores, arriving at Ponta Delgada

*USS Quail towing SC 354, leaving Brest, France.*

on 26 October. The weather was favorable, and they made an average speed of 14.6 knots for the last twenty-seven hours, arriving eighteen hours ahead of the rest of the convoy. Lt. Dole pulled SC 354 up to the pier and tied up alongside the tanker USS *Arethusa* (AO 7).

Their stop in the Azores was a pleasant interlude. "Sure am getting

*Minesweepers USS Teal (front), USS Lapwing (middle), and USS Heron (rear), at Ponta Delgada, Azores, October 1919. (T. Woofenden Collection.)*

my fill of pineapples, mangoes and grapes," Lt. Dole writes home. "It is hot here. The water is warm, and I am going to have a swim this p.m. Am looking forward to swimming in Bermuda when we arrive there."[8] The chaser men enjoyed a last bit of rest before a dangerous and challenging crossing, plagued by high seas and unfavorable weather.

## Bermuda

Two days later the convoy again set sail, SC 354 once again in tow behind USS *Quail*. Rough weather en route to Bermuda made for a difficult time with the towing gear, and multiple repairs had to be made, requiring repeated stops in high seas. On 5 November, while still en route, Lt. Dole cast off the towing gear altogether and SC 354 proceeded under its own power. The weather grew worse, and the high seas flooded the aft store room. While Lt. Dole's crew worked to gather the stores and drain the water, USS *Quail* dropped back to assist SC 46, which was having engine troubles. The convoy carried on, drenched and battered, and finally reached Bermuda on 9 November.

Exhausted, the chaser men began the work of cleaning out the store rooms and making repairs. On 15 November, SC 354 left Bermuda, under tow of USS *Quail*. They were now on the last leg of the journey, anxious finally to be headed for U.S. waters.

The first few days were uneventful, and the convoy proceeded at a good pace. Then Lt. Dole received a message from USS *Panther*: "Bad weather expected. Transfer gas to main tanks if necessary."[9] The sea rose, and the chasers found themselves in a major storm, worse than the weather they had encountered en route to Bermuda. On SC 354, two port covers were broken by the sea, and the hatch over the radio room was split at the deck. Crewman Milton Fogg describes the incident.

> We had some trip while in the North Sea, and *some* trip from Azores to Bermuda, and *some* trip from Bermuda to N.Y. I thought so especially on the last mentioned, when the two ports gave out in the radio room and your part. Say, I wish you could have seen Sterns come flying out of the magazine room when the water came pouring in. He thought sure she was sinking, and I didn't think far away from his thoughts either.[10]

With water gushing in and the crew scrambling to board up the ports, two more port covers were broken. The crew did their best to cover the ports with canvas to keep the sea water from swamping the boat, and held on.

## New York

On 19 November 1919, Lt. Dole reached Thompkinsville, Staten Island, New York, and moored alongside USS *Quail*. The chasers were finally home.

In the following days Lt. Dole made trips to the Brooklyn Navy Yard, carrying Adm. Strauss, the officers of USS *Black Hawk* and other senior officers to the Yard. Of Adm. Strauss, Lt. Dole writes on 23 November 1919, "We haul down his flag tomorrow, and I will watch it go down, the signal that the Minesweeping Detachment is no more."[11]

*Lt. Dole and crew on SC 354, New York, November 24, 1919. Photo by Steinberg. (T. Woofenden Collection.)*

Then SC 354 and the other chasers, along with the minesweepers, steamed up the Hudson River to Brooklyn, and on 24 November, Secretary of the Navy Josephus Daniels performed a review of the Minesweeping Detachment. That evening the men were honored with a Minesweeping Detachment dinner at the Hotel Astor in New York.

Their service nearly over, Lt. Dole and his crew set about the task of preparing the chaser for decommissioning, dismantling the engines, removing all publications and moving all gear up to the deck. The lights were removed from the mast, the pelorus stand and the signal light were removed and all gear was made ready for turning in. All the deck gear was turned in to the salvage office. The engines had been completely dismantled, and all military items removed from the vessel. On 10 December 1919, SC 354 was placed out of commission.

# Epilogue: The Impact of the Submarine Chasers

The American submarine chasers were involved in dozens of pursuits and attacks of enemy submarines, logged countless hours hunting submarines on the barrage lines and in the seaways of Europe, took part in diplomatic missions, assisted in the evacuation of American troops, and served in the post-war minesweeping operations. But how should we measure their overall effectiveness?

We can start by considering how the chasers have been viewed in other works of WWI naval history. Three perspectives are represented: An idealized, rather glamorous view of the chasers as victorious sub-killers, a critical view of the chasers as under-performing, and a view that the chasers aren't notable at all.

The subchaser experience is idealized by several of the men who took part in the effort, as chronicled in such works as *Maverick Navy*, *United States Submarine Chasers*, and *The Splinter Fleet of the Otranto Barrage*, and to some extent in works of a greater scope such as *The Victory at Sea* and *Simsadus: London*. Elements of this perspective are certainly true. The mission was dangerous and difficult; the men who took part are to be praised for coming to the task with such vigor, enthusiasm, patriotism and devotion, particularly given that most of the officers were not regular navy men and had little or no prior experience commanding a vessel; and they encountered and overcame many great obstacles. Other elements are of questionable historical merit. Most tales of the kill, for instance, if not altogether erroneous, are embellished into dramatic narratives that probably bear little resemblance to the actual events.

On the other side of the question are accounts that chalk up the chasers as under-performing, and the strategy of employing them in the ASW effort as, on the whole, ineffective. For instance, Dwight Messimer writes, "The 129 American subchasers (SCs) that served in European and Mediterranean waters were the prettiest, although not the most successful, patrol boats in the Entente force's inventory."[1] And in discussing the naval war in the Adriatic, Paul Halpern similarly remarks, "The submarine chasers never fulfilled the hopes placed in them."[2] Halpern describes the Otranto Barrage overall as similarly disappointing, considering the enormous expense and the small number of confirmed kills.

Typically in this view the credit for addressing the threat of the U-boats is placed with the convoy system and the destroyers and other larger vessels that accumulated much higher kill statistics, and with naval intelligence from intercepted transmissions and spies. The chasers are merely a curious footnote, an interesting experiment in early ASW tactics. In many accounts the chasers are not even mentioned.

On its face, this critical view is defensible. Clearly submarines penetrated the barrage lines in spite of the vigilance of the chasers, and the British Admiralty didn't credit the chasers with any kills. In many accounts of subchaser pursuits and attacks it is quite evident that there was no kill. Maybe history will ultimately corroborate some of the claims of kills by chasers. At least a few of the attacks seem like good candidates, and new information from divers and researchers is coming to light on an ongoing basis. But if the question is whether or not the chasers were successful on the whole in sinking submarines, then even a few kills to their credit wouldn't be enough to warrant an affirmative answer.

Surely this isn't the right question. If the chasers had an impact on the outcome of the war, then the critical view of their effectiveness in sinking subs may be legitimate but not particularly illuminating or important. The overarching objective, after all, was to defeat the enemy, not to sink subs.

The more interesting question is to what degree the chasers affected the outcome of the war. My personal view is that the chasers may be credited with having been an important element of the Allied victory, and that it is probably reasonable to view them, in company with the other small vessels armed with the new listening devices, as having turned the tide of the war. The argument is not that the chasers single-handedly won the war, or that they were somehow more capable than the larger warships, or that they contributed more than Naval Intelligence. The chasers arrived rather late to the war; they were out-gunned not only by the larger warships but by many of the submarines they were hunting; and the kind of intelligence gathered by listeners was important in the immediate time and place when pursuing a particular submarine, but not especially durable in its strategic value. But the U-boat offensive presented the real danger of the enemy starving England into submission, and to win the war thus required neutralizing the U-boat. I would argue that the entry of small ASW vessels into the arena of war and their use of new ASW tactics and equipment sufficiently hampered the U-boat to tip the scales in favor of the Allies: that in fact the chasers were highly effective in addressing the threat posed by the U-boat offensive.

There are two categories of evidence to consider: direct evidence of the effectiveness of the chasers in hampering the U-boats, and the evaluation of the effectiveness of the chasers by naval authorities.

**Hampering the U-boats**

Prior to the arrival of the American submarine chasers, the Allied forces had already worked to establish what Adm. Sims calls "a defensive offensive" approach to the submarine menace in the form of the convoy system. "It compelled the submarine to encounter its most formidable antagonist, the destroyer, and risk destruction every time that it attacked merchant vessels."[3] But this left unaddressed the need to detect enemy subs. As Adm. Sims points out, "Though the convoy, the mine-fields, the mystery ships, the airplane, and several other methods of fighting the under-water boat had been developed, the submarine could still utilize that one great quality of invisibility which made any final method of attacking it such a difficult problem."[4] Put simply, if you can't see the U-boat, you can't pursue it.

The submarine chasers became the eyes of the ASW effort. The new detection instruments developed by the Americans, such as the electronic K Tube device and the S.C. Tube hydrophones, represented significant technological advances over the existing listening devices in use by the British; and the 110' chasers presented an ideal vehicle for deployment of these new technologies and tactics. The chasers were well suited in a number of key respects. They were small, seaworthy and adequately fast; they could handle the repeated, rapid stops and starts needed for listening and pursuing; they required comparatively minimal crews, facilitating the capability to man a large fleet; and they could be built quickly, providing the U.S. Navy with a significant force of ASW vessels in a short time frame.

In effect, the chasers helped to bring the war to the U-boats. Tacticians could now add to their arsenal the prospect of detecting U-boats in strategic locations such as in the Strait of Otranto or along the English coast, instead of relying on luring them into range of the destroyers by presenting them with attractive clusters of target Allied vessels.

The effect of the chasers' presence can be seen in several measures. First is the actual log of detections and pursuits. We can mark off some number of these as erroneous detections, and certainly the log itself bears out the view that detecting a submarine usually didn't lead to destroying one. But the eyewitness accounts and reports of pursuits and attacks present an overall picture of a relentless hunt for the enemy with a large number of contacts, and thus a direct reduction in the ability of the submarine to run unfettered past these seaway checkpoints.

A related consideration is the tactic employed by enemy submarine commanders of "playing dead" by resting silently on the bottom in hopes that the pursuer would abandon the search and go away. That this tactic was used by enemy submarine commanders in the presence of chasers probably can't be conclusively demonstrated. But reports from listeners of submarines falling silent and subsequent reports of the target submarines safely reaching some port present rather strong evidence that the tactic was in fact used in the presence of chasers. For, even if we factor in listener error, we must bear in mind that chasers worked in three-vessel units. While not useful in determining the depth of a submarine, the listening devices were sensitive enough to determine the presence of a submarine; and for all three groups of listeners simultaneously to lose track of the sound seems rather implausible.

Of course we might view this tactic, assuming it was in fact used in the presence of chasers, as a clever way to defeat the chasers, a measure of the chasers' limitations rather than a testament to their tactical value. But at the same time it would be a corroboration of the view that the chasers posed a real threat, for why would the submarines waste time idling on the sea bed if the chasers could easily be passed by? Moreover the act itself, sitting inactive on the bottom of the ocean, constitutes a reduction in the effectiveness of the submarine's tour of duty, delaying its arrival at the target destination and thus reducing the enemy's overall opportunity to sink Allied shipping.

A more compelling piece of evidence can be seen in the reports by enemy submarine commanders after the war. Lt. Dole's account of conversations with Austrian submarine commanders, for instance, paints a picture of an enemy force taking pains to circumnavigate the chasers. The Austrian commanders, in this account, viewed the chasers as having the potential to detect, chase and destroy them, and were thus ordered to avoid them. This alone, if the account is accurate, is evidence of the effectiveness of the chasers in hampering the enemy, both physically and mentally.

In his book *The Victory at Sea*, Adm. Sims describes reports from Austrian naval officers regarding the arrival of the chasers on the barrage line, corroborating Lt. Dole's account, and supporting the notion that the chasers were highly effective in hampering the U-boats. "These little boats, the Austrians now informed us, were responsible for a mutiny in the Austrian submarine force. Two weeks after their arrival it was impossible to compel an Austrian crew to take a vessel through the straits, and from that time until the ending of the war not a single Austrian submarine ventured on such a voyage."[5]

German submarine commander Ernst Hashagen provides a first-hand account of the psychological effect of the ASW efforts, in a passage describing the conditions faced by the U-boat commanders in 1918:

> They pursue and fight us on the surface, through fog and storm, from the air and in the depths of the sea, on the coasts and in the open. It is as though the very sea had gone over to the enemy; it seems as though electrified, so violently do attack and defense rage upon it. Every wave is a foe. The coastal

lights are false: the sea-marks treacherous. They listen-in for us, to hear the distant beat of our screws; and feel for us with electric fingers along the seabed. ... It paid now to chase a submarine at a distance. Before, that had been pointless: now they could fasten on our tracks. Under water they could feel for us, listen, grope, and hunt. Under water they could kill us, too.[6]

Ens. John Langdon Leighton, an Intelligence officer under Adm. Sims, describes the practical effect in terms of the presence of enemy subs in areas patrolled by the chasers. "Plymouth and its vicinity were favorite areas for submarines, for five submarines per month usually would visit this region. In May, before the chasers began to operate, there were sixty-five sightings of, sinkings by, and attacks by, submarines within 100 miles of Plymouth. In July, after they had been operating for two months, there were only forty-five sightings of, sinkings by, and attacks by, submarines within the same distance of Plymouth ... As months went by, submarine activity in the Channel became less and less."[7]

It might be reasonable to question one or two of these bits of evidence. Maybe the Austrian commanders were looking to curry favor with the victors through flattery, and embellished their sense of fear of the chasers. Maybe Hashagen's sense of the growing Allied ASW threat is an apologia for the German loss. Maybe none of the attack reports involved any real threat to a submarine. Maybe the movement of enemy subs away from waters patrolled by chasers was purely coincidental. But these bits of information come from different sources and different types of sources: from chaser men, from Navy Intelligence officers, from navy commanders, from allies and from the enemy. The more likely picture is the more obvious one, that the chasers, armed with depth bombs and equipped with hydrophone detection devices, presented a formidable and palpable threat, hampering the enemy both physically and psychologically, curbing the free reign of the U-boat.

## The Navy's Regard for the Chasers

In WWI, ASW was a new and untested kind of warfare. The German submarine offensive marked the beginning of the era of submarine warfare as a serious tactical concern and the emergence of the science of ASW to combat it. Formative tactical notions lacked a foundation in actual practice. Some efforts appear in hindsight as rather ill-advised, such as the installation of deck guns on small boats like the chasers. In theory, small, fast boats could pursue a sub on the surface and sink it with gunfire, and a 3"/23-caliber deck gun would be more than adequate to pierce the hull of a sub. But the notion of chasers hunting subs on the surface didn't materialize. Most of the hunts involved detection and pursuit of submerged submarines; moreover a little vessel rolling and pitching in even moderate seas wasn't an effective base for the accurate use of a deck gun, even with an excellent marksman on board. This was a lesson learned in the war, evidenced by the removal of the deck guns prior to service in mine sweeping duties, in which the chasers followed behind the sweepers and sank stray mines with rifle fire. Even against a target that didn't shoot back, a deck gun on a chaser wasn't of much use.

There were also a number of less-than-ideal practical aspects of the chasers that resulted from the limitations inherent in the rapid construction of the fleet: the engines required considerable maintenance and were difficult to operate, the highest speed obtainable wasn't particularly impressive, the fuel capacity was limited, and so on. Overall, the chasers were hard to operate, stressful on the officers and crew, and limited in their range.

Yet if we consider how naval authorities viewed the chasers, a much different picture emerges and rises above these limitations and improvisations, that of a set of unique assets that provided tacticians with an entirely new range of motion. Bear in mind that when the U.S. entered the war we weren't starting at the very beginning of ASW. The science of detecting underwater sounds was already a known concern, and the first array of listening devices was already in the field. The task at hand in 1917 was to improve the technology and facilitate its deployment, so that instead of being restricted to the strategy of luring the enemy into strike range by amassing Allied vessels into convoys, naval authorities could consider offensive measures and provide targeted protection of strategic ports and seaways.

Against this background, American scientists had been improving on the existing designs of listening devices and developing new and better alternatives, and the American submarine chasers provided the means of deployment. Adm. Sims puts it this way: "The sea qualities which the subchaser displayed, and the development of listening devices which made it possible to detect all kinds of sounds under water at a considerable distance, immediately laid before us the possibility of a direct offensive against the submarine. It became apparent that these listening devices could be used to greatest advantage on these little craft."[8]

Adm. Sims had high praise for the results of the chaser divisions. But even more telling of his regard for the chaser is his summary remark, "Had it not been that the war ended before enough destroyers could be spared from convoy duty to assist, with their greater speed and offensive power, hunting groups of these tiny craft, it is certain that they would soon have become a still more important factor in destroying submarines and interfering with their operation."[9] Not only were the chasers effective in his view, but they had just started to show their potential.

The most compelling evidence of the high regard for the subchasers may be the fact that twenty years later the U.S. Navy still regarded the chaser as an important part of ASW: 438 chasers were built for duty in WWII.[10] Moreover, this wasn't a case of "we have them, so we have to use them." Almost all of the WWI chasers had been decommissioned and sold, yet for the WWII effort, the navy once again arrived at the strategic decision to build a fleet of chasers and use them against the submarine menace.

Naturally the navy improved upon the design of the vessels and upon the scientific equipment used in ASW. But the continued support for the tactical value of chasers is evidence that navy authorities viewed them as a valuable component of naval strategy.

A final question one might pose is why, if the chasers were of such great value, have they not received due billing in the annals of American naval history? There are several ways one might answer this. First, there was no steady path from concept to impeccable implementation, so perhaps the chasers' contribution didn't seem entirely clear at the time. The chasers were new, untested and unrefined, and ASW by subchaser simply hadn't yet come into its own. It was a growing, developing strategy, and the chasers were a first-stage effort. Second, while the submarine menace was a critical component of WWI, the land engagement was by far the more weighty story, millions of soldiers killed in a relentless, heartless meat-grinder, a story of tragedy and death rising to enormous proportions. The sea engagement, however critical, takes a back seat; and the little chasers fall in behind the large, powerful gun ships in stature.

Another explanation, and perhaps a more useful one, is that the men of the chasers were not giants in their day. There were no Admirals among them, and in fact rather few Lieutenants. There were some regular U.S. Navy men, but most were young Naval Reservists or newly enlisted men, eager to offer their service – ready, as Lt. Dole puts it, "to make the last sacrifice."

Lt. Dole's service on the chasers is representative of the widest span of service: Only a few other chaser officers match his record for capability, duration of service, miles run, engagements and variety of experience. In this sense, we might regard him as a representative character of the World War I subchaser man. Yet for all his devotion, courage and leadership, he makes an unlikely war hero. He was a Naval Reservist, a skilled navigator and an effective officer. But in temperament he was closer to academician than hero. His writing on the Northern Russia Expedition is more travel literature than war story, his perspective on Durazzo and the other glorified accounts of the chasers unglamorously practical. After the war he returned to civilian life, coaching young men in wrestling at Milton Academy in Massachusetts, and teaching economics at St. Lawrence University in New York. He served the world of academia as faithfully as he had served the navy, and as humbly and quietly.

He died at age 43, the official cause of death listed as heart failure, but nobody in the family accepted that diagnosis. His father believed that he had returned from the war having suffered permanent damage to his circulatory system from the time he spent under water in the frigid winter of 1917-1918 clearing the subchaser propellers of wire, and the overall harsh environment of his tour of duty on the chasers. Other family members believed that he died of complications from a smallpox vaccine. But whatever the cause, he died having consistently and unselfishly offered his service to those around him. A posthumous account of his service tells the story of Lt. Dole receiving his Navy Cross in the mail one day at Milton Academy: He opened the package, noted its contents, and quietly and modestly slipped it into his pocket. Did this really happen? Who knows. But it is the kind of thing Lt. Dole would do.

Along with Lt. Dole, thousands of men served on the chasers with the same dedication and passion for their work, relentlessly hunting the steel sharks of the sea. Some continued to serve in the Armed Forces; others returned to civilian life as did Lt. Dole. None became famous American heroes by virtue of their service in the chaser fleet. In fact most of their stories of service on the submarine chasers in WWI now lie packed away in boxes or are lost, maybe a word or two passed down through a few generations about how grandfather hunted submarines.

Lt. Dole offered one final bit of service to the navy in this regard, by saving the documents and photos generated during his tours of duty and keeping them safe. In telling the story of the chasers, based on his remarkable collection, I have endeavored not just to show my respect for the man, but perhaps even more so to show my respect for the kind of man. These were admirable young Americans, willing to offer their selfless service because it was the right thing to do, role models that serve us equally well today as in 1918.

We might do well to view the story of the WWI chasers as a story of men first, and a story of perilous times at sea in the early days of ASW second. So dig those boxes out of the attic, those boxes left behind by men of the chasers and other navy vessels, by men of the infantry, and by men of the other Armed Forces who served in the war. Study their lives and service, honor their sacrifice, and let the example of our ancestors who served in the Great War be an example for us and our children.

# Appendix I – Distribution of Submarine Chasers

Lt. Dole saw many ports during his tour of duty on the chasers, including Corfu, Greece; Lisbon, Portugal; Inverness, Scotland; Archangel, Russia; Kirkwall, Scotland; and Lervig, Norway. He served in three major undertakings involving subchasers – the Otranto Barrage, the Northern Russia Expedition and the work of the North Sea Minesweeping Detachment – placing him in company with a small group of men with the most extensive submarine chaser experience.

But the impact of the chasers was wider still. The WWI submarine chaser program resulted in the construction of 441 subchasers. Of these, one hundred were built for France, and four were transferred to Cuba just prior to the Armistice. Including the four transferred to Cuba, 303 were completed and launched as U.S.N. vessels, and can therefore be counted as the U.S. war time force. Thirty-eight chasers were completed after the Armistice and thus played no role in the war.

The distribution of the war time U.S. submarine chaser forces is as follows:

**Service in Europe at Subchaser Bases.** 133 subchasers crossed the Atlantic for the purpose of engaging in ASW in Europe, some of these vessels having served along the coast of the U.S. prior to being assigned to overseas bases. The three major bases of operations for subchasers overseas were:

**Base 27, Plymouth, England** (Submarine Chaser Detachment One)
**Base 25, Corfu, Greece** (Submarine Chaser Detachment Two)
**Base 6, Queenstown, Ireland** (Cobh) (Submarine Chaser Detachment Three)

A total of 102 subchasers served at one or more of these three bases: thirty-six at Corfu, sixty-six at Plymouth, and of the chasers at Plymouth, thirty were transferred to Queenstown. More were en route to bases in Europe when the Armistice was signed: eighteen arrived at Gibraltar on 11 November 1918, and twelve arrived at Ponta Delgada, Azores, on 12 November. One chaser, SC 219, was lost to fire at Ponta Delgada on 19 October 1918, and thus didn't reach its assigned base.

Chasers based at Queenstown and at Plymouth engaged in concentrated ASW efforts similar to the efforts of the chasers based at Corfu. More information on this service is provided in Appendix II (Plymouth) and in Appendix III (Queenstown). The service of the chasers at Corfu is covered in chapters 4 and 5.

**Service at Other European Bases.** Several other overseas ports were host to chasers at one time or another, including Brest (Base 7), Gibraltar (Base 9) and Ponta Delgada, Azores (Base 13). No regular chaser ASW operations were associated with these bases, although attacks on enemy submarines were reported by chasers while en route to other stations. A notable example is an attack by SC 227 and SC 331 in the vicinity of Gibraltar on 11 November 1918. While there is no confirmation of the sinking of a submarine in this incident, it has the distinction of being the last reported attack by an American submarine chaser in WWI.

**Service on the Atlantic Coast.** As new chasers were completed, they were launched and commissioned at locations along the coast of the U.S., and about half were assigned to U.S. coastal bases, many of them in the northeast. Service on the north Atlantic coast included ASW tactical training, preparation of the vessels for active ASW operations, patrol duties and live ASW operations. Twelve chasers served along the south Atlantic coast, performing ASW operations, patrol and convoy duties. More information on Atlantic coast service is provided in Appendix IV.

**Service on the Pacific Coast.** Thirteen chasers were assigned to the Pacific Fleet, and performed duties including survey work and patrols on the Pacific coast of the U.S. and along the Mexican and Central American coasts.[1] More information on Pacific coast service is provided in Appendix V.

**Service in Alaska.** Two chasers, SC 309 and SC 310, performed duties in Alaskan waters[2] including patrol and enforcement of fishery regulations.

## Appendix II – Submarine Chaser Service at Plymouth, England

The submarine chasers of Detachment One, stationed at Base 27, were active from the earliest arrivals at Plymouth in May 1918 until the Armistice on 11 November 1918. On 16 June 1918, Adm. Sims placed Comdr. Lyman A. Cotten in charge of the Plymouth subchaser detachment.[3] Under his command on 16 June were destroyer USS *Aylwin* (DD 47) and eighteen submarine chasers, at this time organized into units called "groups." These were:

Group 13: SC 177, SC 143 and SC 148
Group 14: SC 226, SC 224 and SC 351
Group 15: SC 35, SC 34 and SC 97
Group 16: SC 36, SC 321 and SC 98
Group 17: SC 37, SC 38 and SC 40
Group 18: SC 137, SC 258 and SC 41

On 30 June 1918, destroyer USS *Parker* (DD 48) and twenty-three additional chasers arrived for service at Plymouth:

Group 19: SC 259, SC 83 and SC 87
Group 20: SC 84, SC 85 and SC 86
Group 21: SC 100 and SC 101
Group 22: SC 99, SC 260 and SC 322
Group 23: SC 354, SC 257 and SC 352
Group 24: SC 39, SC 252 and SC 262
Group 25: SC 323, SC 325 and SC 220
Group 26: SC 91, SC 221 and SC 222

SC 103 was later assigned to Group 21. On 27 July 1918 the detachment was reorganized into "Hunting Units," thereafter referred to as "units" rather than "groups," as follows:

Unit 1: SC 177, SC 143 and SC 148
Unit 2: SC 226, SC 224 and SC 351
Unit 3: SC 35, SC 34 and SC 97
Unit 4: SC 36, SC 321 and SC 98
Unit 5: SC 37, SC 38 and SC 40
Unit 6: SC 137, SC 258 and SC 41
Unit 7: SC 259, SC 83 and SC 87
Unit 8: SC 84, SC 85 and SC 86

Unit 9: SC 100, SC 101 and SC 103
Unit 10: SC 99, SC 260 and SC 322
Unit 11: SC 354, SC 257 and SC 352
Unit 12: SC 39, SC 252 and SC 262
Unit 13: SC 323, SC 325 and SC 220
Unit 14: SC 91, SC 221 and SC 222

On 11 August 1918, eight more units were assigned to Base 27, bringing the total to sixty-six chasers:

Unit 15: SC 342, SC 343 and SC 346
Unit 16: SC 344, SC 345 and SC 1
Unit 17: SC 271, SC 164 and SC 356
Unit 18: SC 272, SC 181 and SC 182
Unit 19: SC 206, SC 207 and SC 208
Unit 20: SC 45, SC 47 and SC 48
Unit 21: SC 178, SC 329 and SC 254
Unit 22: SC 110, SC 44 and SC 46

Of these, thirty were transferred to Queenstown, Base 6, arriving there on 21 August 1918.[4]

During service at Plymouth, chasers engaged in the following pursuits and attacks of enemy submarines:

**30 May 1918, 10:50 p.m.**

SC 143 and SC 177 were on drifting patrol when Ens. Moffat, commanding officer of SC 143, saw a vessel that appeared to be a submarine. Ens. Moffat reported the sighting to SC 177, and Lt. R.N. Griffin on SC 177 saw the vessel as well; then a listener on the C tubes reported making sound contact. The submarine appeared to be approaching the chasers. Soon after, three depth charges were deployed, but without a visible effect on the submarine. The chasers then turned toward the location of the submarine and searchlights were used, but proved ineffective. Contact with the submarine was lost, and both chasers stopped to listen.

Sound contact was again made, indicating that the submarine was on a bearing away from SC 143. SC 177 proceeded toward the projected location, and shortly after, crewmen on SC 143 observed a small submarine heading toward them, presumably having heard SC 177's engines and having changed course to move away. The sub passed within an estimated 200 yards, and SC 143 pursued at full speed. The chaser overshot the mark and crossed the enemy's bow at a considerable distance ahead. A depth charge was dropped, but the detonation was not close enough to affect the enemy sub. SC 143 then turned and fired the Y-gun, the detonations obscuring the submarine.

At 11:55 p.m. the chasers anchored and lowered tubes. Sounds of light hammering or possibly an anchor cable were detected for about 15 minutes, then sound contact was lost. At 1:30 a.m. the chasers detected the sound of a propeller near SC 143. Since SC 143 had only one depth charge left, SC 177 pursued and dropped a charge. The sound was again detected after the detonation, moving away. The chasers continued to listen, SC 143 at anchor and SC 177 drifting. No further contact was made.[5]

**10 July 1918, 10:05 a.m.**
Group 20 (SC 84, SC 85 and SC 86) detected a submarine five miles south of St. Anthony Head. The unit engaged in a chase and attacked at 1:10 p.m., deploying seven depth charges. Sound contact was then made for about 30 seconds, after which no further contact was made. While the listeners believed that the sound indicated that the submarine's engines had been damaged, there was no other evidence of damage to a submarine.[6]

**11 July 1918, 12:30 p.m.**
Group 24 (SC 39, SC 252 and SC 262) detected an enemy submarine five miles southeast of Eddystone Light. The weather conditions were adverse for listening, and the chasers made several runs trying to gain a positive, clear fix on the sub. At 2:30 p.m. the unit dropped seven depth charges and SC 252 reported streaks of oil in the water, but sound contact was once more made, indicating that the sub was not destroyed.

The unit continued to hunt, and at 7:55 p.m. a periscope was sighted. Listening results suggested that the chasers had overshot the mark on more than one occasion. The hunt progressed into the night. At 4:50 a.m. on 12 July a fix was obtained, but a British destroyer entered the scene and interfered with the attack approach. Several more sound contacts were made, and another spread of depth charges was dropped at 12:00 noon. Sound contact was once again made after the attack. As weather conditions worsened, the chasers had increasing difficulty making sound contact, and the chase was called off at 2:00 p.m.[7]

**14 July 1918, 1:55 a.m.**
Two chasers of Group 25, SC 323 and SC 220, detected a submarine ten miles south of the Lizard. The chasers engaged in a chase until 4:44 a.m., when sound contact was lost. It was surmised that this was the same submarine that had been attacked on 10 July, and that "as no vessel was attacked by this submarine, it is probable that she approached the vicinity of Falmouth and the Lizard for the purpose of laying mines, but was forced to abandon her operations by the actions of the Sub Chasers, as sweeping in these areas indicate that no mines had actually been laid."[8]

**31 July 1918, 7:15 p.m.**
Two chasers of Group 22, SC 99 and SC 322, were on patrol on 30 July 1918. SC 260, the third chaser of Unit 10, had returned to base due to illness on board, and was not involved in the hunt. "Hammering and signaling" were detected, and the chasers engaged in a running patrol, losing sound contact, regaining contact at 4:30 p.m., and once more losing contact shortly thereafter.

At 9:30 a. m. on 31 July, a periscope was sighted on the port quarter of SC 99 at a distance of 300 yards. The chasers engaged in drifting patrol for several hours and attacked at 7:15 p.m., dropping a total of seven depth charges. An oil patch was found, but there was no evidence of damage to a submarine.[9]

**5 August 1918, 6:45 a.m.**
SC 342 (prior to arriving at Base 27) launched an attack on an enemy submarine off the coast of France at 6:45 a.m., firing the Y-gun and dropping one charge off the stern, with no visible results. At 8:15 a.m. the chaser sighted a periscope and at 8:20 attacked a second time, again firing the Y-gun and dropping a charge off the stern. Streaks of oil were observed on the water. There was no evidence of damage to a submarine.[10]

**23 August 1918, 2:21 p.m.**
Unit 4 (SC 36, SC 98 and SC 321) detected a submarine and waged

an attack, dropping ten depth charges with no result. The unit attacked again at 8:12 p.m., dropping five depth charges. There was no evidence of damage to a submarine.[11]

**2 September 1918, 2:16 p.m.**

USS *Parker* and Unit 4 (SC 36, SC 98 and SC 321) detected a submarine on the surface, near Lat. N 47° 57', Long. W 9° 20'. The submarine dived, and USS *Parker* waged a depth charge attack, after which the chasers made sound contact immediately. The chasers engaged in a chase and attacked about two hours later with a spread of twelve depth charges. There was no evidence of damage to the submarine.[12]

**6 September 1918, 11:45 a.m.**

Unit 2 (SC 226, SC 224 and SC 351), Unit 6 (SC 137, SC 41 and SC 258) and Unit 10 (SC 99, SC 260 and SC 322) made sound contact with an enemy submarine near Lat. N 50° 17', Long. W 5° 46', the sound of the engine leading the listeners to believe that the submarine had already been damaged. Unit 2 attacked with a spread of nine depth charges, after which sound contact was once again made, the engine of the submarine seeming to be further damaged. Unit 2 delivered a second attack at 12:28 a.m., dropping a spread of eight depth charges. The charge launched from the starboard barrel of the Y-gun on SC 226 fell close aboard, damaging all three engines so that the chaser had to be towed to base. Unit 6 then made sound contact and delivered a third attack, with no visible result.

The chase continued until about 6:00 p.m., with units 6 and 10 dropping charges ahead of and behind the detected location of the submarine. Bottoming noises were then detected at times for several hours. The following day chasers remained near the site, but no further sound contact was made.[13]

In several unconfirmed reports and later accounts of this incident, listeners are reported to have detected revolver shots after the attack, interpreted as a case of submarine crewmen committing suicide; however there is no mention of this in the Base 27 subchaser war diary. In one unconfirmed report of the incident, crewman Thomas G. Sweet of SC 260 claims that the submarine targeted in this incident was later raised by the British.

**27 October 1918, 6:50 p.m.**
Unit 6 (SC 137, SC 41 and SC 258) detected a submarine and engaged in a chase, delivering an attack of three depth charges at 1:20 a.m. on 28 October. Unit 1 (SC 177, SC 143 and SC 148) delivered a second attack of six depth charges. Sound contact was lost due to sound interference from other vessels. There was no evidence of damage to a submarine.[14]

## Appendix III – Submarine Chaser Service at Queenstown, Ireland

Thirty chasers previously stationed at Plymouth arrived at Queenstown, Ireland (Cobh), on 21 August 1918, forming a presence at this base similar to that at Corfu (where 36 chasers were stationed), although of a shorter duration.[15] The chasers transferred to Queenstown, under the command of Capt. A. J. Hepburn, were assigned to units as follows:

Unit 13: SC 271, SC 164 and SC 356
Unit 14: SC 272, SC 181 and SC 182
Unit 15: SC 342, SC 343 and SC 346
Unit 16: SC 344, SC 345 and SC 1
Unit 17: SC 323, SC 325 and SC 220
Unit 18: SC 91, SC 221 and SC 222
Unit 19: SC 206, SC 207 and SC 208
Unit 20: SC 45, SC 47 and SC 48
Unit 21: SC 178, SC 329 and SC 254
Unit 22: SC 110, SC 44 and SC 46

The chasers at Queenstown were active in ASW from the third week of August 1918, until the Armistice on 11 November, and engaged in the following pursuits and attacks:

**25 September 1918, 7:30 p.m.**
Unit 13 (SC 271, SC 164 and SC 356) and SC 181 detected a submarine off Barrels Lightship, at Lat. N 51° 40', Long. W 7° 13'. The chase continued, sound contact being lost and regained several times. On the morning of 26 September contact was lost altogether. No attack was waged.[16]

**29 September 1918, 5:47 a.m.**
Unit 22 (SC 110, SC 44 and SC 46) detected a submarine at Lat. N 53° 44', Long. W 5° 47'. At 6:44 a.m. sound contact was lost. Between 7:41 and 7:52 six depth charges were dropped in a spread across the suspected area, for the purpose of causing the submarine to move and disclose its location. No further sound contact was made.[17]

**30 September 1918, 3:50 p.m.**
SC 164 made sight contact with a submarine eight miles southwest of Tuskar. The submarine submerged immediately. Unit 13 (SC 271,

SC 164 and SC 356) and SC 181 engaged in a chase, but no further contact was made.[18]

**11 October 1918, 12:45 p.m.**
Unit 19 (SC 206, SC 207 and SC 208) and Unit 20 (SC 45, SC 47 and SC 48) were on patrol when SC 48 discovered an oil patch and detected a submarine. Under the command of SC 206, the division engaged in a chase. Sound contact was lost when a destroyer and two trawlers approached. No further contact was made.[19]

**13 October 1918, 6:40 a.m.**
Unit 18 (SC 91, SC 221 and SC 222) was on patrol when SC 91 sighted a periscope close off the starboard bow and dropped a pattern of five depth charges. SC 221 also dropped a depth charge. SC 91 and SC 221 then reported a "swishing sound" and hammering sounds, but were unable to obtain a fix. SC 222, also in the vicinity, reported damage to listening devices caused by the depth charge explosions. The sounds detected by SC 91 and SC 221 diminished and finally stopped. At 10:30 the chasers engaged in a running hunt, but no further contact was made.[20]

**16 October 1918, 5:05 p.m.**
At 4:20 p.m. SC 46 received a report by radio of the location of an enemy submarine and proceeded to the coordinates. At 4:55, SC 46 sighted a periscope on the starboard beam and fired the Y-gun. The starboard charge was reported to have landed in close proximity to the submarine. SC 178 then fired its Y-gun and dropped two depth charges off the stern on an oil slick. After the attack, sound contact was made by SC 178, the distance estimated at 500 yards. A second attack was made, two charges dropped by SC 178 and one by SC 46. No further sound contact was made.[21]

**22 October 1918, 1:30 p.m.**
Unit 22 (SC 110, SC 44 and SC 46) made sound contact with a submarine seven miles from Coningbeg Light Vessel. The unit dropped a pattern of five depth charges on an oil slick identified by dirigible SSZ-53, then began following an oil wake, dropping more charges. The wake terminated at a point at which the dirigible dropped two bombs. The chaser crews observed oil coming to the surface for two hours at this location, and at 4:00 p.m. observed another oil trail.

The unit engaged in a second chase, dropping eleven depth charges at Lat. N 52° 00', Long. W 6° 29'. The dirigible dropped one bomb at this location. The chasers buoyed the location and dropped a pattern of five depth charges over the area. SC 46 trailed for the submarine, but the trailing wire snagged and separated before any detection could be made. Oil continued to rise at the spot throughout the night, but no further sound contact was made. There was no evidence collected of damage to a submarine.[22]

**27 October 1918, 7:00 a.m.**
Unit 20 (SC 45, SC 47 and SC 48) was ordered to the location of a depth charge attack, and instituted a drifting patrol. SC 45 reported making sound contact with an enemy submarine at about 9:35 a.m. near Codling Lightship. Several runs were made, as the wing boats were unable to make sound contact. At 9:49 SC 45 and SC 47 were able to obtain fixes on the sound. The unit continued to make short runs while closing their formation, and at 9:59 estimated the submarine to be 400 yards away. At 10:03 an attack was made, a total of twenty-four depth charges deployed. Sound contact continued after the attack, and was lost due to sound interference from other surface vessels at about 10:30 a.m.[23]

# Appendix IV – Submarine Chaser Service on the Atlantic Coast

The service range of chasers spanned the Atlantic coast from Nova Scotia to the Gulf of Mexico. Most of the chasers were assigned to U.S. Naval Districts at one time or another, particularly during ASW training. Some of these chasers were given longer-term assignments working with hunting units on the Atlantic coast including the USS *Salem* (CS 3) Group, the USS *Jouett* (DD 41) Group, the USS *Henley* (DD 39) Group and the USS *Patterson* (DD 36) Group. Six chasers, SC 51, SC 183, SC 240, SC 241, SC 242 and SC 247 were sent to Nova Scotia, and performed patrol and escort duties.

**The USS *Jouett* Group.** Early work of the chasers stationed along the north Atlantic coast included testing of new ASW equipment and techniques. The USS *Jouett* Group, under Capt. J. T. Tompkins, commanding officer of USS *Jouett*, was assigned to the Experimental Board at the submarine base in New London, Connecticut, and engaged in testing of submarine detection devices, tactical maneuvers with subchaser units, patrols and ASW operations. This special group was comprised initially of USS *Jouett*, USS *Henley*, USS *Perkins* (DD 26) and thirty-three submarine chasers arranged in Divisions as follows:[24]

Division L: SC 134, SC 136, SC 190, SC 191, SC 223 and SC 332
Division M: SC 132, SC 133, SC 219, SC 331, SC 353 and SC 355
Division N: SC 42, SC 102, SC 105, SC 135, SC 180 and SC 330
Division O: SC 68, SC 69, SC 70, SC 145, SC 189 and SC 339
Division P: SC 210, SC 211, SC 212, SC 213, SC 340 and SC 341
Tactical Group: SC 6, SC 214 and SC 253

The chaser force attached to the USS *Jouett* Group was reduced on 9 June 1918, nine chasers reassigned to other locations and the remaining twenty-four placed under the command of Comdr. William P. Cronan on USS *Jouett*.

**The USS *Henley* Group.** On 4 September 1918 all but six of the chasers in the USS *Jouett* Group were reassigned to the First Naval District, and three additional chasers (Group C, below) were assigned to the group. On 25 September Comdr. Cronan transferred to USS *Henley*, which became flagship for the group. The subchasers attached to the USS *Henley* Group were:

Group A: SC 6, SC 133 and SC 134
Group B: SC 42, SC 102 and SC 105
Group C: SC 263, SC 266 and SC 269

**The USS *Patterson* Group.** On 22 August 1918, Lt. Alfred Y. Lanphier took command of USS *Patterson* and assumed command of twelve submarine chasers, SC 22, SC 23, SC 111, SC 121, SC 186, SC 188, SC 203, SC 209, SC 232, SC 234, SC 245 and SC 270. In September, SC 119 and SC 122 also served in this group. The USS *Patterson* Group engaged in patrol and ASW operations along the Atlantic coast.[25]

**The USS *Salem* Group.** A special hunting squadron under the command of Capt. S.V. Graham on the cruiser USS *Salem* was established to patrol the Gulf of Mexico and the surrounding region, and performed training exercises, patrols and ASW operations.[26] Twelve subchasers were assigned to the USS *Salem* Group, and arranged into Groups as follows:

Group A: SC 320, SC 261 and SC 104
Group B: SC 2, SC 3 and SC 4
Group C: SC 68, SC 70 and SC 339
Group D: SC 69, SC 145 and SC 189

**Canal Zone (Base 15).** Twelve submarine chasers, SC 279 through SC 290, served in the Panama Canal region. Most of this force patrolled the region around the Atlantic entrance of the canal. Four chasers patrolled the region around the Pacific entrance. Three chasers, SC 288, SC 289 and SC 290, were reassigned to convoy duty in September 1918, and sailed for Guantanamo, Cuba; Key West, Florida, and other ports.

Chasers assigned to service on the Atlantic coast of the U.S. engaged in detections and attacks of submarines, including the following:

**9 June 1918, 5:00 a.m.**
SC 234 was on escort duty with USS *South Carolina*, bound for Delaware Bay. Between 5:00 and 5:15 a.m. a periscope and part of the conning tower of an enemy submarine were sighted about 500 yards away. USS *South Carolina* opened fire, and the subchaser headed for the target. Depth charges were fired from the chaser's Y-gun, but the charge fired to the port side failed to detonate. There was no evidence of damage to the submarine.[27]

**17 June 1918, 9:45 p.m.**
Serving in the USS *Jouett* Group, submarine chasers in Division L (SC 223, SC 191, SC 134, SC 136, SC 332 and SC 190) detected a

submarine and engaged in a chase. Chasers in Division M (SC 132, SC 219, SC 331, SC 355, SC 133 and SC 353) also picked up the sound, and joined in the chase. Sound bearings indicated that the submarine was following a zigzag pattern to avoid the subchasers. Due to a fuel shortage, the chasers were ordered to abandon the chase at about midnight. No attack was waged.[28]

**1 July 1918, 3:40 p.m.**
En route to Dartmouth Cove, Nova Scotia, SC 241 sighted a torpedo heading in the direction of a freighter, and altered course to avoid its path. At 3:45 p.m. a submarine was sighted on the starboard bow, 200 to 300 yards away, in heavy fog, running parallel to the course of the chaser. At a distance of about thirty-three yards, SC 241 fired the Y-gun, one depth charge reported to have landed about ten yards from the periscope. The submarine submerged, and heavy oil was observed on the surface. There was no evidence of damage to a submarine.[29]

**3 September 1918, 3:15 p.m.**
Serving in the USS *Patterson* Group, submarine chaser SC 234 sighted a periscope 1,000 to 1,500 feet away, and SC 234, SC 245 and SC 121 dropped a pattern of 11 depth charges at Lat. N 36° 34', Long. W 75° 24'. USS *Patterson* then dropped six depth charges on an area where oil was seen rising to the surface. An anchor buoy was dropped to mark the location, and chasers engaged in listening for the rest of the day. No sound contact was made, and there was no evidence of damage to a submarine.[30]

**24 September 1918, midnight.**
Serving in the USS *Patterson* group, submarine chaser SC 234 made sound contact with an enemy submarine on a northward course at Lat. N 36° 26', Long. W 73° 46'. A depth charge attack was made, and the sound ceased. A slight oil slick appeared, but there was no evidence of damage to a submarine.[31]

## Appendix V – Submarine Chaser Service on the Pacific Coast

A small force of chasers served along the Pacific coast of the U.S. and farther south. These included SC 301, SC 302, SC 303, SC 304, SC 305, SC 306, SC 307, SC 308, SC 311 and SC 312, assigned to perform a survey in the region of Amapala, Honduras. SC 273, SC 274 and SC 275 were later added to this group, and performed patrols along coast of Mexico and Central America. Some were later reassigned to service along the Atlantic coast. Four of these chasers – SC 274, SC 302, SC 311 and SC 312 – were prepped for, and transferred to, the Cuban government in November 1918.[32]

Additionally, four subchasers performed patrol duties around the Pacific entrance of the Panama Canal (see Appendix IV).

# Bibliography

## Books

Buranelli, Prosper. *Maggie of the Suicide Fleet.* New York: Doubleday, Doran & Company, 1930.

Chambers, Hilary R. *United States Submarine Chasers.* New York: The Knickerbocker Press, 1920.

Clark, William Bell. *When the U-Boats Came to America.* Boston: Little, Brown and Company, 1929.

Daniels, Josephus. *Our Navy at War.* Washington, DC: Pictorial Bureau, 1922.

Grant, Robert M. *U-Boat Hunters.* Annapolis: Naval Institute Press, 2003.

Grant, Robert M. *U-Boat Intelligence 1914 – 1918.* Hamden: Archon Books, 1969.

Halliday, Ernest. *The Ignorant Armies.* New York: Harper & Brother, Publishers, 1958.

Halpern, Paul G. *A Naval History of World War I.* Annapolis: Naval Institute Press, 1994.

Hashagen, Ernst. *U-Boats Westward.* Translated from the German by Lieutenant-Commander Vesey Ross. New York: G.P. Putnam's Sons, 1931.

Kemp, Paul, *U-Boats Destroyed.* London: Arms & Armour, 1997.

Knox, Dudley W., *A History of the United States Navy.* New York: G. Putnam's Sons, 1948.

Leighton, John Langdon. *Simasadus London: The American Navy in Europe.* New York: Henry Holt and Company, 1920.

Massie, Robert. *Castles of Steel: Britain, Germany, and the Winning of the Great War at Sea.* New York: Random House, 2003.

Messimer, Dwight R. *Find and Destroy – Antisubmarine Warfare in World War I.* Annapolis: Naval Institute Press, 2001.

Millholland, Ray. *The Splinter Fleet of the Otranto Barrage.* New York: Bobbs Merrill Company, 1936.

Mine Force, United States Atlantic Fleet. *The Northern Barrage.* Edited by All Hands. Annapolis: U.S. Naval Institute, 1919.

Moffat, Alexander. *Maverick Navy.* Middletown: Wesleyan University Press, 1976.

Nutting, William Washburn. *The Cinderellas of the Fleet.* Jersey City: Standard Motor Construction Company, 1920.

Perry, Lawrence. *Our Navy in the War.* New York: Charles Scribner's Sons, 1918.

Sims, William Sowden. *The Victory At Sea*. New York: Doubleday, Page & Company, 1920.

Standard Motor Construction Company. *100-Foot Submarine Chaser – Instructions, Care and Operation of Machinery Plant*. New York: Thomson & Company Printers, 1917.

Strakhovsky, Leonid I. *Intervention at Archangel, The Story of Allied Intervention and Russian Counter-Revolution in North Russia, 1918-1920*. Princeton: Princeton University Press, 1944.

Sutphen, Henry R. *Building Submarine Chasers by Standardized Methods*. From: The Society of Automotive Engineers, Inc., Transactions, Part II, New York, 1917.

Treadwell, Theodore R. *Splinter Fleet – The Wooden Subchasers of World War II*. Annapolis: Naval Institute Press, 2000.

U.S. Naval Department, Historical Section. *American Ship Casualties of the World War*. Washington, D.C.: Washington Government Printing Office, 1923.

U.S. Navy Department, Mine Force, North Sea Minesweeping Detachment. *Sweeping the North Sea Mine Barrage*. 1919.

U.S. Navy Department, Office of Naval Records and Library. *Publication Number 1 – German Submarine Activities on the Atlantic Coast of the United States and Canada*. Washington, D.C.: Washington Government Printing Office, 1920.

U.S. Navy Department, Office of Naval Records and Library, Historical Section. *Publication Number 4: "The Northern Barrage" (Taking Up the Mines)*. Washington. D.C.: Government Printing Office, 1920.

U.S. Navy Department, Office of Naval Records and Library, Historical Section. *Publication Number 5, History of the Bureau of Engineering, Navy Department During the World War*. Washington, D.C.: Government Printing Office, 1922.

U.S. Navy Department, Office of Records Administration, Administrative Office, Navy Department, *The American Naval Mission in the Adriatic, 1918-1921*, Prepared by Dr. A.C. Davidonis, September, 1943.

Willoughby, Malcolm F. *Yankton, Yacht and Man-of-War*. Cambridge: Crimson Publishing Company, 1935.

**Periodicals**

Dole, George S. "Farthest North in a Submarine Chaser." *Motorboat*, June 1920. (Also in Nutting, *Cinderellas of the Fleet*.)

Fernandez, Gerard. "A Lemon of a Trip." *The Log, newsletter of the Submarine*

*Chaser Club of America.* Vol. II No. 6, June 1921.
Loomis, Al. "What Were the Faults of the Sub-Chasers?" *Motor Boating.* December 1919.

**Typescripts**

Barbier, Lt. deVasseau. *La traversée del'Atlantique par les Chasseurs de Sous Marins contruits en Amérique.* Ecole de Guerre Navale, 1922-1923.
Clephane, Lewis P. *History of the Submarine Chasers in the World War.* Washington Government Printing Office, 1920.
McBride, L.B. *Submarine Chasers.* Navy Department, Bureau of Construction and Repair, 1920.
Post, Charles A. *Navy Life Aboard the SC 40.*
West, Stephen.Crane. *Let Her Go East.* National Archives, Washington, D.C., 1922.

**Primary Source Documents, G.S. Dole Collection**

*110-ft. Submarine Chasers; Sale of; Vessels to be stripped of Military Fittings and Arms*, 19 January 1919.
*Advance Memorandum No. 1 on Tactics.* Naval District Base, New London, CT.
*Battle Signal Book for Submarine Chasers Operating in English Channel.* (Operational document.)
Cotten, Captain Lyman A. *Instructions and Doctrine for Sub Chaser Detachment One.*
Hepburn, A.J. *Memorandum for C.O.'s of Chasers*, 2 November 1918.
*Instructions for Minesweeping Detachment. Mine Force, U.S. Atlantic Fleet.* 19 May 1919.
*Instructions for the Guidance of the Engineer Force.* Submarine Chaser Force, State Pier, New London, CT. 14 February 1918.
*Internal Organization for 100 Foot Submarine Chasers Attached to the Submarine Chaser Force, Squadrons 2, 3, 4, and 5.* (Organizational document.)
*Details of Chasing of Sub Chasers.* (Tactical document).
Dole, George S. *G.S. Dole Letters.* (Personal correspondence).
Lanphier, Alfred Y. *Description of Listening Apparatus and Signals for Submarine Chasers.*
*Minesweeping Orders for the Minesweeping Detachment*, Mine Force, U.S. Atlantic Fleet, 31 May 1919.

Sextant Journal, SC 93. (Journal of sextant readings).

Store Invoices, SC 354. Supply Officer, U.S. Navy Yard, New York, 1917 to 1919.

*Submarine Hunting by Submarine Chasers*. (Tactical document.) 20 August 1918.

U.S. Navy Department, Bureau of Supplies and Accounts. *Sale of Vessels by the Navy at Minimum Prices*. 1919.

**Primary Source Documents, Other**

Cairns, Claude F. *Detection of Ships*. Archives of the Raytheon Corporation, Waltham, MA. 25 October 1917.

Fay, H.J.W., *Anti Submarine Devices Developed at Nahant*. Bound volumes of period photographic prints and captions. Submarine Signal Company, Archives of the Raytheon Corporation, Waltham, MA.

Lord Mersey, S*hipping Casualties. (Loss of the Steamship "Lusitania"): Report of a formal investigation into the circumstances attending the foundering on 7th May, 1915, of the British steamship "Lusitania."* 17 July 1915. Darling and Son, Ltd., Bacon Street, E. London.

Mine Force, U.S. Atlantic Fleet, Minesweeping Division, *Detachment Instructions*, 19 April 1919. National Archives, Washington, D.C.

*Movements of Submarine Chasers*, July 1, 1918 – 1940. National Archives, Washington D.C.

Navy Subject File, 1911 – 1927: AN-Northern Mine Barrage, AP-Mining Operations, OS-U.S. Navy Vessels (Subchaser Files), and WA6-Russia. Naval Records Collection of the Office of Naval Records & Library, National Archives, Washington, D.C.

SC 93 Deck Log, 24 December 1917 – 1 May 1919. National Archives, Washington, D.C.

SC 354 Deck Log, 2 March 1918 – 12 June 1920. National Archives, Washington. D.C.

*Trip of USS Leonidas' Convoy from Bermuda to Ponta Delgada, Azores*, in S.C. Subject Files, 1911 to 1927, National Archives, Washington, D.C.

*War Diary of SC 77*. U.S. Naval Forces Operating in European Waters, Pola, Austria. Naval Records Collection, Office of Naval Records. National Archives, Washington, D.C.

*War Diary of First Squadron* and *War Diary of Second Squadron*, U.S. Submarine Chasers, Otranto Barrage Detachment. Naval Records Collection, Office of Naval Records. National Archives, Washington, D.C.

*War Diary, Subchaser Detachment One*. (Base 27). Naval Records Collection,

Office of Naval Records. National Archives, Washington, D.C.

*War Diary, Subchaser Detachment Two* (Base. 25), Naval Records Collection, Office of Naval Records. National Archives, Washington, D.C.

*War Diary, Subchaser Detachment Three* (Base 6). Naval Records Collection, Office of Naval Records. National Archives, Washington, D.C.

*War Diary, USS Jouett*. Naval Records Collection, Office of Naval Records. National Archives, Washington, D.C.

*War Diary, USS Patterson*. Naval Records Collection, Office of Naval Records. National Archives, Washington, D.C.

Williams, Lawrence E. Personal correspondence. Collection of Capt. Lawrence B. Brenner, USNR.

## Maps / Charts

*Corfu Road (KERKYRA)*, Surveyed by Thomas A. Hull, Master R.N. Under the direction of Commander A.L. Mansell, HMS Firefly, 1863. London, Published at the Admiralty, Under the Superintendence of Captn. G.H. Richards R.N. Hydrographer.

*Durazzo Bay to Corfu Including the Coast of Italy from Cape St. Maria di Leuca to Brindisi.* Nautical chart. Hydrographic Department of the Admiralty, 8th Feb.,1918, under the Superintendence of Rear Admiral J.F. Parry, C.B. Hydrographer.

# Notes

## Notes : Author's Notes

1. G.S. Dole Letters, 29 April 1918.
2. Lord Mersey, *Shipping Casualties. (Loss of the Steamship "Lusitania")*. The count varies from one source to another. For instance, Robert Massie, in *Castles of Steel*, indicates 1,201 lives lost including 126 U.S. citizens.
3. Sims, *The Victory at Sea*, page 199.

## Notes: Prologue

1. Sextant journal, SC 93.
2. Details of the chase on 24 October from *War Diary, First Squadron, U.S. Submarine Chasers, Detachment Two* and from SC 93 Deck Log.
3. Reports of Williams, Murphy, Cormier and Tessman from the folder on SC 92 in *Navy Subject File, 1911 – 1927* (Subchaser Files).

## Notes: Chapter 1 – Building the Chaser Fleet

1. Leighton, *Simasadus London: The American Navy in Europe*, page 3.
2. Leighton, page 13.
3. From *Submarine Hunting by Submarine Chasers*.
4. Sims, *The Victory At Sea*, page 206. See also Treadwell, *Splinter Fleet – The Wooden Subchasers of World War II*, page 10.
5. Clephane, *History of the Submarine Chasers in the World War*, page 10.
6. *Movements of Submarine Chasers*. Information on transfer of chasers to Cuba in *Navy Subject File, 1911 – 1927* (Subchaser Files).
7. Clephane, page 15.
8. SC 90 was delivered by Elco on 6 November 1917; SC 93 on 21 November, and SC 92 probably about the same date. See *Movements of Submarine Chasers*.
9. G.S. Dole Letters, 15 December 1917.
10. *Trip of USS Leonidas' Convoy from Bermuda to Ponta Delgada, Azores*.
11. Sutphen, *Building Submarine Chasers by Standardized Methods*, page 151.
12. Navy Department, *Publication Number 5, History of the Bureau of Engineering, Navy Department During the World War*, pages 33-34.
13. Navy Department, *Publication Number 5, History of the Bureau of Engineering, Navy Department During the World War*, page 34.

14. Circular letter D-2, Navy Department, Bureau of Steam Engineering, Washington, D.C., 2 July 1919. G.S. Dole Collection.
15. *100-Foot Submarine Chaser – Instructions, Care and Operation of Machinery Plant*, page 13.
16. SC 93 Deck Log, 13 January 1918.
17. G.S. Dole Letters, 15 February 1918.
18. G.S. Dole Letters, 17 October 1917.
19. Cadet School training documents, including *Examination for Ensign – Deck Duties / Navigation*, Navy Yard, Boston, 22 August 1917. G.S. Dole Collection.
20. Undated poem from Milton Academy. G.S. Dole Collection.
21. G.S. Dole Letters, 15 December 1917.
22. G.S. Dole Letters, 15 December 1917.
23. G.S. Dole Letters, 30 December 1917.
24. The crew had grown from 18 to 20 men by Christmas, for a total of 22 including the officers.
25. Memorandum, *Schedule of Lectures*, issued by E.E. Spafford, 27 January 1918, Submarine Chaser Base, New London, Connecticut. G.S. Dole Collection.
26. Detachment 4, Squadron 5, Patrol Force, Movement Order No. 1. G.S. Dole Collection
27. Deck Log, SC 90. National Archives, Washington, D.C.

**Notes: Chapter 2 – Antisubmarine Warfare**

1. G.S. Dole Letters, 7 July 1918.
2. Cotten, *Instructions and Doctrine for Sub Chaser Detachment One*.
3. Lanphier, *Description of Listening Apparatus and Signals for Submarine Chasers*.
4. Cairns, *Detection of Ships*, pages 3-4.
5. Fay, *Anti Submarine Devices Developed at Nahant*, caption to photograph 74-186.
6. Hepburn, *Memorandum for C.O.'s of Chasers*.
7. Clephane, *History of the Submarine Chasers in the World War*, page 128.
8. *General Situation and Patrol Operations*, from tactical document credited to E.C.S. Parker. G.S. Dole Collection.
9. *Preliminary Communication Order for U.S. Sm. C., Otranto Detachment (Corfu)*, Page 4. G.S. Dole Collection.
10. Cotten, page 5.
11. Tactics of short runs/not over-shooting the sub, and staggered stop from

*Submarine Hunting by Submarine Chasers*.
12. Cotten, page 6.
13. Cotten, page 9.
14. Stations and duties from *Details of Chasing of Sub Chasers*.
15. U.S. Navy Department, *Publication Number 5, History of the Bureau of Engineering, Navy Department During the World War*, page 37.

**Notes: Chapter 3 – Crossing the Atlantic**

1. G.S. Dole Letters, 2 March 1918.
2. G.S. Dole Letters, 2 March 1918.
3. Moffat, *Maverick Navy*, page 49.
4. Moffat, page 51.
5. Moffat, page 57.
6. The ship behind the chasers is probably HMS *Mutine*, which served as a depot ship in Bermuda.
7. U.S.S.C. #93, *Report to Senior Officer Present*, H.M. Dockyard, Bermuda, 3 March 1918. G.S. Dole Collection.
8. Information and sketch on fueling arrangement from Cotten, L.A., File No. 20-248-1, U.S. Receiving Barracks, Naval District Base, State Pier, New London, Conn., 9 April 1918. G.S. Dole Collection.
9. U.S. Submarine Chaser #349, *Guard Duty notice*, 3 March 1918. G.S. Dole Collection.
10. USS *Wadena*, Liberty notice, 4 March 1918. G.S. Dole Collection.
11. USS *Wadena*, *Notice on Signal Books, Ciphers, Codes, Calls, etc.*, 4 March 1918. G.S. Dole Collection.
12. USS *Yacona*, notice of 7 March 1918. G.S. Dole Collection.
13. G.S. Dole Letters, 10 March 1918.
14. G.S. Dole Letters, 15 March 1918.
15. *Orders for Drills at Sea*, issued from USS *Yacona*, H.M. Dockyard, Bermuda, 21 March 1918. G.S. Dole Collection.
16. Memo on subject *Prevention of Submarine Devices from falling into the hands of the enemy*, T.G. Ellyson, U.S. Receiving Barrack, Naval District Base, State Pier, New London, Conn., 20 April 1918. G.S. Dole Collection.
17. Clephane, *History of the Submarine Chasers in the World War*, page 19.
18. G.S. Dole Letters, 28 April 1918.
19. G.S. Dole Letters, 28 April 1918.
20. G.S. Dole Letters, addendum to 28 April 1918 letter.
21. G.S. Dole Letters, 25 May 1918.

22. Fernandez, *A Lemon of a Trip.*

**Notes: Chapter 4 – American Bay**

1. G.S. Dole Letters, 2 June 1918.
2. Clephane, *History of the Submarine Chasers in the World War*, page 127.
3. Chambers, *United States Submarine Chasers*, page 40.
4. Section of nautical chart, *Durazzo Bay to Corfu Including the Coast of Italy from Cape St. Maria di Leuca to Brindisi.*
5. G.S. Dole Letters, 8 June 1918.
6. Information on construction of Base 25 from Clephane, pages 127-128.
7. Section of nautical chart, *Corfu Road (KERKYRA).*
8. Loomis, *What Were the Faults of the Sub-Chasers?*
9. G.S. Dole Letters, 7 June 1918.
10. Chaser movements from Clephane, pages 128-129.
11. *War Diary of First Squadron* and *War Diary of Second Squadron*, U.S. Submarine Chasers, Otranto Barrage Detachment.
12. Clephane, page 129. Note: Clephane omits SC 244 in the list, but indicates that nine chasers were in the first hunt. Presumably the missing chaser in the list is SC 244, the third chaser in Unit D.
13. Memorandum, USS *Leonidas*, U.S. Naval Base 25, 11 June 1918. G.S. Dole Collection.

**Notes: Chapter 5 – On the Otranto Barrage**

1. G.S. Dole Letters, 7 July 1918.
2. *War Diary, U.S. Naval Base No. 25*, 25 August 1918. See also Chambers, *United States Submarine Chasers*, page 60.
3. SC 93 Deck Log, 11 June 1918.
4. SC 93 Deck Log, 11 June 1918.
5. SC 93 Deck Log, 15 June 1918.
6. G.S. Dole Letters, 7 July 1918.
7. G.S. Dole Letters, 21 June 1918.
8. G.S. Dole Letters, 17 July 1918.
9. G.S. Dole Letters, 17 July 1918.
10. G.S. Dole Letters, 26 July 1918.
11. Deck Log, SC 354.
12. G.S. Dole Letters, 23 August 1918.
13. SC 93 Deck Log.
14. G.S. Dole Letters, 4 September 1918.

15. G.S. Dole Letters, 4 September 1918.
16. Leighton, *Simasadus London: The American Navy in Europe*, page 127.
17. G.S. Dole Letters, 4 September 1918.
18. Leighton, page 132.
19. Leighton, appendix pages 165 and 167.
20. Log Book of SC 93. Location from *No. 1: Routes to Stations* document, G.S. Dole Collection. *War Diary, U.S. Naval Base No. 25* indicates that nine depth charges were dropped during hunt No. 1.
21. *War Diary, U.S. Naval Base No. 25*, Volume I.
22. *War Diary, U.S. Naval Base No. 25*, Volume I.
23. *Navy Subject File, 1911 – 1927* (Subchaser Files), folder on SC 90.
24. *Navy Subject File, 1911 – 1927* (Subchaser Files), folder on SC 78.
25. *Navy Subject File, 1911 – 1927* (Subchaser Files), folder on SC 90.
26. *War Diary, U.S. Naval Base No. 25*, Volume II.
27. *War Diary of Second Squadron*.
28. *War Diary of First Squadron*.
29. *War Diary of Second Squadron*.
30. *War Diary of Second Squadron*; also see *War Diary, U.S. Naval Base No. 25*, Volume III, which indicates deployment of three charges rather than two. The former includes a more detailed account of this attack.
31. *War Diary of Second Squadron*.
32. *War Diary of First Squadron*.
33. *War Diary of Second Squadron*.
34. *War Diary of Second Squadron*.
35. *War Diary of First Squadron*.
36. Log Book of SC 93; *Navy Subject File, 1911 – 1927* (Subchaser Files), folders on SC 90, SC 92 and SC 93; Sextant Journal, SC 93. See also *War Diary, U.S. Naval Base No. 25*, Volume V and W*ar Diary of First Squadron*.
37. *War Diary, U.S. Naval Base No. 25*, Volume III.
38. See Chambers, *United States Submarine Chasers*, Chapter X.
39. Sims, *The Victory At Sea*, page 236.
40. West, *Let Her Go East*.
41. West, *Let Her Go East*.
42. Chambers, *United States Submarine Chasers*, Chapter X.
43. West, *Let Her Go East*.
44. Millholland, *The Splinter Fleet of the Otranto Barrage*, pages 223-224.
45. Millholland, page 238.
46. Halpern, *A Naval History of World War I*, page 176.
47. G.S. Dole Letters, 11 November 1918.

48. G.S. Dole Letters, 18 November 1918.
49. G.S. Dole Letters, 29 November 1918.
50. Special Report by E.E. Spafford, appended to *War Diary, U.S. Naval Base No. 25*, page 3.
51. Halpern, page 176.
52. G.S. Dole Letters, 18 October 1918.
53. Deck Log, SC 93.
54. G.S. Dole Letters, 11 November 1918.
55. G.S. Dole Letters, 18 November 1918.
56. G.S. Dole Letters, 11 November 1918.

**Notes: Chapter 6 – Post-War Diplomacy and Travels**

1. G.S. Dole Letters, 29 November 1918, describing events at Cattaro.
2. G.S. Dole Letters, 29 November 1918.
3. Special Report by E.E. Spafford, appended to *War Diary, U.S. Naval Base No. 25*, page 2-3.
4. Special Report, page 4.
5. Special Report, page 5.
6. G.S. Dole Letters, 21 November 1918.
7. G.S. Dole Letters, 29 November 1918.
8. Chambers, *United States Submarine Chasers*, Chapter XI.
9. G.S. Dole Letters, 29 November 1918.
10. War Diary of SC 77.
11. Special Report, page 11.
12. G.S. Dole Letters, 29 November 1918.
13. Navy Department, *The American Mission in the Adriatic, 1918-1921*, page 4.
14. War Diary of SC 77. See also G.S. Dole Letters, 29 November 1918.
15. G.S. Dole Letters, 3 December 1918.
16. G.S. Dole Letters, 3 December 1918.
17. G.S. Dole Letters, 3 December 1918.
18. G.S. Dole Letters, 9 December 1918.
19. G.S. Dole Letters, 12 December 1918.
20. G.S. Dole Letters, 1 January 1919.
21. G.S. Dole Letters, 16 January 1919.
22. G.S. Dole Letters, 17 January 1919.
23. G.S. Dole Letters, 27 January 1919.
24. G.S. Dole Letters, 17 February 1919.
25. *110-ft. Submarine Chasers; Sale of; Vessels to be stripped of Military Fittings and Arms.*

26. *Report of Destruction of Secret and Confidential Publications Distributed by Code and Signal Division*, 12 February 1919. G.S. Dole Collection.
27. G.S. Dole Letters, 17 February 1919.
28. G.S. Dole Letters, 1 March 1919.
29. G.S. Dole Letters, 12 March 1919.
30. G.S. Dole Letters, 23 March 1919.

**Notes: Chapter 7 – The Northern Russia Expedition**

1. G.S. Dole Letters, 4 April 1919.
2. Transcript of telegram received from Department of State, 3 August 1918. National Archives, Washington, D.C.
3. Strakhovsky, *Intervention at Archangel*, pages 257-258.
4. Halliday, *The Ignorant Armies*, pages 24-25.
5. Operations Memo, Josephus Daniels, 3 October 1918. National Archives, Washington, D.C.
6. Message from Benson, Received Amnavpar, Paris, 1 March 1919. National Archives, Washington, D.C.
7. Cablegram, 16 March 1919, to Adm. Benson from Adm. Sims. National Archives, Washington, D.C.
8. Operations memo, 26 March 1919. National Archives, Washington, D.C.
9. *Volunteers for Russian Service*, memo of 25 March 1919, C.P. Nelson. G.S. Dole Collection.
10. G.S. Dole Letters, 26 March 1919.
11. G.S. Dole Letters, 4 April 1919.
12. *Operation Order No. 4, Northern Russia Detachment*, 14 May 1919. G.S. Dole Collection.
13. U.S.S.C. 354, *Report to Secretary of the Navy*, 3 July 1919. G.S. Dole Collection.
14. Ordinance invoices, G.S. Dole Collection.
15. G.S. Dole Letters, 20 April 1919.
16. G.S. Dole Letters, 27 April 1919.
17. Cablegram, 11 April 1919, from Adm. McCully to Adm. Sims. National Archives, Washington, D.C.
18. Deck Log, SC 354. National Archives, Washington, D.C.
19. Letter to the President of the United States from Adm. Benson, 1 May 1919. National Archives, Washington, D.C.
20. Letter of response from President Woodrow Wilson to Adm. Benson, 2 May 1919. National Archives, Washington, D.C.
21. SIMSADUS memo, 7 May 1919. National Archives, Washington, D.C.

22. G.S. Dole Letters, 1 June 1919.
23. Operation Order No. 1, 5 June 1919. G.S. Dole Collection.
24. Dole, George S. *Farthest North in a Submarine Chaser.*
25. SC 354 Deck Log. National Archives, Washington, D.C.
26. Dole, George S. *Farthest North in a Submarine Chaser.*
27. G.S. Dole Letters, 13 June 1919.
28. SC 354 Deck Log. National Archives, Washington, D.C.
29. G.S. Dole Letters, 13 June 1919.
30. Williams, personal correspondence, 23 June 1919.
31. Memo to Adm. Benson from Gilbert Close, Confidential Secretary to the President, 7 June 1919. National Archives, Washington, D.C.
32. *Policy on Northern Russia.* Document circulated by Adm. McCully, 24 April 1919. National Archives, Washington, D.C.
33. *Disposition and Employment of Forces* memo, 14 June 1919. National Archives, Washington, D.C.
34. Dole, *Farthest North in a Submarine Chaser.*
35. G.S. Dole Letters, 2 July 1919.
36. G.S. Dole Letters, 4 July 1919.
37. G.S. Dole Letters, 4 July 1919.
38. Opnav memo from Adm. Knapp, 29 June 1919. National Archives, Washington, D.C.
39. G.S. Dole Letters, 24 July 1919.
40. G.S. Dole Letters, 20 July 1919.

## Notes: Chapter 8 – Mine Sweeping in the North Sea

1. G.S. Dole Letters, 31 August 1919.
2. SC 354 Deck Log.
3. *Minesweeping Orders for the Minesweeping Detachment*, page 14.
4. *Minesweeping Orders for the Minesweeping Detachment*, pages 16-18.
5. Mine sweeping tactics from documents in *Navy Subject File, 1911 – 1927*, AP-Mining Operations and AN-Northern Mine Barrage, particularly summary reports on the first through the seventh minesweeping operations. Also *Publication Number 4: The Northern Barrage (Taking Up the Mines).*
6. *Mine Force, U.S. Atlantic Fleet, Minesweeping Division, Detachment Instructions*, 19 April 1919, Page 2. National Archives, Washington, D.C.
7. From chart: *Vessels Operating with Mine Force, North Sea Minesweeping Detachment.* Navy Subject File, 1911 – 1927.
8. *Publication Number 4: The Northern Barrage (Taking Up the Mines)*, page 42.

9. Post, *Navy Life Aboard the SC 40*, pages 16-17.
10. G.S. Dole Letters, 30 July 1919.
11. G.S. Dole Letters, 4 August 1919.
12. Incident reports from documents in *Navy Subject File, 1911 – 1927*.
13. SC 354 Deck Log.
14. G.S. Dole Letters, 31 August 1919.
15. G.S. Dole Letters, 31 August 1919.

**Notes: Chapter 9 – Homeward Bound**

1. G.S. Dole Letters, 27 October 1919.
2. Memo from Admiral Strauss, Commander, Mine Force, 4 September 1919. G.S. Dole Collection.
3. Memo from W.K. Harrill, by direction of Commander, Mine Force, 4 September 1919. G.S. Dole Collection.
4. Detachment Formation memo, USS *Panther*, 4 September 1919. G.S. Dole Collection. Also Deck Log, SC 354.
5. Operation Order from USS *Black Hawk*. G.S. Dole Collection.
6. Detachment Order No. 15, USS *Panther*, 13 October 1919. G.S. Dole Collection.
7. Deck Log, SC 354.
8. G.S. Dole Letters, 27 October 1919.
9. Deck Log, SC 354, 18 November 1919.
10. Letter to Lt. Dole from Milton Fogg, 25 January 1921. G.S. Dole Collection.
11. G.S. Dole Letters, 23 November 1919.

**Notes: Epilogue: The Impact of the Chasers**

1. Messimer, *Find and Destroy – Antisubmarine Warfare in World War I*, page 125.
2. Halpern, *A Naval History of World War I*, page 399.
3. Sims, *The Victory at Sea*, page 199.
4. Sims, page 199.
5. Sims, page 231.
6. Hashagen, *U-Boats Westward*, pages 215 and 217.
7. Leighton, *Simsadus: London*, page 84.
8. Sims, page 210.
9. Sims, page 198.
10. Treadwell, web page: http://www.splinterfleet.org/sfspec.php

**Notes: Appendices I to V**

1. Clephane, *History of the Submarine Chasers in the World War*, page 81.
2. Clephane, page 76.
3. *War Diary, Subchaser Detachment One, Base 27*, page 1.
4. Chaser movements from *War Diary, Subchaser Detachment One* and *War Diary, Subchaser Detachment Three*.
5. *Navy Subject File, 1911 – 1927* (Subchaser Files).
6. *War Diary, Subchaser Detachment One, Base 27*, page 7.
7. *Navy Subject File, 1911 – 1927* (Subchaser Files). Also *War Diary, Subchaser Detachment One, Base 27*, page 7.
8. *War Diary, Subchaser Detachment One, Base 27*, page 9.
9. *Navy Subject File, 1911 – 1927* (Subchaser Files).
10. *Navy Subject File, 1911 – 1927* (Subchaser Files).
11. *War Diary, Subchaser Detachment One*, Base 27, page 22.
12. *War Diary, Subchaser Detachment One*, Base 27, page 26.
13. *S.C. Subject Files, 1911 to 1927*. Also War Diary, Subchaser Detachment One, Base 27, pages 26-27.
14. *War Diary, Subchaser Detachment One*, Base 27, page 38.
15. Clephane, page 100.
16. *War Diary, Subchaser Detachment Three*.
17. *War Diary, Subchaser Detachment Three*.
18. *War Diary, Subchaser Detachment Three*.
19. *War Diary, Subchaser Detachment Three*.
20. *Navy Subject File, 1911 – 1927* (Subchaser Files). Also *War Diary, Subchaser Detachment Three*.
21. *Navy Subject File, 1911 – 1927* (Subchaser Files).
22. *War Diary, Subchaser Detachment Three*.
23. *Navy Subject File, 1911 – 1927* (Subchaser Files). Also *War Diary, Subchaser Detachment Three*.
24. *War Diary, USS Jouett*.
25. *War Diary, USS Patterson*.
26. Clephane, page 82.
27. *Navy Subject File, 1911 – 1927* (Subchaser Files).
28. *War Diary, USS Jouett*.
29. *Navy Subject File, 1911 – 1927* (Subchaser Files).
30. *War Diary, USS Patterson*.
31. *War Diary, USS Patterson*.
32. Clephane, page 81.

# Index

Photos/illustrations in **boldface**.

60-degree method 52-53, **53**
Adriatic Sea 3, 77, 108
aircraft 6, 48, 82, 86, 88, 96, 97, 175
Aldrich, Lt. G. F. **133**
American Bay 6, 77-82, **78**, **79**, **80**, **81**, **83**, 86-87, 88, 90
Amapala, Honduras 195
anchored patrol 48
antenna sweeping 152
antisubmarine warfare (ASW) 2, 4, 5, 12, 25, 26, 36-60, 92, 124, 173-175, 176-177, 178-179, 181-182, 192
*Arethusa* (AO 7) 169
Archangel, Russia 4, 120, 121, 123, 124, 131, 139, **139**, 140, 141, 144, 181
Arctic Sea 136, 138, 147
armament, of subchasers 3, 12, 60, 119
ash can 54, 87
Astor Hotel 171
attack pattern **54** 54-55
Austrian warships, transfer of 108
Austrian submarine commanders 114-115, 176
aviation base, French 88, **89**
*Aylwin* (DD 47) 183
Azores **13**, 70-73, **71**, 120, 125, 168-169, **169**, 181, 182
Base 6, Queenstown, Ireland 126, 181, 184
Base 7, Brest (see Brest)
Base 9, Gibraltar (see Gibraltar)
Base 13, Azores (see Ponta Delgada)
Base 15, Canal Zone 193, 195
Base 18, Inverness 127, 130, **148**
Base 25, Corfu 77-83, **80**, **81**, **83**, 86, 88, 91, 108, 110, 126, 181
Base 27, Plymouth 119, 127, 181, 183-187

Bastedo, Lt. Comdr. 99
bearing indicator 7, **17**, **18**, 37, **44**, **45**, 44-47, **49**, 51, 52, 58, 69
Benson, Adm. William S. 123, 129
Bergen Norway 132, **133**
Bermuda 61-69, **64**, 170
*Birchol* 131, 132, **133**, 136
black gang 20, 22
*Black Hawk* 154, 155, **155**, 163, **163**, 165, 171
*Bobolink* 155, 157, **159**
Block Island, NY 31, 34
Blumenthal, Ens. Hugo W. 104-105
Bolsheviks 121-124, **144**
Boness, Lt. P.W. **133**
Borgeson, Lt. Oscar 6-7, 47-49, 52-53, **55**, 57-58, 92, 95
Brest, France 127, 129, 140, 168, **169**, 182
Brindisi, Italy 98, 101, **101**
*British Light* **73**
Brooklyn Navy Yard 14, 171
Bruce, Lt. Frank 157
Bullard, Rear Adm. W.H. 108
buoy division 160-162
Bureau of Navigation 32
Bureau of Steam Engineering 15, 60
C-Tube hydrophone (see S.C. Tube)
Caledonian Canal 127, **128**
Cape Pali, Albania 98
Cape St. Maria di Leucca, Italy 6, **7**, 97
Cattaro, Montenegro 105, 107, 108, 110-112, **111**, **112**
Catinelli, Rear Adm. A. 104-105, 111
Chambers, Ens. Hilary R. 77, 82, 101, 110
China, rumor of trip to 108, 113-115
Christiana (Oslo), Norway 144-145, **146**

211

Clay, Lt. W.G. 131, **133**
Clephane, Capt. Lewis 77
Codling Lightship 191
Comeni Head, Corfu 77, **79**
Compensator, K Tube 39, **40**, 41-42, 70
*Conde* 139
Coningbeg Light Vessel 190
convoy system 2, 15, 25, **43**, 61, 63, 71, 82, 173, 175, 178, 182, 193
Construction Corps 12
Corfu, Greece 6, 48, 77-83, **78**, 86, 106, **106**, **107**, 181
Cormier, Jeffrey, seaman 8
Cotten, Capt. Lyman A. 36, 57, 183
course protractor 47
Cronan, Comdr. William P. 192
Cuba 13, 181, 193, 195
*Curlew* 155, 158
*Cyclops* 139
Daniels, Josephus 171
deck gun 3, 6, 12, **14**, **17**, **19**, 36, 56, 119, 127, 128, 132, 147, 177-178
depth charge 3, 7, 8, 12, 16, 18, 19, 36, 47, 53, 54, 55, **55**, 56, 57, 87, **87**, 102, 119
depth charge racks 87, **87**
*Des Moines* (C-15) 124, 129, 130, 139, **139**
Devonport, England 163, 165-166, **166**, 168
Dole, Lt. George S.
    collection of 4-5
    Durazzo engagement 103
    Lieutenant (j.g.) rank awarded 92
    Minesweeping Detachment **171**
    Navy Cross 4
    Northern Russia Expedition 124, 131, **133**, **137**
    Olympic wrestling 3-4, 27
    service of 179-180
    sextant readings 6
    submarine attack 8, 87, 91-92
    USNRF 3
    Yale, 3, 4
Dole, Henry Clinton 25
Dole, Louis A. 4
Durazzo, bombardment of 93, 98-106, **99**, **100**, **101**
duties, of officers and crew 57-60, 69-70
drifting patrol 48, 185, 186, 191
Dvina River 123, 129, 132, 139, 143
Eagle boats 124, 130, 139, **139**, 140, 141
Eddystone Light 185
*Eider* 155, 158
Elco, Bayonne, NJ 13
electric protective device 149-150
*Elerol* 130
engines, of subchasers 3, 15, 23-25, **19**, **20**, **21**, **22**, **23**, 61-62, 63-64, 66, 119, 156, 159, 171, 178, 187
evidence of a kill 8, 47, 57, 92, 93, 102, 103
Falconer, Lt. Comdr. W.M. 35, 66
*Felix Taussig* 13
Fernandez, Gerard 75
Fiume, Dalmatian coast 108
*Flamingo* 155, 158
flu 119
Fogg, Milton 170
Ford Motor Company 124
*Fram* 109
France 13, 118-119, **118**, 121, 127, 140, 168, **169**, 181, 186
Frognesvettern Inn, Christiana **145**
Fuglo Island, Norway 134, **134**
Furer, Comdr. Julius A. 12
Fustipidima Point, Corfu 77-78, **79**
Gallipoli, Italy **90**, 91
Gibraltar 73, **73**, 103, 118, 119, 181, 182
Govino Bay, Corfu 77, **89**
Graham, Capt. S.V. 193
Granton, Scotland **165**, 166
Griffin, Rear Adm. Robert S. 60
Griffin, Lt. Comdr. R.M. 132, **133**, 138, 141

# Index

Griffin, Lt. R.N. 184
Guantanamo, Cuba 193
Gulf of Mexico 192, 193
Halliday, Ernest 121
Halpern, Paul G. 103, 104, 105, 173
Hamilton, Bermuda 66-67
Hashagen, Ernst 176-177
hearing lights 50
*Henley* 192
    USS *Henley* Group 192
*Heron* 155, **169**
Holmengraa, Norway 131, 132
inland waterways, Norway 135-138
Inverness, Scotland 120, 124, 126, 127, **129**, 130, **130**, 131, **131**, 136, **148**, 181
Ionian Sea 6
Italy 6, 77, 86, **90**, 91, 97, 98, 103, **117**, 117
    post-war tensions 107-109, 112-113, 115
    sales of subchasers to 118
*Jouett* (DD 41) 192
    USS *Jouett* Group 192, 193
Jugoslavia (Yugoslavia) 109, 111-113
K Tube hydrophone 6, 39, **40**, **41**, **42**, 41-43, 67, 69, 70, 95, 119, 175
Kego Island 143-144, **144**
Kem, Russia 140, 141
Keret Bay, Russia 140, 141
Key West, Florida 193
King, Comdr. Frank 158
*Kingfisher* 155, 159
Kirkwall, Orkney Islands 147, 154, 156, 157, 159, 162-163, **163**, 181
Kola inlet 138
Knapp, Adm. Harry S. 129
Lanphier, Lt. Alfred Y. 36, 193
*Lapwing* **151**, 1698
La Spezia, Italy **117** 117
Leighton, Ens. John Langdon 10, 93, 177
Leovy, Lt. George J. **133**

lemons 74-76
Lervig, Norway 161, **161**, *181*
Lerwick, Shetland Islands 132, 159
*Leonidas* (AD 7) 65, 70, 73, 75, 77, 81, **81**, 82, 83, 87, 88, 95, 106, 124
Lissa, Albania 108
Lisbon, Portugal 119-120, **120**, 126-127, 168, 181
listening period 8, 15, 48-49, 76, 96, 98
Lizard 186
Loftin, Lt. Comdr. 105, 108, 111
longitudinal sweeping 152
Loomis, Alfred F. 79, 81
*Lusitania* (HMS Lusitania) 1, 10
Lyons-Atlas Company, Indianapolis, IN 20
machine guns 3, **16**, **18**, 58, 119, 127
malaria 77, 88
*Malay* (USN patrol vessel) 4, 25, **26**
Malta 73-76, **74**, 115-117, **116**
Mandukio, Corfu 78, 88
*Matzouk*, tanker 91, 110
maneuvering lights **18**, 50-51
*Maverick Navy* 26, 62-63, 173
Massachusetts Institute of Technology 26
Mark VI mine 147-151, **148**, **150**, 152
M.B. Tube hydrophone 37, 39, 70
McCully, Rear Adm. Newton A. 122, 123, 127, 129, 139, 140, 141, 144
Meleda, Dalmatian coast 108
Messimer, Dwight 173
Mexico 192, 193, 195
Milford Haven, Wales 127
Millholland, Ray 103, 105
Milton Academy 27, 180
mine sweeping 144, 145, 147-164
    incidents 157-159
Minesweeping Detachment 154-155, 159, 171, 181
minesweeper 149, 151, **151**, **153**, 154-155, **155**, 160, 166, **167**, 168, **169**, 171

213

mine train **148**
ML (British Motor Launch) **11**, 11-12, 13, 15
Moffat, Ens. Alexander 26, 62-64, 184
Mundy, Ens. Joseph H. 6, 8, 47, 49, 52, 57-58, 92
Murmansk, Russia 121, 123, 131, 134, 138
Murphy, John J., seaman 8
Nahant, Boston, MA 37
*Nautilus*, Italian submarine **86**
Navy Cross 4, 180
Nelson, Capt. Charles **55**, 73, 99, 124
Ness River 129
New London, CT 3, 14, 24, 26, **28**, 32, 61, 63, 69, 70, 81, 192
New York 8, 14, 26, **31**, 34, 171, **171**
North Sea mine barrage, 3, 4, 146, 147-164
Northern Russia Expedition 15, 31, 121-146
    chasers initially assigned to 126
    flag officer, Dvina detachment 131, 132
    unit command 131
Nova Scotia 192, 194
Olympics, 1908 London Games 3, 4, 27
*Oriole* 155, 158
*Osprey* 155, 160
Otranto Barrage, 3, 4, 6, 48, 60, 65, 77, 78, 82, 83, **85**, 86-98, **94**, 94-98, 120, 173
Panama Canal (see Base 15)
*Panther* 147, 154, **156**, 156, 159, 165, 166, 168, 170
*Parker* (DD 48) 183, 187
*Patepsco* 155
*Patterson* (DD 36) 192, 193, 194
    USS *Patterson* Special Hunting Group 36, 192, 193, 194
*Patuxent* 155, 157
*Pelican* 155, 158
*Penguin* 155, 159
*Perkins* (DD 26) 192
Plymouth, England (see Base 27)

Point Judith, RI 34
Pola, Austria 108
Ponta Delgada, Azores 70-72, **71**, 168, **169**, 181, 182
Popov Island, Russia 140
Portugal 119-120
position plotter **46**, 46-47, 52, 58, 69
Post, Charles 155-156
*Quail* 155, 168, **169**, 170-171
*Radetzky* 109
radio telegraph 49, 52, 60
radio telephone 7, 46, **50**, **51**, 51-52, **59**, 60, **68**, 69, 119, 160
*Rail* 155, 158
*Richard Bulkeley* 155, 158
Richardson, Ens. C. Read **133**
running patrol 48-49, 186
Russian Revolution 4, 121
*Sacramento* (AG 19) 123, 124, 130, 141
Saint Anthony Head 185
Saint Lawrence University 180
*Salem* (CS 3) 70, 193
    USS *Salem* Group 192, 193
San Miguel Island, Azores **71**, 71, 168
*Sanderling* 155, 159
S.C. Tube hydrophone 37-38, **38**, **39**, 175
*Seagull* 155, 159
Serb camp, Corfu 88, **90**
sextant readings 6, 27, 62, 73, **137**
shape signals **49**, 50, 119
Sicily 91, 117
silent running 54, 175
Sims, Adm. William Sowden 2, 10, 123, 127, 129, 175, 176, 178, 183
Snow, Ens. Frank A. 29, 67, **68**, 119, 124-125
Solovetski Island, Russia 140-141, **141**, **142**
Soro Sound, Norway 138
*South Carolina* 193
Spafford, Lt. Comdr. E.E. 105, 108-111, 112-

113
Spalato, Dalmatian coast 108, 109, 112-115, **113**, **114**
*Splinter Fleet*, Millholland 103, 173
squares 83, 93
SSZ-53 190
Standard Motor Construction Company 15, 20, 22
steel sharks: frontispiece, 4, 72, 180
Strait of Otranto 3, 6, **7**, 84, **85**, 92, 93
Strauss, Rear Adm. 164, 165
Strakhovsky, Leonid 121
Swasey. Lt. Comdr. Albert Loring 12
Subchaser Club of America 75, 104
Subchaser Post newsletter **31**
submarine chasers
    attacks and pursuits 94-98, 100-103, 184-188, 189-191, 193-194
    construction of 12-25
    design of 11, 16-19, 29
    Division C, New York **31**
    Divisions L-P and Tactical Group, USS *Jouett* Group 192
    engines 15, **20**, **21** 20-25, 63-64
    employment of 11
    fires in 13, 23, 119
    France, built for 13, 181
    fueling at sea 25, **65**, 65-66
    fuel consumption 63, 81
    Groups A-C, USS *Henley* Group 192
    Groups A-D, USS *Salem* Group 193
    Groups 13 to 26, Plymouth 183
    heat plant 22, 30
    hull markings 15, 126
    losses of, 13, 181
    mine sweeping 153-154, 156, 159-163, **160**, **161**, **162**, **163**
    organization of 47-48
    sailing of 135-136, **135**, **136**
    sale of, overseas 118-119, 120, 165
    seaworthiness of 14, 29, 30-31, 34, 70, 145
    tactics of 48-57
    target practice 141-142, **143**
    towed by minesweepers 166, **167**, **169**
    transport duties 111, 114, 141, 143
SC-1 126, 184, 189
SC-2 193
SC-3 193
SC-4 193
SC-6 192
SC-22 193
SC-23 193
SC-34 183
SC-35 183
SC-36 183, 186, 187
SC-37 154, 158, 168, 183
SC-38 154, 158, 159, 183
SC-39 183, 184, 185
SC-40 154, 156, 183
SC-41 183, 187, 188
SC-42 192
SC-44 154, 184, 189, 190
SC-45 **23**, 154, 184, 189, 190, 191
SC-46 154, 158, 168, 170, 184, 189, 190, 191
SC-47 154, 158, 184, 189, 190, 191
SC-48 154, 165, **166**, 168, 184, 189, 190, 191
SC-51 192
SC-58 13
SC-60 13
SC-68 192, 193
SC-69 192, 193
SC-70 192, 193
SC-77 82, 83, 95, 97, 111, **120**
SC-78 79, 81, 82, 83, 95, 97, 120
SC-79 82, 83, 95, 97
SC-80 **29**, 82, 83, 104, 111
SC-81 75, 82, 83, **120**

SC-82 82, 83, 96, 120
SC-83 183
SC-84 183, 185
SC-85 183, 185
SC-86 183, 185
SC-87 183
SC-90 6-7, 13, 24, 35, **44**, 47, 65, 70, 82, **83**, 87, 91, 94, 95, 98, **118**, 126
SC-91 183, 184, 189, 190
SC-92 6-8, 13, 35, 47, **74**, 81, 82, **83**, 87, 91, 94, 95, 98, **118**
SC-93 3, 4, 6-8, 13-14, 24, 25, **28**, 29, 32-35, **42**, 47, 60, 67, **74**, 81, 82, **83**, 87, **87**, 91, 94, 95, 98, 115, **118**, 124, **125**, 125
SC-94 82, 95, 120
SC-95 **12**, 82, 83, 94, 95, 98, 126, 131, **131**, **133**, 135, **136**, **139**, 140, 154, 165, **165**, **166**, 168
SC-96 82, 83
SC-97 183
SC-98 126-127, 183, 186, 187
SC-99 183, 184, 186, 187
SC-100 183, 184
SC-101 183, 184
SC-102 192
SC-103 183, 184
SC-104 193
SC-105 192
SC-110 154, 168, 184, 189, 190
SC-111 193
SC-117 13
SC-119 193
SC-121 193, 194
SC-122 193
SC-124 82, 96, 97
SC-125 82, 96, 97
SC-127 82, 96, 97
SC-128 77, 82, 97, 98, 101-102, 110, 120

SC-129 82, 97, 98, 101-102
SC-130 82, 83, 96, 98
SC-131 82, 83, 96
SC-132 13, 192, 194
SC 133 192, 194
SC-134 192, 193
SC-135 192
SC-136 192, 193
SC-137 126-127, 183, 187, 188
SC-143 24, 26, 35, 62, 183, 184-185, 188
SC-145 192, 193
SC-147 81, 82, 83, 95, 97
SC-148 35, 183, 188
SC-151 **13**, 82, 95
SC-164 154, 157, 184, 189, 190
SC-177 35, 183, 184-185, 188
SC-178 67, 154, 184, 189. 190
SC-179 82, 83, 94, 95, 98, **101**, 120
SC-180 192
SC-181 154, 168, 184. 189, 190
SC-182 154, 184, 189
SC-183 192
SC-186 193
SC-187 13
SC-188 193
SC-189 192, 193
SC-190 192, 193
SC-191 192, 193
SC-203 193
SC-206 154, 184, 189, 190
SC-207 154, **163**, 168, 184, 189, 190
SC-208 154, 157, **163**, 165, **166**, 168, 184, 189, 190
SC-209 13, 193
SC-210 192
SC-211 192
SC-212 192
SC-213 192
SC-214 192

SC-215 82, 97, 98, 101-103, 120
SC-216 82, 83, 96, **120**
SC-217 82, 83, 96
SC-219 13, 181, 192, 194
SC-220 183, 184, 186, 189
SC-221 183, 184, 189, 190
SC-222 183, 184, 189, 190
SC-223 192, 193
SC-224 183, 187
SC-225 35, 82, 98, 103, 110
SC-226 183, 187
SC-227 82, 95, 182
SC-232 193
SC-234 193, 194
SC-240 192
SC-241 192, 194
SC-242 192
SC-244 35, 67, 81, 82, **87**, 98, 110
SC-245 193, 194
SC-247 192
SC-248 82, 83, 96, 109, 120
SC-252 183, 184, 185
SC-253 192
SC-254 154, 184, 189
SC-255 35, 67, **74**, 81, 82, 96
SC-256 13, 35, 82, 96, 119, 124, 126, 131, **131**, **133**, 140, 154, 165, **166**, 168
SC-257 126-127, 183, 184
SC-258 126-127, 183, 187, 188
SC-259 154, 165, **166**, 168, 183
SC-260 183, 184, 186, 187
SC-261 193
SC-262 126-127, 183, 184, 185
SC-263 192
SC-266 192
SC-269 192
SC-270 193
SC-271 126, 184, 189
SC-272 154, 184, 189

SC-273 195
SC-274 195
SC-275 195
SC-279 193
SC-280 193
SC-281 193
SC-182 193
SC-183 193
SC-184 193
SC-185 193
SC-186 193
SC-187 193
SC-188 193
SC-189 193
SC-290 193
SC-301 195
SC-302 195
SC-303 195
SC-304 195
SC-305 195
SC-306 195
SC-307 195
SC-308 195
SC-309 182
SC-310 182
SC-311 195
SC-312 195
SC-320 193
SC-321 126-127, 183, 186, 187
SC-322 183, 184, 187
SC-323 183, 184, 186, 189
SC-324 82, 83, 95, 97, 98
SC-325 183, 184, 189
SC-327 35, **74**, 81, 82, 91, 98, 120
SC-329 154, 168, 184, 189
SC-330 192
SC-331 182, 192, 194
SC-332 192, 193
SC-337 81, 82, 83, 95, 97, 98
SC-338 82, 83, 94, 95, 98

SC-339 192, 193
SC-340 192
SC-341 192
SC-342 184, 186, 189
SC-343 13, 184, 189
SC-344 **120**, 184, 189
SC-345 184, 189
SC-346 184, 189
SC-349 35, 81, 82, 96
SC-351 183, 187
SC-352 183
SC-353 192, 194
SC-354 4, 124-129, **125**, **126**, 126-127, 130, 131, **131**, 133, **135**, 138, 139, 140-142, **141**, **143**, 144, 147, 154, 155, 156-157, 159-163, **161**, 165, **165**, 166, **166**, 168, **169**, 170-172, **171**, 183, 184
SC-355 192, 194
SC-356 154, 184, 189, 190
Units 1-22, Plymouth 183-184
Units 13-22, Queenstown 189
Unit A 82, 96, 97, 108, 110
Unit B 82, 97, 98, 99, 110
Unit C 82, 83, 96, 108, 110
Unit D 82, 83, 98, 110
Unit E 6-8, 13, 47-49, 52, 82, **83**, 87, 92, 94, 95, 98, 110
Unit F 82, 95, 108
Unit G 83, 93, 94, 95, 98, 108, 110
Unit H 83, 95, 97, 98, 110
Unit I 83, 95, 97, 108
Unit J 83, 108
Unit K 83, 96, 98, 110
Unit L 83, 96, 108
Submarine Signal Company 37-43
Swasey, Lt. Comdr. Albert Loring 12
Sweet, Thomas G. 187
*Tanager* 155, 158
*Teal* 155, 157, **169**

Tessman, Gordon Ellis, ship's cook 8
Thornbush Dockyard 130, **130**
Tompkins, Capt. J.T. 192
transverse sweeping 152
trailing wire **43**, 43-44, 56, 69, 119, 177, 191
Tromso, Norway 136, 138
*Turkey* 155, 157
Tuskar 189
*Tyne* 161, **161**
U-boat
   U-20 1
   U-126 **3**
   UB-92 **1**, **2**
   UC, 22-70 type 8
   UC-III 119
   UE-2 **3**, 119
unrestricted submarine warfare 1, 2, 10
U.S. Naval Districts 192
U.S. Naval Reserve 3, 12, 25, 179
Valetta, Malta 74
Vardo, Norway 138
Villefranche, France **118** 118
*Wadena* (SP 158) 35, 66
*Weymouth*, **100**, 101, 105
West, Stephen Crane 98-100, 102-103
Western Electric radio telephone (see radio telephone)
White Russians (Tzarists) 121
White Sea 120, **122**, 124, 127, 138, 139-144
Williams, Edward J, Coxswain 8
Williams, Ens. Lawrence E. 133, 139
Wilson, President Woodrow 1, 112, 121-123, 129
wing boats 6, 8, 46, 47, 52-58, 97, 191
wrestling 3, 4, 27, 180
Y-gun 3, 12, **16**, **18**, 55, **55**, **56**, 69, 119, 127, 185, 186, 187, 190, 193
*Yacona* (SP 617) 66, 57
*Yankton* 122, 123, 134, 138, **138**, 141
*Zriski* 109

Made in United States
Orlando, FL
20 February 2023